Helen Grace is Research Associate in the Department of Gender and Cultural Studies and Research Affiliate, Sydney College of the Arts, University of Sydney. Previously she established the MA Programme in Visual Culture Studies at the Chinese University of Hong Kong. Most recently she was Visiting Professor at National Central University in Taiwan.

Amy Chan Kit-Sze is Associate Professor in the English Department, Director of the Master of Arts Programme in Interdisciplinary Cultural Studies and Associate Director of the Technoscience Culture Research and Development Center, Hong Kong Shue Yan University.

Wong Kin Yuen is Professor in and Head of the Department of English Language and Literature and Director of the Technoscience Culture Research and Development Center at Hong Kong Shue Yan University.

EDITED BY HELEN GRACE, AMY CHAN KIT-SZE AND WONG KIN YUEN

TECHNOVISUALITY

CULTURAL RE-ENCHANTMENT AND THE EXPERIENCE OF TECHNOLOGY

I.B. TAURIS
LONDON · NEW YORK

Published in 2016 by
I.B.Tauris & Co. Ltd
London • New York
www.ibtauris.com

International Library of Visual Culture 21

ISBN: 978 1 78453 034 1
eISBN: 978 0 85773 919 3
ePDF: 978 0 85772 563 9

A full CIP record for this book is available from the British Library
A full CIP record is available from the Library of Congress

Library of Congress Catalog Card Number: available

Typeset by Aptara

Contents

Section 3: Experiencing

List of Illustrations

Contributors

Chris Berry is Professor of Film Studies at King's College, London. His academic research is grounded in work on cinema and other screen-based media. His primary publications include: *Cinema and the National: China on Screen* (2006), *Postsocialist Cinema in Post-Mao China: The Cultural Revolution after the Cultural Revolution* (2004), *The New Chinese Documentary Film Movement: For the Public Record* (2010), *Electronic Elsewheres: Media, Technology, and the Experience of Social Space* (2010), *Cultural Studies and Cultural Industries in Northeast Asia: What a Difference a Region Makes* (2009), *TV China* (edited with Ying Zhu, 2008), *Chinese Films in Focus II* (2008), and *Island on the Edge: Taiwan New Cinema and After* (2005).

Amy Chan Kit-Sze is an associate professor of the English department at Hong Kong Shue Yan University. She is also the Director of the Master of Arts Programme in Interdisciplinary Cultural Studies and the Associate Director of the Technoscience Culture Research and Development Centre at HKSYU. She holds a PhD in intercultural studies and her research interests include: cultural studies, technoscience culture, gender studies, literary studies and science fiction. She is particularly interested in exploring the intersections of Deleuzian philosophy, technoscience culture and Chinese culture and philosophy. She has co-edited *Science Fiction and the Prediction of the Future* (2011) and *World Weavers: Globalization, Science Fiction, and the Cybernetic Revolution* (2005).

Sean Cubitt is Professor of Film and Television and co-head of the Department of Media and Communications at Goldsmiths, University of London; Professorial Fellow of the University of Melbourne and Honorary Professor of the University of Dundee. His publications include *Timeshift: On Video Culture* (1991), *Videography: Video Media as Art and Culture* (1993), *Digital Aesthetics* (1998), *Simulation and Social Theory* (2000), *The Cinema Effect* (2005), *EcoMedia* (2005) and *The Practice of Light* (2014). He has recently co-edited *Rewind: British Artists' Video in the 1970s & 1980s* (2012), *Relive: Media Art Histories* (2013), *Ecocinema: Theory and Practice* (2012), and *Digital Light* (2015). He is the series editor for Leonardo Books at MIT Press. His current research is on environmental impacts of digital media and on media arts and their history.

Helen Grace established the MA Programme in Visual Culture Studies in the Department of Cultural and Religious Studies, Chinese University of Hong Kong; most recently she has been a visiting professor at National Central University, Taiwan on a National Science Council Fellowship. She is an associate in the Department of Gender and Cultural Studies and Research Affiliate, Sydney College of the Arts, University of Sydney. Her most recent book is *Culture, Aesthetics and Affect in Ubiquitous Media: The Prosaic Image* (2014). She is author of the CD-ROM, *Before Utopia: A Non-official History of the Present* (2000) and co-author of *Home/World: Space, Community and Marginality in Sydney's West* (1997). She edited the collection *Aesthesia and the Economy of the Senses* (1996) and co-edited *Planet Diana: Cultural Studies and Global Mourning* (1997). She is an award-winning filmmaker, photographer and new media producer and her works are included in the collections of the National Gallery of Australia, the Art Gallery of New South Wales, the Art Gallery of South Australia and Artbank.

Janet Harbord is Professor of Film Studies at Queen Mary University of London. She is the author of several books on film and philosophies of screen technologies in the digital age, including *Chris Marker: La Jetée* (2009), *The Evolution of Film: Rethinking Film Studies* (2007) and *Film Cultures* (2002), and editor of *Temporalities: Autobiography and Everyday Life* (with J. Campbell, 2002) and *Psycho-politics and Cultural Desires* (with J. Campbell, 1998).

Veronica Hollinger is Professor of Cultural Studies at Trent University in Ontario, Canada. She is a long-time co-editor of the journal *Science Fiction Studies*, and co-editor of five scholarly collections, the most recent of which is *Parabolas of Science Fiction* (2013). She has published many essays on feminist science fiction, on cyberfiction, on theories of post-modernism and post-humanism, and on recent developments in science fiction theory and criticism.

Michelle Huang Tsung-yi is Professor in the Department of Geography, National Taiwan University and currently Associate Professor, Department of Cultural and Religious Studies, Chinese University of Hong Kong. Her research over the last ten years has been concerned with identifying, investigating and creatively revealing new urban phenomena that have radically transformed the urban landscape and everyday life in East Asian metropolises through interdisciplinary critical perspectives. Her books include *Walking Between Slums and Skyscrapers: Illusions of Open Space in Hong Kong, Tokyo and Shanghai* (2004) and *Articulating New Cultural Identities: Self-Writing of East Asian Global City-regions* (2008).

Nevena Ivanova is currently a postgraduate fellow at the School of Creative Media, City University of Hong Kong, working on ontogenesis of emerging technologies. She earned her PhD in Philosophy of New Media in 2011, from Tokyo University's Graduate School of Interdisciplinary Information Studies.

Chi-she Li teaches in the Department of Foreign Languages and Literatures, National Taiwan University. His research interests include cultural globalization and the novel. He has published studies on neoliberalism, late Victorian fiction, cosmopolitanism and East Asian cinema.

Felix Loi Ho Man received his BA and MPhil in Cultural Studies from the Chinese University of Hong Kong. He is currently a research assistant in the Department of Literature and Cultural Studies and sessional lecturer in the Department of Curriculum and Instruction, Hong Kong Institute of Education.

D. N. Rodowick is The Glen A. Lloyd Distinguished Service Professor in the Division of the Humanities at the University of Chicago. His research interests include aesthetics and the philosophy of art, the history of film theory, philosophical approaches to contemporary art and culture, and the impact of new technologies on contemporary society. He is the author of seven books and an edited collection including *Philosophy's Artful Conversation* (2015), *Elegy for Theory* (2014) and *The Virtual Life of Film* (2007). Rodowick is also a curator, and an award-winning experimental filmmaker and video artist. With Victor Burgin, he was recently awarded a Mellon Collaborative Fellowship at the Richard and Mary L. Gray Center for Arts and Inquiry, University of Chicago, to produce a new video work, *Overlay*.

Eivind Røssaak is Associate Professor in Film and Media Studies at the Department of Research and Collections, National Library of Norway, Oslo. He has been a visiting associate professor at the Cinema and Media Studies Department, University of Chicago and Fellow at the Cinema Department, New York University and USC, Los Angeles. His books include: *Memories in Motion* (forthcoming), *Between Stillness and Motion: Film, Photography, Algorithms* (editor, 2011), *The Archive in Motion* (editor, 2010), *The Still/Moving Image: Cinema and the Arts* (2010), *Selviakttakelse: En tendens i kunst og litteratur* (On Observations of the Self in Art and Literature, 2005), *Kyssing og slåssing* (Four Chapters on Film, 2004), *Sic: Fra litteraturens randsone* (Mapping the Margins of Art, 2001), and *Det postmoderne og de intellektuelle* (1998).

Wong Kin-Yuen is Professor, Head of the Department of English Language and Literature and Director, Technoscience Culture Research and Development Center, Hong Kong Shue Yan University. His research interests are in technoscience culture, ecology and environmental ethics, science fiction, urban studies and consumer culture and he has written widely in these areas in Chinese and English. He has co-edited with Gary Westfahl and Amy Chan Kit-Sze *Science Fiction and the Prediction of the Future* (2011) and *World Weavers: Globalization, Science Fiction, and the Cybernetic Revolution* (2005).

Introduction
Experiencing Wonder: Technovisuality and Cultural Re-enchantment

Helen Grace

> If we want to give meaning any depth, we have to permit our glance to travel over the surface, and thus to reconstruct abstracted dimensions.[1]

The chapters in this book arise from an interdisciplinary project entitled *Technovisuality and Cultural Re-enchantment*, initiated in Hong Kong in 2008 and bringing together established and young scholars from art history, literature, film studies, philosophy and technocultural studies, from the UK and Europe, Canada, the US, Australia, from Taiwan, Japan, Hong Kong and Mainland China. The project set out to find fresh insights beyond the exhaustion of certain debates about visuality and the image, within what appears to be a general crisis of nature – and of the economy. We wanted to tackle these issues from an intercultural perspective so that we could be open to the energy that arises in the unpredictable moments of exchange between different frameworks, all seeking answers to contemporary questions.

When we began the project, we were ourselves captured by the word we had coined to describe the phenomenon we wanted to explore. 'Technovisuality' seemed to invoke for us a broad sweep of possibilities in contemporary life: cinematography's magical world and the camera's eye; the enchantment of/in mediated visualization; the history and development of digital images and the way a nuanced relationship is established between the human and the nonhuman, technoscience and philosophy; imagescape as a new ecology; online gaming as a spectacular showcase of cultural enchantment; classical Eastern philosophy and contemporary theories of visualization within an interdisciplinary and intercultural framework; science fiction and film as artefacts of cultural re-enchantment; architecture and virtuality – or virtual life in general.

In coining the word 'technovisuality', we wanted to explore the paradoxical space between technoscience's relatively unquestioned visualism and an ambivalence directed to the visual in contemporary cultural criticism and technocultural studies. This ambivalence sometimes amounts to a decidedly anti-visualist stance; for example, the former is explored in the work of a number of writers,[2] and the latter is outlined and reflected in critiques such as those by Jay[3] and Levin.[4] We were also aware of a desire to move beyond a sense of disenchantment with the world that is a characteristic of political discourse, allowing only a negative – and defeated – relation to daily life and struggles.

This negativity is not new; Sean Cubitt reminds us that disenchantment was already a Romantic attitude by the beginning of the Industrial Revolution, and a recent exhibition in China, entitled 'Disenchantment of Chinese Imagination',[5] and recent work in eco-criticism and Chinese cinema,[6] remind us that disenchantment does not belong to the negative dialectics of European thought alone – and there is a great deal to be pessimistic about. However, our aim was to enable fresh ways of thinking the world beyond the exhaustion of some familiar approaches.

In his essay 'The Future of the Image', Jacques Rancière writes of the contemporary state of the image: we are told on the one hand, that there is no longer any reality but only images, and on the other, that there are no longer images but only 'a reality representing itself to itself'. This impasse gives way in turn to a vicious circle or dead-end: 'If there is now nothing but images, there is nothing other than the image. And if there is nothing but the image, the very notion of the image becomes devoid of content.'[7] Philosophically this situation represents a state of exhaustion, and so, to think more productively of the image and of visuality as a space of potential, beyond exhaustion and disenchantment, we need to turn elsewhere.

One way forward might be to look more closely at the concept of the image; the distinction which Hans Belting[8] makes between visuality and pictoriality is helpful here, because it hinges upon a relatively unacknowledged legacy of Renaissance visual thought – that of Arab optics.

Alhazen's optics focused on light's linearity, but Renaissance perspective connects the movement of light to the eye, to the body, to the depiction of the world, producing icons and idols, the mimetic and the pictorial.

Abstraction – as opposed to depiction – in art is concerned with the possibility of communication beyond the limits of analogy and likeness, so it is helpful to distinguish visual and pictorial theory. We can say that *visual* theory is concerned with the characteristics of light; it is more conceptual, concerned with abstractions – lines, geometry, pattern, numbers, mathematics. *Pictorial* theory, on the other hand, is concerned with form, shape, outline – the results of light's characteristics as it plays on surface and is perceived by the eye; it involves a body to body interaction – and the appropriation of scientific theory for artistic purpose. The concept of the image may thus act as a bridge between visual and pictorial theory, inviting us to extend the insights of art history, in order to address the 'question of technology'.[9]

In thinking through these issues of abstraction and expression, it is tempting to agree with Friedrich Kittler's (2006) claim that 'we need to unfold the essential unity of writing, number, image and tone'.[10] If different signifying or notational systems have produced their own worlds, separate from one another – writing, mathematics, visual art, music (as if they are different cultures) – it has become more urgent to find ways in which these worlds can speak to each other. To explore the directions such conversations might take, we want to mention here the work of Vilém Flusser, a cybernetic thinker as well as a poetic thinker, someone who takes on the question of the technological and applies imaginative thought to it, in such a way as to suggest possibilities of re-enchantment beyond the limits of Weber's sense of the disenchantment of the world under the impact of scientific rationality.[11] Flusser's *Towards a Philosophy of Photography* is remarkably prescient in foreseeing the impact of what we are here calling 'technovisuality' – an extension of Flusser's concept of the 'technical image'.

According to Vilém Flusser, surfaces have become more important to us than lines in daily life, so that pictures, in a sense (and we will explore the limits of this sense), have become more important than words. This claim seems too simple a statement – and as we read through these essays on technovisuality, we will begin to see its depth. The city is certainly a place in which surfaces proliferate: from the vast planes of new architecture and advertising, to the huge images projected on animated screens, demanding our attention. We are surrounded by teletext messages (words, numbers): moving inexorably from right to left on LED displays everywhere, signalling news, market prices, weather; moving images on television screens, even on buses and trains; the tiny images of the mobile phone screen or games consoles. And the bodies of citizens and non-citizens are also screens, attracting our attention, sometimes projecting counter-images – animated versions and variants of the fashion or celebrity images that capture our gaze in our movement through the space of the city.

If we are teachers, we complain all the time that our students do not read the wonderful texts we so carefully select for them, though they have an extraordinary capacity to process images and information flows, absorbing complex concepts with a lightness that the weight of our thought may sometimes envy.

For Flusser, this development from line to surface does not at all represent a simple shift from the predominance of the word to the predominance of the image, but involves a spiral movement – from image (or imaginal thought) to concept (conceptual thought) to image (a new form of both imaginal and conceptual thought), suggesting 'a being-in-the-world so radically new that its manifold impacts are difficult to grasp'.[12] He associates this new mode of being with the invention of the 'technical image' (the image produced by an apparatus – camera, computer, and so on). The 'technical image' forms a 'third-degree abstraction', beyond the first-degree abstraction of a traditional image (let's say, a cave painting), that is itself abstracted from the concrete world; the technical image is the indirect result of second-level abstraction (such as applied scientific texts) – a product of technology.

Of course, writing is also technology, but in Flusser's account, linear writing represents the moment when the circular time of magic is transcoded into the linear time of history. So it is the 'technical image' that is the basis of a generalized form of seeing we are calling 'technovisuality', a form that is machinic as well as organic.

Flusser does not claim privilege for the technical image, but sees a limitation of the imagistic world:

> Man forgets that he produces images in order to find his way in the world; he now tries to find his way in images. He no longer deciphers his own images, but lives in their function. Imagination has become hallucination.[13]

There is a shadow here of Plato's denigration of the image in the simile of the cave, in this sense of the deception of the image, that may be quite familiar to us. In another more fearful commentary on the image, Julia Kristeva identified a new 'malady of the soul' associated with the proliferation of images. Mistrustful of the sheer mass of visual overstimulation (she sees the image as 'the new opium of the people'), she is fearful of the way that image proliferation obliterates psychic space, resulting, for her, in all the problems of the world – 'ulcers, cancers, eczemas, and so on. Acts of violence such as terrorism, vandalism, torching cars in the suburbs … drugs.' She worries that 'conflict is drowned out in the experience of an oceanic pleasure that disconnects individuals both from themselves and from others'.[14]

In proposing the idea of technovisuality, we are less inclined to have a catastrophic opinion of visuality, and we would suggest that perhaps too much power is attributed to the image in such accounts. A key feature of image proliferation is that the vast number of images and surfaces that surround us do not represent the increasing power of the image, but its opposite. Each image screams for attention, but no image, however powerful, can hold our gaze for long – this is a shift in the supposed 'power' of the image. We are engaged in a constant process of self-imaging alongside – and partly countering – constant processes of external surveillance; databanks can track us, and ostensibly keep us in their sights, but data-loss and 'bit-rot' also occur. Though we do not wish to deny the realities of contemporary 'control societies',[15] we seek gaps and ruptures in the tightly-controlled borders of totalizing power, trying to pass under the radar. Although, as good subjects and citizens, we may be ready to take up the task of self-surveillance under a panoptic gaze, the history of panopticism as imperial vision is equally a history of resistance and evasion – recall a key principle of a Foucauldian model of power.

In fact, the image has never been more unstable, so we seem to be in an era of the hyper-inflation of the image. Eras of hyper-inflation involve massive devaluations of currency and people,[16] and in a world in which the image has become currency, it too has suffered the fate of devaluation, the result of having been too heavily geared. In any case, the ever-presence of the image in contemporary visual space is not the result of an aesthetic move, but of a technological one; the graphical user interface, as an *engineered* development, began to replace command-line interfaces from the middle of the 1960s, leading to the ubiquity of visual interfaces and 'user-friendliness'.[17] But these are now being displaced by increasingly affective interfaces, based on touch – for example, as the iPhone and touchscreens further displace the power of sight – or they are becoming entirely instrumentalized and machinized in possibilities, such as 'Eye Scroll' and 'Eye Pause'.[18]

We might remember Groupe Dziga Vertov's slogan on a blackboard in *Le Vent d'Est* (1970): 'Ce n'est pas un image juste, c'est juste an image'. There is thus a pragmatism of the image in Godard's comment – and his work – in which the limitations of *le mot juste* are partially transferred to the image. It then becomes not so much a question of the search for the 'just image' but rather, the simple truth that each picture is 'just an image'.[19]

Within the more speculative discourse of technovisuality, the visual is not being enlarged but rather reduced – eclipsed, we might say – in thought and expression. If a critical view problematized vision as being a philosophically privileged sense,[20] we argue that it has now become merely an entry point for a consideration of the other senses, especially in the ways in which we are immersed in and by new media technologies. Vision and visuality are therefore displaced from the eyes and from opticality, becoming instead embodied; the senses and the mind coalesce, each helping the other – the body sees, hears, feels in a more generalized aesthesis. So we might more properly speak of the 'postvisual' as a space of operation of a new ethics.

Rey Chow introduces this possibility of an 'ethics of postvisuality' in writing of Zhang Yimou's *Happy Times* (幸福时光 *Xìngfú Shíguāng*, 2000), making the point that 'the ethics to which "high" theory has held itself is often inextricable from a particular negative relation to the visual as such'.[21] Hers is a useful relocation of the place of vision within the widespread critique and denunciation of visuality in recent thought and an emphasis on the importance of other senses. Philosophically this is registered in the Levinasian emphasis on touch,[22] and it is also found in new media theory's emphasis on affect[23] and in the sound theory argument that it is auditory experience that is capable of providing a better register of experience in general.[24] In other words, the denunciation of vision has resulted in a general claim on behalf of other senses (or rather, their proponents) to the privileged relation to truth, which sight was once thought to occupy.

Let us then consider the spheres of operation of technovisuality in a general way. We can agree that daily life is increasingly mediated by technology, and remorseless visual stimuli in everyday technovisual forms have now become the very incarnation of what it means to be human. While technovisuality points to the visual as object and site of social interaction, it is also very much about embodiment and how we transform information and knowledge ('infoledge') into material and aesthetic forms. Bergson[25] thinks of the body itself as an image among other images, hence the theory of perception as affect.[26] Such processes of technical and biological symbiosis entail cultural re-enchantment occurring where nature and nurture overlap, where becomings – through circuits of intensity – occur between humans and machines, humans and nonhumans.

Think of cinematography, digital images in all media, video games, scientific data visualization, info-aesthetics, virtual environments (even utopian architectural projections in real-estate development proposals) – all could be summed up as manifestations of what in film theory[27] and philosophy[28] has been called the Figural. These elaborations of the Figural in philosophy and film theory build on Lyotard,[29] responding to new hieroglyphic and ideographic forms of textuality under the impact of new media, encapsulating an epoch of formal hybridity that breaks markedly with the concept of formal purity in modernism.

Technovisuality programmes more and more intelligence into the very fabric of a new ecology of wonders. In a return to magical thinking for an age beyond belief, images have become animated and are now thought to be able to think and have desires themselves.[30]

Within the spaces of visuality, cultural re-enchantment also points to eco-consciousness, warning us of our ecological violence, requiring the re-enchantment of nature by recovering a sense of the sacred as a means of survival. Here, Latour's network,[31] Prigogine and Stengers' affirmation of the fabulous in the nature of swerving matter,[32] the quantum enigma in new physics, might be drawn upon in leading us towards what Laszlo calls the re-enchantment of the cosmos.[33]

There is nothing unnatural about technology; like cyberpunk, technology is certainly within us. Hence technology does not have to limit itself to those 'technological devices' of which Heidegger is wary[34]. In a sense, visualization has always been technological since the beginning of time as a kind of primordial mechanism which has, according to Heidegger, not too much to do with 'the technological'. Here Oriental philosophy provides an alternative perspective of how cultural re-enchantment can be tied to technovision in a broad sense.

The chapters in this volume endeavour to draw the readers' attention to the fact that modern technovisual forms can work both ways. Either they tend to impinge on our daily life through cinematography, digital images in all media and video games, so much so that we are numbed to such a flooding of signs, or they could take the form of, say, scientific data visualization, virtual environments or enhancement of atoms or cells, to the extent of never failing to amaze us in our social interaction with them. However, the kind of cultural re-enchantment most of the essays in this collection have in mind concerns the ways in which technovisuality can work wonders, not so much fascinating us through special effects (such as 3D movies) as reminding us how we have drifted away from any sense of wonder, or worse, how we have kept wonder away from mental, social and environmental registers: the 'three ecologies' as Guattari has it.

Whether it is the camera screen as reflection of life through a machine, or cosmic telescopic/microscopic visual devices in quantum physics and medical imaging, we are sure that technovisuality has inherent impacts on our eventful sense of being enchanted. The task before us, therefore, is to rediscover a sense of sublimity by re-enchanting both the kind of techno-visuals of our mediated experience of the world *and* that world itself, the world from which we have all been estranged for too long. One of the ways we can move forward is to recognize afresh that technology does not have to be unnatural – and Deleuze reminds us that 'artifice is fully a part of nature'.[35] Such a discovery itself can already be seen as a continuum between technovisuality and cultural re-enchantment.

Everywhere we are immersed in video-telephonic mobile visuals, and the capacity of what and how much our body can feel is certainly a subject for research in what Luciana Parisi calls a 'technoecology'.[36] For Deleuze and Guattari, a machinic involution has been at work to bring a new ecology of symbiosis between biology/body and cybernetic/new media. The new media have evolved, by the way, from Kittler's new media as information systems which themselves 'are faster than human perception' to the digital dubbing of the analogical resulting in a nuanced becoming of micro and macro perceptions.[37] What Donna Haraway has suggested as the seamless bioinformatics among animals, humans and machines has become more imminent than ever.[38] Such a particle-wave folding of things 'behooves subjects to look at all matter from a different angle',[39] a kind of 'absolute deterritorialization' that affirms a new protoaesthetics 'from vertigo or dizziness to luminous life'.[40] We would agree, therefore, that it is on this level of machinic intricacies of the technovisual that a sense of cultural re-enchantment becomes inevitable.

* * * * *

If the concept of 'technovisuality' is loosely and imprecisely understood as a self-referencing emergent concept, it is certainly understood and experienced in technocultural studies by virtue of its ubiquitous presence in daily life. This presence is registered in all of the instances already cited – the widespread use of electronic images, games consoles, mobile phones, high end animation and computer graphics in entertainment, and the insistence of images in public and commercial space – and the blurring and convergence of the lines between public and private, between commercial 'for profit' and public 'not-for-profit'.[41] Additionally, newly emerging technoscience – cloning, biogenetic engineering, quantum mechanics – requires the 'evidence' of visuality, frequently in animated simulations, because of the sheer 'invisibility' of nano technologies. The lines between science and science fiction converge, and we come to terms with these transformations of the everyday largely through fiction, cinema, animation, computer mediated communication devices, interactive social networking and so on.

In the following chapters, three takes on these possibilities are considered. In the first section, entitled 'Wondering', we present a series of philosophical speculations on technovisuality and cultural re-enchantment; in the second, entitled 'Perceiving', we have grouped chapters on different ways of conceiving/perceiving worlds; and in the third, entitled 'Experiencing', a series of chapters examine specific instances/experiences of and encounters with technovisuality in contemporary spaces.

Wong Kin-Yuen focuses on Deleuze's action-image and time-image, only this time the two types of image are used to demonstrate a kind of primordial natural technovisuality to be found in Chinese eco-poetics. Wong comes to the conclusion that all those who are enchanted by modern-day technovisuality are people with a universal desire to 'climb up another flight of stairs', to raise themselves up onto another 'plateau' in a thousand ecologies, so as to have 'a thousand-mile eye' on the world, as a Tang poet has suggested. Thus for Wong, technovisuality should not be restricted to modernity and post-modernity but belongs within the long history of human imagination, that cannot be so easily periodized in terms of the modern, pre and post.

This is a perspective that comes from within Wong's long – and highly original – engagement with the sense of time's circularity, rather than its linearity, a perspective to be found more in Chinese than Western philosophy (though his work draws upon the resonances of this sense of time in recent Western philosophy as well). His 'experiment with new arguments' presents a detailed play on signs, meanings, concepts and percepts, reading/looking closely at a group of well-known Tang dynasty poems. We might note that Tang dynasty poetry has lasted longer than Tang dynasty science – or politics – and that poetry itself has this long and important history of imagining the world, prior to and alongside technological realizations of imagination. These concerns are part of a longer term project in which Wong is engaged – to re-imagine the 'eventfulness' of our relation with nature in different cultures and histories, within an overall eco-ethics.

D. N. Rodowick's chapter, 'The World, Time' sets out the ethical dimensions of our speculations, beginning with a question from Kracauer: 'how do movies solicit and sustain the possibility of ethical thought?' In answering, he cuts through Spinoza's univocity of Being, Nietzsche's eternal return, all the while basing his discussion on Deleuze's two Cinema books. The thesis of this chapter highlights a deep ethical thinking: 'the problem of choosing a mode of existence defined by the possibility of choice'. By drawing upon classical and modernist films as examples, Rodowick delineates a number of affect-images, locating them in terms of the movement-image (sensory movement or sequential action) and the time-image (the force of the virtual but direct time), respectively. Without using the word 'enchantment', Rodowick in actual fact discovers a sense of wonder as 'the subtle way out' towards a shock to thought – and even the un-thought – bringing together world, life, choice and force, under the frame of a Deleuzian ethics expressed through cinema.

In her chapter, Veronica Hollinger extends this idea in considering the ways that cyberfiction re-enchants the human subject itself, imagining a technological transcendence of the human – or rather, the imagination of the human within a technocultural landscape as a kind of 'second nature', beginning with the literary invention of cyberspace in William Gibson's 1984 *Neuromancer*.

For Hollinger, the 'technologies of enchantment' in science fiction start with narratives on how we are 'trapped in the scene of the screen' as an 'absence', reflecting a lack of enchantment of 'authentic presence'. However, Hollinger duly points out that science fiction is a unique genre that harbours a 'complex interplay of enchantment and disenchantment' yielding, as always, a 'sense of wonder' in the midst of, say, the technovisuality of cyberspace. Finally, Hollinger refers to newly emerging 'singularity fiction' to execute an expansion of the concept of 'technovisual re-enchantment of the future' by highlighting how post-human subjects are at home in a vast, intelligent as well as 'natural' universe. Here the motto is 'we will be different', and, having co-evolved with technovisuality, we as human subjects, have become a figure of wonder – re-enchantment ourselves.

In considering the birth of wonder in the database economy, Sean Cubitt begins by suggesting that we need to understand how the world has become disenchanted before we can understand how we might re-enchant it. In shifting from epistemology to ontology, he explores the possibility of escaping the limits of the present in order to confront it in its potentiality, via a consideration of three examples from cinema and new media. Cubitt traces the history of epistemology in the West by naming three of its stages: the medieval secret, the professionalism of science and the private database, the last which he regards as an 'emergent hegemony'.

By focusing on the triadic structure of human/nature/technology developed in his earlier work, Cubitt discusses three recent screen works, sharing with us his elegant, subtle and perceptual reading of them. The purpose is to show how a sense of wonder can be created by technovisuality, and this succeeds in turning epistemology towards ontology, in re-engaging *poesis* and *techne*, and also in temporalizing space. Here Cubitt emphasizes a perceiving experience which registers movement, force and rhythm towards a 'synthetic enchantment' – an event in Deleuze's sense. This opens up a kind of public space of the virtual and the becoming, or in Cubitt's words, a world of 'what is not the case'. Such a re-enchanting process brings together the perceiver and the perceived in a multiplicity that multiplies within the infinite speed of soundscape and 'machinic rhythms', in an active synthesis of the new and emergent network culture in which we live.

In the first chapter of Section 2, Eivind Røssaak discusses the emergence of what he calls the 'performative archive' in the context of a proliferation of alternative archives. So, we are in an era of transformations of the archive and archival strategies in art and philosophy that radically shift the structure and function of classical archives. Whereas the authority of the archive was originally based on some principle of neutrality (such as chronology), the performative archive involves a more open playful or ambiguous relation to the principle of selection. From Foucault's sense of the archive as 'the border of time that surrounds our presence' to Kittler's new *aufschreibesysteme* (literally, 'system for inscription' and inaccurately translated as 'discourse network'), the archive's mutation suggests a new 'reign of the real' in the recirculation – remixing – of fragments of the everyday. But the limit point of the new accumulations of data revolves around a dream – that of total storage, a dream that, in any case, was always inherent in the idea of the archive.

Amy Chan Kit-Sze presents a reading of Tibetan Buddhist mandalas as visualizations of the universe, drawing upon Deleuze's arguments about thinking in and through the figural in *What is Philosophy*? She refers to quantum physics' more recent speculations on the nature of the universe as a cyclical concept, requiring an endless sequence of 'Big Bangs' and 'Big Crunches' – centrifugal and centripetal forces – that parallel the cosmologies of religions.

Leading on from this chapter, Nevena Ivanova continues these concerns with technovisual enchantment in her chapter on the recent video installations of Bill Viola and his creation of what she calls the 'meditation-image'. Such images require active transformation in the viewer's consciousness; they are not merely formed as a property of the video image, but might be regarded as a special type of affection-image viewed in extremely slow motion. It is this engagement of perception, requiring the immersion of the audience, that is emblematic of the type of technovisuality and cultural re-enchantment that the project as a whole discussed and debated.

In Section 3, the three chapters engage more directly with the *experience* of technovisuality, in embodied encounters with the city and with the biopolitical impacts of rapid economic restructure in East Asia, as reflected in cinema.

Chris Berry and Janet Harbord begin their discussion of a research project on public screens in London, Cairo and Shanghai by referring to Rem Koolhaas's definition of the Generic City as that which is left over after sections of urban life have crossed over into cyberspace. In presenting an account of their London-based research here, the focus on the use of advanced screen technologies in public space – a relatively neglected field in 'screen studies' – and they consider how the experience of location itself is increasingly imbricated in virtual worlds. Part Situationist-*dérive*, part speculation on the nature of contemporary urban experience, their focus is on three areas: archive, surveillance and attention in their very nuanced reading of a number of London sites.

Continuing some of these concerns into the space of Hong Kong, Felix Loi proposes a reconsideration of consumption via an investigation of visual experience and, in particular, the special kind of technovisuality that is a key aspect of media globalization and global consumption. His focus on the 'domestication' of shopping malls in Hong Kong explores the experience of a phenomenon designed for tourists but appropriated by locals, because of its inescapability and the peculiarity of public/private development via the operations of the MTR Corporation's simultaneous infrastructure and property development. He compares the specific intensification of consumption in shopping malls with the very different consumption experience of an even greater intensity of flows in the streets of Mong Kok. He argues that the open streets of Mong Kok present a space for greater public engagement, where an organic transience presents a dynamic resistance to the globalized spectacle of shopping malls selling luxury goods.

Michelle Huang and Chi-she Li draw upon the model of the *bildungsroman* (as technological form). They note the rise of the novel of individual formation within the massive transformation of Europe in the nineteenth century as a space within which the experience of change and crisis inherent to modernity is registered. Heroes and heroines of *bildung* narratives develop the mental strength to overcome the challenges of the external world, allowing for the growth and adaptation of subjects to the social transformations in which they are immersed. In different experiences of modernity – and their examples are in the analyses of contemporary cinema in Hong Kong, Taiwan and Japan – there is another side to this in the production of uselessness, of dropouts, the unemployed for whom the myth of progress has no traction. This is perhaps less an image of enchantment, but it does make sense of certain very interesting features of youth cultures, especially in Asia, which have been relatively unexplored and do not make sense within cultural studies' models of 'sub-cultures'.

These three 'takes' on technovisuality and re-enchantment – speculation ('wondering'), imagination ('perceiving') and the physical encounter with technologies and their effects ('experiencing') – allow us to speculate on the impacts of the technical image as mediated relation to the world, reminding us too that 'the world is more than human projection or construction, more than the categories we impose on it, more than the meanings we impute to it'.[42]

Acknowledgments

Brautigan, Richard. From *All Watched Over by Machines of Loving Grace* by Richard Brautigan. Copyright © 1967 by Richard Brautigan. Reprinted with the permission of the estate of Richard Brautigan, all rights reserved.

D. N. Rodowick's 'The World, Time' was first published in Rodowick (ed.), *Afterimages of Gilles Deleuze's Film Philosophy*, Minneapolis: University of Minnesota Press, 2010, and is used with permission.

Notes

1 V. Flusser, 2000, *Towards a Philosophy of Photography*, London: Reaktion Books, 6.

2 See, D. Ihde, 1979, *Technics and Praxis*, Dordrecht, Holland and Boston: D. Reidel Publishing Company; D. Ihde, 1999, *Expanding Hermeneutics: Visualism in Science*, Evanston, IL: Northwestern University Press; P. L. Galison, 1997, *Image and Logic: A Material Culture of Microphysics*, Chicago: University of Chicago Press; L. Daston and P. Galison, 2010, *Objectivity,* New York: Zone Books; L. Cartwright, 1995, *Screening the Body: Tracing Medicine's Visual Culture,* Minneapolis: University of Minnesota Press.

3 M. Jay, 1993, *Downcast Eyes: The Denigration of Vision in Twentieth-Century French Philosophy*, Oakland, CA: University of California Press.

4 D. M. Levin (ed.), 2003, *Modernity: the Hegemony of Vision*, New York: University of California Press.

5 The exhibition was the first in a series of themed shows as part of the 4th Guangzhou Triennial 2012. For further detail, see the Guangzhou Museum of Art Triennial website, www.gdmoa.org/zhanlan/threeyear/Thefourth/23/en/Mediareports/22140.jsp accessed 31 March 2012.

6 S. H. Lu and M. Jiayan (eds), 2009, *Chinese Ecocinema in the Age of Environmental Challenge*, Hong Kong: Hong Kong University Press.

7 J. Rancière, 2007, *The Future of the Image*, London: Verso, 1.

8 H. Belting, 2008, 'Arab mathematics and Renaissance Western Art', *European Review*, 16:2, 183–90.

9 For a summary of the significance of what has been called the 'pictorial turn' or the 'iconic turn' and the concept of 'image science' in freshly approaching the nature of the image, see 2009 special issue of *Culture, Theory and Critique*, 50, 2–3. See, in particular, contributions by M. Jay, L. Liu and J. Rancière; for an excellent account of the development of 'image science', see G. Boehm and W. J. T. Mitchell, 2009, 'Pictorial versus iconic turn: Two letters' in *Culture, Theory and Critique*, 50:2–3, 103–121. Mitchell was a key figure for us in our Technovisuality event in Hong Kong in November 2008, providing the opening keynote ('Clonophobia: The techno-magic of the biocybernetic image') in a small moment of technological 'wonder' as everyday 'telepresence'. 'Teleconferences' are of course unremarkable, but we choose to regard the phenomenon here with a small sense of thrill and triumph, that links worked across space and time. It can also be noted that telepresence has the effect of converting participants into images, framed in mid-shot, rendered in iconic fashion, like the images they are themselves discussing. Although the frame composition of these encounters of telepresence may owe its currency to television, the framing conventions are somewhat older than this, drawing upon the histories of painting, sculpture and cinema, now extended into new media and animation. And so we find ourselves in the expression of thought itself, converted into animated images, transcending the very limitations of the image that Plato had conceived.

10 F. Kittler, 2006, 'Number and numeral' in *Theory, Culture & Society*, London, Thousand Oaks and New Delhi: Sage, 23: 7–8, 51–61.

11 M. Weber, 2009, *From Max Weber: Essays in Sociology*, Abingdon: Routledge.

12 V. Flusser, 2002, 'Line and surface' in A. Ströhl (ed.), *Writings*, Minneapolis: University of Minnesota Press.

13 Flusser, *Towards a Philosophy of Photography*, 7.

14 J. Kristeva, 2003, 'The future of a defeat: Interview with Arnaud Spire', *Parallax*, 9: 2, 21–6; first published *L'Humanite´* 2 July 2001.

15 G. Deleuze, 1992, 'Postscript on societies of control', *October* 59, Winter, 3–7.

16 E. Canetti, 1984, *Crowds and Power* New York: Farrar, Straus and Giroux.

17 S. Pold, 2005, 'Interface realisms: The interface as aesthetic form', *Postmodern Culture* 15:2, January.

18 In 2013, Samsung announced the addition of new 'smart scroll' and 'smart pause' software in its Galaxy S IV mobile phone that would allow eye control of screen scrolling, enabled by infra-red sensors tracking eye movement. Some months earlier it filed to trademark the name 'Eye Scroll' in Europe as well as 'Eye Pause', a technique that automatically

pauses video when the user's attention shifts from the screen. Both techniques suggest the increasing level of absorption of the body itself into machinic processes, as the eye in this case replaces the finger, and becomes itself a pause button.

19 H. Hartley, 1994, 'In images we trust: Hal Hartley interviews Jean-Luc Godard', *Filmmaker* 3:1, Autumn, 14, 16–18, 55–6.

20 Levin, 2003, *Modernity and the Hegemony of Vision.*

21 R. Chow, 2004, 'Towards an ethics of postvisuality: Some thoughts on the recent work of Zhang Yimou', *Poetics Today*, 25:4, 673–88.

22 C. Vasseleu, 1998, *Textures of Light: Vision and Touch in Irigaray, Levinas and Merleau-Ponty*, Abingdon: Routledge.

23 M. Hansen, 2006, *New Philosophy for New Media*, Cambridge, MA: MIT Press.

24 D. Kahn, 1999, *Noise, Water, Meat: A History of Sound in the Arts*, Cambridge, MA: MIT Press.

25 H. Bergson, 1991, *Matter and Memory* (1896), New York: Zone Books.

26 M. Hansen, 2000, *Embodying Technesis: Technology beyond Writing*, Ann Arbor: University of Michigan Press.

27 N. Brenez, 1998, *De la figure en géneral et du corps en particulier: L'invention figurative au cinema*, Paris: De Boeck Universite.

28 D. N. Rodowick, 2001, *Reading the Figural, or, Philosophy after the New Media*, Durham, NC: Duke University Press.

29 J. F. Lyotard, 1971, *Discours, Figure*, Paris: Klincksieck.

30 W. J. T. Mitchell, 2005, *What Do Pictures Want? The Lives and Loves of Images*, Chicago: University of Chicago Press.

31 B. Latour, 2005, *Reassembling the Social: An Introduction to Actor-Network-Theory*, Oxford: Oxford University Press.

32 I. Prigogine.and I. Stengers, 1984, *Order out of Chaos: Man's New Dialogue with Nature*, New York: Bantam.

33 E. Laszlo, 2006, *Science and the Re-enchantment of the Cosmos: The Rise of the Integral Vision of Reality*, Rochester, VT: Inner Traditions; E. Laszlo, 2006, *Science and the Akashic Field: An Integral Theory of Everything*, Rochester, VT: Inner Traditions.

34 M. Heidegger, 1977, *The Question Concerning Technology and Other Essays*, New York: Harper Row.

35 G. Deleuze, 1988, *Spinoza: Practical Philosophy*, San Francisco: City Lights Books, 124.

36 L. Parisi, 2009, 'Technoecologies of sensation' in B. Herzogenrath (ed.), *Deleuze/Guattari & Ecology*, London: Palgrave Macmillan, 182–99.

37 A. Murphie, 2002, 'Putting the virtual back into VR' in B. Massumi (ed.), *A Shock to Thought: Expression after Deleuze and Guattari*, New York and London: Routledge, 188–214.

38 D. Haraway, 1991, 'A cyborg manifesto: Science, technology, and socialist-feminism in the late twentieth century' in *Simians, Cyborgs and Women: The Reinvention of Nature,* New York: Routledge, 149–81.

39 G. Deleuze, 1993, *The Fold: Leibniz and the Baroque*, foreword and trans. T. Conley, Minneapolis: University of Minnesota Press, xiv.

40 Ibid. 92.

41 In 2008 in Hong Kong, a dispute arose over the use of public space when it became known that a property management company had been renting a part of the Times Square piazza – designated public space in rental agreements – to Starbucks and collecting rent over a number of years. See C. Loh, 2008, 'Reclaiming the city' *South China Morning Post,* 10 April; P. Hui, 2008, 'Luxury estate owners demand "public" podium back' *South China Morning Post,* 14 April; H. Wu, 2008, 'Developers back review of policies covering public space', *South China Morning Post*, 23 April; N. Gentle, 2008, 'Mall sued over public space rents', *South China Morning Post,* 18 June A1; O. Wong, and J. Ng, 2008, 'Bid to resolve conflict over open space', *South China Morning Post*, 27 August. For more discussion of this, see Loi Ho Man in this collection.

42 Jay, 'Magical Nominalism: Photography and the Re-enchantment of the World' in *Culture, Theory and Critique,* 50: 2–3 (special issue), 165–83: 181.

Section 1

Wondering

1

The 'Thousand-Mile Eye' and the Image-less Elephant: Imag(in)ing the Universe in Eco-poetics and Philosophy

Wong Kin Yuen

The concept of 'technovisuality' does not have to be limited to modern times. Yes, all of us must have been fascinated by the wonders that modern technology such as cinema can do to our way of seeing things. So a sense of 'cultural re-enchantment' should already be in place, if we care to look back at the very virtuality embedded in the history of human perception, and how it has always been made possible by technology itself. This chapter, therefore, proposes to reconstruct a 'plateau' on which the classical 'seeing', as attested to by Chinese landscape poetry, can be 'precessed'[1] together with the contemporary philosophy of cinema, and particularly with Deleuze's movement-image and time-image in his two cinema books.

This chapter argues that the classical Chinese concepts of technology, perception, imaging and so on, all have characteristics pertaining to a cinematic process, which can in turn contribute to our further understanding of Deleuze's philosophical cinema.[2] Deleuze's theory of the cinema can also be read into his ecoethics, which can be further substantiated by its counterpart in a Chinese cinematic poetics of nature that I will outline here. By 'highlighting' (here as an image of physics, image and thought) such an odd coupling – indeed, a monstrous cross-breed[3] – between, say, the Daoist and Buddhist philosophy of the natural wilderness, on the one side, and Deleuzian becomings, primordial difference, intensive science, territory-milieu, affects and so on, on the other, my ultimate aim in this chapter is to extract an ecological problematic 'field' of certain 'transversal communication' between the human and the nonhuman.

We may start by remarking that there is nothing unnatural about technology, or we can say that there is actually such a thing as 'natural technology' in the world; as Deleuze writes, 'Artifice is fully a part of Nature.'[4] To a certain extent, visuality has always been technological since the beginning of time, if we take technology to mean primordially 'machinic' in the Deleuzian sense. Visuality is possible only by a process in which the mechanism of perception, body, object, the Bergsonian image, light and movement all have a part to play within the perceptual 'field'. From Bergson, Deleuze thinks of cinema as a machine that can make use of the matter of the brain (memory) to construct a better brain, to 'make a machine to triumph over mechanism'.[5] In terms of modern science, the 'natural link' between vision and light can be seen as a source of amazement; we can be re-enchanted by the enigma of quantum physics where the visual field becomes an ocean of forces, particles, molecules, action at a distance, non-locality and wave-function.

This enigma has now succeeded in reminding us of the existence of 'natural technology' which has always been there. After all, the whole of Deleuze's geophilosophy focuses on 'machinic thinking', since his 'ethics aims to vitalize technology' in order 'to open up and potentialize science and technology to the internal evolution of matter all the way down'.[6] It would be too linear for us to say that humans invented tools and language, since it is in fact a kind of non-linear, 'nuanced' dynamics that has been at work. After Heidegger delineated it as the essence that has a revealing power of things, technology is now taken as something that is not on a par with 'the technological'. It may not be life itself, but it can be considered at least as 'both an extension of life's potential – so that writing is an extension of the brain – and a transformation of life'.[7] After all, 'the mechanic is the cosmic artisan: a homemade atomic bomb'.[8]

As for the Chinese *ji* 機, technology seems to be the fundamental technicity of all things. Signifying the very Dao of life, its intensive and obscure 'distribution' of cosmic energy and life-forces could well be something like Deleuze's desiring machine. In both *Zhuangzi* 《莊子》 and *Liezi* 《列子》, we already have the phrase 'species have *ji*' 種有幾,

designating a process of biological transmutations with technicity, hence the famous phrase, 'the myriad things all come out of *ji* and all go into *ji*'. This is followed by the *Confucian Commentary* (*Xici Zhuan*) 《繫辭傳》 of *Yijing* 《易經》 where we see 'by *ji*, it's the minuteness of motion' 幾者，動之微; and then 'knowing *ji*, what a wonder'. 知幾其神乎! Besides *tianji* 天機 (heavenly technicity) and *shengji* 生機 (life machine), all have retained the element of *ji* as a cosmic pattern or tendency as the primordial mechanism of life-giving force, not unlike the Deleuzian sense of cutting and imaging. Here, for both the Chinese *ji* and Deleuze's desiring machine, technology is 'any repeatable or regular practice that maximizes the efficiency of life itself'.[9]

The Chinese *ji*, scientifically speaking, is also a threshold, a 'critical' or 'tipping point' of phase transition in a complexity moment where order and disorder transform each other at the edge of chaos. It works parallel to the Chinese concepts of *shu* 數 、 (numbers), *li* 理 、 (reason), *qi* 氣 、 (breath), *xiang* 象 (phenomena); all of these reach back to the *xiang shu* 象數, expounded in *Yijing*. *Ji* can actually be the technoscientific approach to ecoethics within Dawkins' idea of memeplexes. *Ji* refers to those minute changes at a critical moment of divergences and bifurcations where living and nonliving things interact in what biologists call 'intercellular oscillations'.[10] By and large, *ji* can finally be considered to echo Deleuze's idea of 'dark-precursor', 'abstract machine', 'line of flight' and 'quasi-causal operator',[11] and Deleuze is clear on this when he says:

> This state of affairs is adequately expressed by certain physical concepts: *coupling* between heterogeneous systems, from which is derived an *internal resonance* within the system, and from which in turn is derived a *forced movement*, the amplitude of which exceeds that of the basic series themselves.[12]

Remember Fenollosa and Ezra Pound and their fascination with the Chinese ideographs? Along with the modernist poetics of imagism, Chinese poetry became known to the West for its being remarkably pictorial and imagistic, with spot-lighting, using super-positions on overlapping planes within one single character and among characters, arrayed say, between couplets. Remember the character *ma* 馬 (horse), and how the Orientalists were amazed by its dynamic rendering of both form and movement all at once? Well, they would have been truly enchanted, had they been informed about the visual perspicuity of the character *xiang* 象 here in our case. *Xiang* in ancient forms started out as vividly pictorial, as one looks at an elephant on the side. *Xiang* retains the montage cuts of imaging for both shape and action, forming the kind of cinematic technology that so inspired Eisenstein.[13]

Xiang xing 象形 (from elephant form to resembling form) as a term points back to itself as the origin of the ideograph, the kind of drawing or inscription approximating the myriad things. It expressively demonstrates the very act of constructing Chinese language in a technical way, on the one hand, and directly relates itself to the montage structure as imaging forth the universe and the emergence of thought, on the other, since things, lines and colours are the roots of thought. With its pictorial and sound systems, the Chinese ideogram should be qualified as Deleuze and Guattari's 'sign' in *A Thousand Plateaus*. Stephen Zepke points out:

> Signs do not, on this account, appear as signifiers or as representations, but as particular assemblages of material forces and functions stratified into relations of content and expression. This understanding of the sign is therefore ontological, because it puts the sign back into contact with the material and vital plane of consistency that constitutes it.[14]

When the Chinese think of thinking, they can go back to the process where a heart (心 xīn) is always fashioned as the base support of appearance or form (*xiang* 想).

But how did an elephant enlarge its reference to such a cosmic dimension? What was the path of transition for *xiang* to mean both an elephant as a noun, and as a verb, comparing, analogizing and symbolizing at a later stage? Finally, together with *ying* as *ying xiang* 影象, how are we going to turn this Chinese image of imaging, or rather image of becoming-image, into both movement-image and time-image as expounded by Deleuze? For answers, we would need to refer back to two different versions of the familiar proverb of the 'Four Blind Men Touching an Elephant'. This popular story unjustly puts down affects and percepts by assuming the reliability of affections and perceptions, by having the blind men volunteer their opinion on the 'whole' of an elephant too hastily. Ironically, this proverb unwittingly touches on the possibility that with things that get too big for human comprehension, imagination (virtual images) can come to perception's aid. In fact, in the classic *Han Feizi*《韓非子》,[15] it is noted that, since ancient people rarely got to see the living elephant, they had to resort to conjecture of its form from its dead bones, hence what they did in their imagining was from then on called '*xiang*' (translation mine). Two elephants put together, as it were, as in the expression *xiang xiang* 象象, now come to mean 'to describe by analogy the universal phenomena, the former being a verb and the latter, *hsien xiang* 現象, the noun, *phenomenon* itself. What is more interesting is that the analogical nature of such has been made clear by the concept of *xiang wǎng* 象罔 in *Zhuangzi* (shapeless or formless Image).[16] In this parable, the personified 'Knowing', 'Seeing' and 'Debating' all failed to retrieve the Dark Pearl (truth) that the Yellow Emperor had left behind. Finally, the Fuzzy Image was sent, achieving what the other greater powers had failed to do.

Here, the elephant-becoming-image is transformed into the Dao itself, becoming imperceptible as a zone of indetermination. As we will see later, this Daoist concept is close to Deleuze's simulacrum as an image of, say, human art, since as a copy, it 'harbors a positive power which denies the original and the copy, the model and reproduction'.[17] Rodowick explains that 'Simulacra are better understood as heterocosmic forces rather than utopian worlds. Between each measure of time there is an infinite movement, so many possible worlds and immanent modes of existence, that we must recover from time's passing.'[18]

Xiang Wǎng has been annotated by scholars as an image of tracelessness, *xiang* being not-nothing and *wǎng* not-something. This leads us to the lesser known Buddhist version of the 'Four Blind Men' recorded in *Nirvana Sutra*《涅槃經》. There, the King gathers a crowd and then asks each blind man: 'What does the elephant resemble?' Note here that the format of the question already moves away from positing any trace of entirety in reality. Then the King turns to the crowd: 'You good people, do you see? As those blind men did not speak of the whole elephant, it is also not true that they didn't speak of it; the different shapes of the elephant they described cannot be the whole of the elephant, nevertheless there's no elephant other than this one' (translation mine). The moral of this parable on the knowability of *xiang* is of course in line with Nagarjuna's philosophy of Emptiness and the Middle Way, which have 'an unmistakable resonance' with 'the new physics of quantum mechanics'.[19]

When Buddhism deals with perception, generally speaking, it has a fundamental doctrine of 'dependent arising, according to which phenomena arise in interdependence with each other'.[20] At this point of our discussion, it should not be too difficult for us to understand such a view of perception as a thought-image of time in a Deleuzian sense, since the mutually nuanced involvement or dependent arising between the environment and the perceptual consciousness takes place in time, or in duration as such, within a process of becoming-virtual. *Xiang Wāng* is also close to Bergson's matter which 'is an aggregate of images'. Bergson is against both realism and idealism, when he points out: 'And by "image" we mean a certain existence which is more than that which the idealist calls a *representation*, but less than that which the realist calls a *thing* – an existence placed halfway between the "thing" and the representation.[21]

With a basic understanding of the development of *ying-xiang* (from shadow-elephant to shapeless imaging), and also of how the Chinese 'machine', as natural technology, becomes a source of wonder, one would have guessed by now that the English word 'camera' is logically translated into Chinese either as *xiang ji* 像機 (photographing machine) or *shè ying ji* 攝影機 (image-gathering machine). *Ying* from the ancient Oracle-Bone inscription uses the radical (itself a separate character meaning environ/landscape) of a sun above a built structure, animated by three slanted lines of light (景因光而生 – Jǐng yīn guāng ér shēng) on the right. *Ying* is now used to mean 'shadow' or the act of imaging (with 電影 *dianying* – electric shadow – as cinema).[22] We have now established a link between the Chinese image-making process, through an analysis of the etymology of key characters directly relevant to perception, and Deleuze's philosophy of the cinema which emphasizes a folded precession, a matrix of action, movement, thought and time. It is therefore time to illustrate, through analysis of a few poems or poetic lines which are immediately about 'seeing' during a poet-landscape encounter, how a kind of cinematic technology comes to the fore, the kind that can be defined as 'an already established set of relations allowing for ongoing maximization of energy'.[23] My first example is Wang Zhihuan's 王之煥 (688–742) famous 'Ascending the Heron Tower' 登鸛鵲樓:

White sun along mountain end　白日依山盡
Yellow River into sea flows　黃河入海流

Wishing, Wanting to exhaust thousand mile eye (ken of sight) 欲窮千里目
Farther Up one (more) flight tower 更上一層樓

We can see the poet's attempt at a wider perspective, or a proximal comprehension of the inexhaustible otherness, and we also recognize the poet's effort, temporalizing the unbounded or unfathomable space through a montage of what Deleuze calls the movement-image.[24] Here in the Chinese poem, the temporal movement takes the form of Merleau-Ponty's 'synthesis of transition' (*synthese d'horizon*) through an intuitive reliance on bodily motility (the eye and then the whole body) or motor involvement. Following Heidegger's idea of the fore-structure of our being thrown into the world (*Geworfenheit*), Merleau-Ponty posits a primordial and general level or horizon of sedimented situation towards which every new creativity of experience perpetually strives. And also echoing Heidegger's 'ultimate concealedness', Merleau-Ponty's otherness and subjectivity are inexhaustibly vague, ambiguous and indeterminable, since a particular situation at present will never run out of its possibilities of future sedimentations. At the same time, every past sedimented situation can only have been a partial success in permeating the denseness of the subject's otherness, and every future sedimentation opens up other invitations to still further structuring. Thus Merleau-Ponty says:

> It is thus of the essence of the thing and of the world to present themselves as 'open', to send us beyond their determinate manifestations, to promise us always 'something else to see'. This is what is sometimes expressed by saying that the thing and the world are mysterious.[25]

In the first line of the poem, we are presented with a moment of time in which the sun is at the point of totally disappearing behind the mountain. Here, some entity which was at one point within the poet's field of visibility, now beyond his grasp, is receding into the background or horizontal field, becoming at best a potential goal of his attention. In other words, it has become more general, deterritorialized but ambiguous and unfulfilled; and since the horizontal being is 'a being by porosity', it is 'incapable of final determination but is nevertheless pregnant with the structures into which it can be resolved inexhaustibly'.[26] The character *jin* 盡 (end), by the way, functions as a kind of blank (*liu-bei*) 留白, or point of indeterminacy, which is characteristic in many Chinese landscape paintings, where a continuous line of mist is always strategically and dramatically plotted, cutting off the backdrop from the human world. It is a dynamic materialization of emptiness as screen, a connecting through absence, or a frame carved out of space-time,[27] ensuring a 'deterritorialization of the image'.[28] This line of indetermination 'both separates and unites',[29] a mobile cut of duration delinking any fixed schematism. *Jin* is then liberated by *liu* 流 (flow) of the second line; and together the two images form a montage of stop-motion within the dimension of time. In other words, the sunset is being registered by dint of both its haecceity (singularity of here and now), and its becoming a reminder of the pure and virtual memories of the past.

It is the kind of Bergsonian past that 'remains bound up with the present' in duration.[30] This superpositioning of ending and flowing foreshadows a desire of life rather than life itself, since 'there are desiring flows that connect with other flows – eye and light',[31] perpetuating on-coming flows and connections. Deleuze's geophilosophy is such that it does not start out with life and then add to life, movement and duration. 'Rather, it is within blocks of becoming where the image = movement'[32] that create the becoming of life as pulsation and vibration. The character *yi* 依 is a non-active verb meaning 'tacking-along' or 'loosely hanging-on to'. It stabilizes the duration of the setting sun as a framed image of movement=image=perception=action. *Yi* also denotes a gradual, bloc-after bloc disappearing of the sun behind the mountain as a result of the eye's subtraction along with a 'modulation of the object itself'.[33] For Deleuze, subtraction is our attempt at grafting order onto the world, thereby something like a subject is brought forward which does the work of framing, selecting and focusing. Here the poet is prepared for action; and the gap as interval drawn out by *jin*, having caused a delay, allows the subject's brain to 'select their elements, to organize them, or to integrate them into a new movement'.[34]

With an intention to 'exhaust' his visibility of a thousand miles, the poet, now in the second half of the poem, thematizes his situational relation to the grandeur of nature. The significance of the character *yu* 欲 (wanting to) can be explained by Merleau-Ponty when he writes:

> Through my perceptual field, with its spatial horizon, I am present to my surrounding, I co-exist with all the other landscapes which stretch out beyond it, and all these perspectives together form a single temporal wave,

> one of the world's instants … And at the same time, this ubiquity is not strictly real, but is clearly only intentional.[35]

This intention to grasp what is beyond the perceptual field is enacted by a life-force similar to a Deleuzian desiring machine, which gives rise to life as a changing multiplicity of becomings.[36] It is also the life-giving *sheng ji* in Daoism that propels us for an ever broader view on all things in an embedded affect of wonder. The second character *qiong* 窮 (exhaust) reinforces the negating power of *jin* in the first line, only this time it is called upon to affirm the virtuality of perceptual connectivity itself. Here, the poet's desire to exhaust the mechanism of his seeing is being temporalized; and with the unique nature of temporality, the movement towards a more comprehensive view is possible only by recognizing its own character of ever-out-flowing, itself being undulated in a rhythmic 'tacking-on' duration of *yi* in the first line. It is a moment where the poet attempts to seize his 'subjectivation' in 'its dimension of processual creativity'.[37] A thousand-mile eye reaches way beyond our ken of sight, and its technicity is to be forever renewed towards a sense of the whole. For Deleuze, the whole is a set of images interconnected to one another, yielding a kind of relative out-of-field totality:

> The correlation between non-human matter and a superhuman eye is the dialectic itself, because it is also the identity of a community of matter and a communism of man. And montage itself constantly adapts the transformation of movements in the material universe to the internal movement in the eye of the camera: rhythm.[38]

The third line of Wang's poem triggers forth affective action, where 'perceiving things here where they are, I grasp the "virtual action" that they have on me, and simultaneously the "possible action" that I have on them, by diminishing or increasing the distance'.[39] This explains what it means when we say that a painter or poet is always *in* the things she tries to present. The inexhaustibility on which comprehension towards the whole relies is embodied here by the superhuman eye of a thousand miles, since 'the eye is in things, consciousness immanent within the meta-cinema of matter, and what actualizes virtual movement-images is the "centre of indetermination" of a living image, and *interval* or gap in the universal interaction of the matter-flows'.[40]

Following on the montage of visual images, the action-image takes place as the poet decides to 'take another flight up the stairs'. The very function of these steps in a tower reminds us of the famous story of Zhuangzi's debate with his friend about how he knows that the swimming fish is happy. When Zhuangzi gives his final remark 'I know it on the river', he kind of implies that he is standing on a dam or bridge-like structure above the water. To extract morals for the moderns, we would say both the steps of a tower and the wooden structure serve as a platform on which the triadic relatedness of human, technology and nature can be constructed. The emphasis of climbing only one level up at a time is in line with Merleau-Ponty's theory of temporal synthesis, and we can attribute such a choice to its concurrence with the essence of time, which being an 'unbroken chain of the fields of presence' has the 'essential characteristic of being formed only gradually and one step at a time'.[41] Here, 'interval propels what is called thinking, but only insofar as it is preparatory to action: in the interval, a momentary delay, perception is transformed into action, which is to say, a re-action to a given set of images (situation)'.[42] This provoked action translates the perception-images of the first two lines of Wang's poem into 'new images, a process whereby the subject moves to acclimate to the exigencies of situations';[43] and by choosing to go up another flight, the poet is actually converting the 'vibrations' of matter 'into practical deed'.[44] In terms of poetic structure, Wang's poem exhibits a vagary of forms, something like a conflating of Roman Jakobson's metaphorics and metonymics.

We can easily see that the first two lines are in couplet form with spatial juxtaposition as the orientation of the first couplet, whereas the relation between the third and fourth lines becomes temporal, contiguously emplotted in narrative. There is therefore no doubt that this poem as a whole operates under the principle of the movement-image, which emphasizes narrative guided by the sensory motor-schema. Beyond the human perceptual tendency of grasping 'immobile sections of movement', the poem puts bodily action back to a block of becoming within the duration of the cosmos. On the one hand it brings us back to the Daoist and Buddhist idea about 'elephant-phenomena' which are too big for human perception, and on the other, the action taken answers to our need of responding to a montage of natural grandeur, by adapting to the mechanical 'transformation of movement' made possible by the eye of something like a rhythmic camera – or the Chinese *ying xiang*.

This poem, therefore, can be read as the very embodiment of the indistinctive, universal desire in every one of us to move further on to another 'plateau'. It calls us to endlessly immerse ourselves in a mutually reinforcing relationship with our thousand-mile-eye – be it a camera as life machine, cosmic telescope or microscopic visual devices in new physics and medicine – automatically triggering in us a sharpened and intensified sense of being enchanted. The desire to gain an extended vision, a fostering of multiplicity, by the way, is montage itself, since it 'extends (or "ascends") shots by constructing an "out of frame" that they express, their out of frame world being in reciprocal presupposition'.[45] Such a technovisual eye has been the original propeller which pushes contemporary civilization onward, under the law of projection-reciprocation or the feedback loop. We remember one of the early scenes in *2001: Space Odyssey* (1968), where an ape throws into the air a piece of bone used as a weapon, and through a fade-in technique of the montage, it immediately changes into a space-ship, leaving us in awe of the immensity of millions of cyclical machines having been at work in our universe at all times.

Wang Zhi-huan's 'Ascending the Heron Tower' provides us with an exemplar of a Chinese style of the sublime, which can be considered a movement-image touching on time indirectly. However, the poem does not really give too much support to the idea that when we see things, we ourselves are part of the to-be-seen, or seeing seeing together, hence the Daoist concept of *yū wu ji guān* 與物齊觀 ('looking together with things'). There is a potential for the poem to go beyond movement through the poet's 'seeing an image that is continually changing, continually under construction, vibrating in its difference from itself',[46] and such 'attentive' (Bergson's term) seeing has a progressive result 'in creating anew, not only the object perceived, but also the ever-widening systems with which it may be bound up'.[47]

However, taken as a whole, the poem's in-and-out cuttings of vibratory images only invites the poet to undertake action within the sensory motor-schema, the kind of reaction triggered by an interval between an infinity of approachability and the desire to maximize human perceptual power. Deleuze's movement-image presents time indirectly, since movement within a narrative/action structure is oriented towards subtraction. Such subtraction is manifested in the grammatical structure of noun (subject), verb and object (predicate), whereby things get to be perceived through our subtracting from the complexity and fluidity of a pool of ever fluctuating images, something not unlike the Chinese 'shadowy *xiang*'. On the contrary, Deleuze's time-image embodies time itself; it is the kind of time, as pure memory, that does not spatialize itself by linkages or cuts of the montage; it is 'time out of joint and presents itself in the pure state'.[48]

As Aion (the infinite past and future), the time-image belongs to the virtual, 'the indefinite time of the event', a 'time of the pure event or of becoming, which articulates relative speeds and slowness independently of the chronometric or chronological value time assumes in the other modes'.[49] I propose, therefore, to introduce to you yet another Chinese poet, Wang Wei 王維, who is noted for his 'pure eventfulness' grounded in the Buddhist idea of consciousness, in order to illustrate how Chinese ecoethics has embodied the kind of Deleuzian time-image, and by bringing these two approaches together, we can suggest a means of joining forces towards a moment of cultural re-enchantment for the sake of our planet earth.

As a Tang poet and painter, Wang Wei (701–761) is known for his Buddhist inclination, with 'mountain and water' as subject matters and themes in most of his works. Stillness, austere simplicity, emptiness and a 'trancelike consciousness'[50] prevail in his poems, and he often describes his Buddhist practice of meditation towards 'mindfulness', a kind of spotless quietude (*vimala*) achieved through a deep withdrawal into solitude which embodies matter and consciousness. When he writes 'Dust, at an empty pool bend/ Meditation exorcises heart's virulent dragon', there is no doubt that he is in search of *sunyata*; and the lines 'The river flows beyond the sky and earth./ The mountain's colour, between seen and unseen'[51] clearly point to the Middle Way of being and nonbeing. The two lines in another poem: 'Walking to where the water ends / Sitting to look when the cloud rises' designate a kind of Buddhist sense of roundness and fullness (*purna*) without cognition or attainment (*najnām, naprāpthi*), life being a chance encounter, an invention of relation between humans and the molecules of water and rain. They make up an event of becoming in a cosmic duration, the unfolding of complexity of a time-image rather than a transition between events; they register an instant of productivity of intensive changes in the cosmic flow.

For the purpose of performing a more rigorous analysis to bring together the Buddhist sense of consciousness and Deleuzian ecoethics in Wang Wei, I propose to draw upon two famous poems by our Buddhist poet.

'Bird-Singing Stream'

Man at leisure. Cassia flowers fall.
Quiet night. Spring mountain is empty.
Moon rises. Startles – a mountain bird.
It sings at time in the spring stream.

'Deer Enclosure'

Empty mountain: no man is seen,
But voices of men are heard.
Sun's reflection reaches into the woods
And shines upon the green moss.[52] (101)

First, Deleuze's onto-ethologics grants primacy to a kind of territory or environment he calls 'milieu';[53] and in fact in *A Thousand Plateaus*, the authors make a point of their being familiar with what a Chinese poet is like:

> Animal elegance, the camouflage fish, the clandestine: this fish is crisscrossed by abstract lines that resemble nothing, that do not even follow its organic divisions: but thus disorganized, disarticulated, it worlds with the lines of a rock, sand, and plants, becoming imperceptible. The fish is like the Chinese poet: not imitative or structural, but cosmic. Francis Cheng shows that poets do not pursue resemblance, any more than they calculate 'geometric proportions'. They retain, extract only the essential lines and movements of nature.[54]

Wang Wei's 'Bird-Singing Stream' is about movement, the movements inbetween chaos/cosmos/milieus which designate time itself. This is time grasped in its constitutive bifurcation, the time that is directly embodied in a concrescence of vibration and rhythm, iteration and reiteration without obstruction of the heart or hanging on to formal resemblance (*cittavavana*). The first line here juxtaposes a human world with a natural habitat, crisscrossed by differential speeds, namely human at leisure and a more abrupt, but lighter, soundless fall of a flower. Man-at-leisure coincides with Bergson's idea of duration which frees us from practical action; and perception here only hides itself 'by perceiving what a world might be for an organism not in tune with our own rhythms',[55] so as to remind ourselves of the durations of others. Mountains of course have geological *durée*, to the extent that 'they constitute a "slowing-down" of global flows of matter-energy'.[56] Here we have a milieu of man's more relaxed rhythm where the movement of a flower is felt, the two durations affecting and being affected, since the elegance of the fall has been a result of a process of intensive 'abstract' blocks of becoming of natural growth and withering. Colebrook has this to say about Bergson's intuiting nonhuman durations:

> We can move from the perception of an autumnal leaf falling from a tree, to the farmed soil upon which that leaf falls, and then across to a lake where humans playing on a jet-ski disturb the lake's fish. Such a perception is at once located within the human point of view, but also allows for distinct rhythms, durations and imagined points that are beyond the human: The yearly cycles of the natural and agricultural seasons, the broader timescale of an earth and sea that have altered ecologies because of human action.[57]

Every movement of the interplay between leisure and fall prepares for a thematic emergence of 'night quiets itself' in the second line of the poem. My line of argument dictates that the character *jing* 靜, first, is the centre of the poem in terms of the poetics of *yiching* 意境 (imagescape), and second, occupies a position of what Chinese poetics calls 'the eye of a line of poem' 詩眼. This is why I modify Yip's rendering 'Quiet night' to 'night quiets,' thereby unleashing the pure duration of *jing*, to be incorporated as a noun, an adjective and a verb. Bergson[58] tells us that, besides human perception, there is a field beyond which is a centred consciousness, a kind of 'perception that merges with all physical interactions'.[59]

The Chinese 'poetic eye' could have been what Deleuze, drawing upon Bergson, has in mind when he talks of Vertov's 'cine-eye' (*kinoglaz*), where 'the photograph, if photograph there be, is already taken, already developed in the very heart of things'.[60] In *What Is Philosophy*? Deleuze and Guattari quote Raymond Ruyer's ideal of the 'absolute survey' and 'incorporeal predicate', as 'without distance, at ground level, a self-survey, that no chasm, fold or hiatus escapes'.[61] Primarily it is an 'overflight' of consciousness of all living forms, self-shaping and self-enjoying across its own absolute surface.[62] From this Deleuze develops a difference between 'green' as a sensible colour or quality and 'to green' as a noematic colour or attribute: 'the tree greens'. What makes it work is 'a qualitative predicate' and 'the attribute of the thing is the verb: to green, for example, or rather the event expressed by this verb'.[63] Deleuze talks of 'taking a walk' becoming subject to an 'incorporeal effect' in so far as 'it is a way of being'.[64] This is a moment which goes beyond the narrative movement-image as such, since there is no individual subject (noun) which does the seeing (verb). In this meandering, the receptive body is absorbed into the 'any-space-whatever', part of the perceiving power of the to-be-seen. The bodies have become embodiment in the very act of the 'communication of events';[65] by entering into the kind of cosmic time called Aion, bodies are 'virtualized' into the process of becoming-imperceptible in their very durations. We are reminded here of the Chinese *ji* being the minuteness of motion, and we are apt to associate this *ji* with the kind of 'technological seeing' by the eye of poetry, such as in the famous line 'Spring wind *greens* again the south-river shore' 春風又綠江南岸.[66] The character *lü* 綠 here defies categories of parts of speech, turning all life-forms into a temporal panorama of relational, abstract events of animate forces by assuming a role of 'incorporeal predicate'. The colour green here becomes the immediate given of pure affect of colour as a time-image:

> The colour-image does not refer to a particular object, but absorbs all that it can: it is the power which seizes all that happens within its range … Colour is the affect itself, that is, the virtual conjunction of all the objects which it picks up.[67]

In the first two lines of 'Bird-Singing Stream', we can say that milieus are gathered together to form some 'nuanced' relation in time between human and nonhuman worlds by executing travel, a movement and a change, not the corporeal entities one can see by freezing images, but by the dynamic predication which brings forth various durations. By willing the event, the poet releases the energies and arrays them with rhythms in resonance with each other. The third and fourth lines, however, bring the milieu-relations to the Deleuzian 'territory' by staging a deterritorializing event caught in a music-becoming of bird, the two forming a 'single becoming, a single bloc, an a-parallel evolution'.[68] When milieus meet and interact, the differences in speed, intensity and oscillation give rise to haecceity, the this-ness of things. This reminds us of the different *qua* in *Yijing*; when the *yin* and *yang* or *qian* and *kun* meet, you will go through a whole range of ordinary events before you arrive at a critical point, a phase transition which manifests itself as haecceity. Deleuze and Guattari mention the Japanese haiku as example, since this form of poetry excels in consisting 'entirely of relations of movement and rest between molecules or particles, capacities to affect and be affected'.[69] The character *jing* 驚 ('startles') used here requires some explanation: it is another 'eye' of both the poem and the landscape, functioning, on the one hand, as a contrast to the quiet but vibrant night and the rhythmic emptiness of the mountain valley, and on the other, a sudden but gentle outburst of the rising moon, an abrupt threshold crossing at the edge of complexity. Here the moon becomes a face of the landscape, and as Bonta and Protevi explain: Deleuze and Guattari in *A Thousand Plateaus* view 'Mother Earth' as a body which is 'the embeddedness of the face in landscape'; this is to 'present a deterritorialized sense of landscape in discussion of painting in the "Becoming-intense, becoming-animal" plateau. "Put the landscape to flight." '[70]

The third and fourth lines of 'Bird-Singing Stream' present the affects at work when animals are put to action by the cosmic 'moving *ji*' 動機, which is a composite of movement of all matters and particles, waves of light, germinally and molecularly appearing and disappearing, the space-time snaking in from all directions and tendencies guided by the natural affordance, the interplay of milieus displaying all the lines, cuts, folds, the grand total of the results that are 'following the *ji* in accord with change' 隨機應變. Rhythms, flows and resonance are being 'startled' into action, into form. In a confrontation with chaos, the character *shi* 時 (時鳴 *shi ming* sounding from time to time) here constitutes the intervals of the duration of a bird encountering the duration of the moon, plus of course all those vital flows of life energies in the bird territory. *Shi ming* is therefore the 'refrain', a 'periodic repetition',[71] an undulating sound wave of the melodic landscape; it is 'no longer a melody associated with a landscape; the melody itself is a sonorous landscape in counterpoint to a virtual landscape'.[72]

Here the Chinese 'moving *ji*' displays itself as technological seeing, seeing of itself, and it happens that this kind of interweaving of time-image is precisely what Deleuze Guattari call 'the machinic opera'.[73] Biologically and ethologically, what Wang Wei does here in the poem is to weave together the falling flower, the rising moon and the flushing of bird-sound over the stream, to conjoin visual and vocal elements for a phenomenon of 'coupled oscillations as the affectual dynamic of life'.[74] It is a crystal translating of temporal modalities; and insofar as fireflies flash in synchrony, planets orbit in their pulls and pushes, lights and particles entrain themselves towards some rhythmic tugs and turns with natural forces, gravity, all these oscillators under 'some physical or chemical process' allow them 'to influence one another'[75] in wonder. We now understand better why Deleuze and Guattari think that Chinese poets tend to be *cosmic* in their art.

Wang Wei's second poem 'Deer Enclosure' is all about sound and sight, through which affects and percepts are put to work in a process of transversal communication as assemblage of affects, which in turn, serves as our ultimate index for an encounter of Deleuzian and Chinese ecoethics. If human, mountain, forest and moss are the motifs of the poem, the voice, the expansive void, the setting sun and its slanting rays become the counter-motifs. These are of course, Deleuze's opsigns and sonsigns and also the resulting tactisigns.[76] The motifs and counter-motifs would be the two poles of 'reflecting surface and intensive micro-movements',[77] which, through sound and light, are knotted into 'the gest' of images.[78] Interestingly, sound coming from the empty valley causes a deeper level of emptiness than otherwise, and the light reflection on the moss intensifies the profound depth of the dark forest. This gives Buddhism confirmation that emptiness is something to be realized. One can say that Wang Wei achieves in this poem a kind of Buddhist substrate consciousness, as manifested in an expansive quietude. In Chinese classics, mountains are the place where the *qi* 氣 (vital breath air) gets to spread itself and to give rise to life; and they are also the natural forces for foldedness which hides the carrying capacity and affordance of the natural wilderness. This could also be supported by Heidegger's notion of a clearing where 'letting-be' can be enacted. Human beings achieve a sense of freedom 'by situating themselves within the expanse of world openness, within the space allocated for dwelling'.[79]

The usual question for the poem would be: if in this empty mountain no one is seen, who then is doing the 'not seeing' anyone? The usual answer is that it is of course the poet, the persona who is presenting the 'not seeing'. This answer, however, does not take note that the mountain could well be taken as a non-subject subject, and the 'not seeing' as a predicate of the line. Moreover, in the Chinese poetics of silence, human voices heard and unheard at the same time amount to creating a certain primordial sense of quietude in the environment. Such a quietude resembles the Heideggerian notion of the materiality of language 'not so much in the vocalization of sounds but, if anything, in the receding of those sounds: silence'.[80] The empty mountain here is in a state of chaos at the stage that order might spontaneously emerge; and human beings mentioned but not seen designate the 'emptiness' into which a world is being worlded. This is of course the grounding of 'one's proximities and zones of indiscernibility' that Deleuze and Guattari talk about, and all these motifs and counter-motifs can be subsumed under their concept of 'becoming-imperceptible'. Deleuze and Guattari would look at the brain as rhizomatic, an acentred network or system of affecting and being affected with emergent properties.[81]

In conjunction with ideas such as lines of flight, quasi-causal operation, milieu and territory, the becoming-imperceptible in art would be for the artist to reduce herself 'to an abstract line, a trait, in order to find one's zone of indiscernibility with other traits'.[82] In other words, the poet, and in our case Wang Wei, cuts himself into a zero degree perception, entering into the absolute survey in an utmost reclusive state of mind, a moment of movement of micro-becomings triggered by *sheng ji* itself. Lines counter lines to produce what the Chinese talk so much about – 'leaving it blank' 留白 and 'expansive emptiness' 空靈 in a state of non-gaining (*tasmad aprāptitvād*). This requires the poet to be absent in presence, to be there and not there under the law of *nihsvabhāva*. Singularities are always retained in the multitude of lines. The 'voices vaguely heard' are to reinforce the micro-percepts rather than perceptions, the latter would only stop the flows by 'imaging' processes, the halos or auras around things.[83] Here we have the mountain, the woods to be covered by sound waves and light waves, and the one who does not see anyone and only hears vaguely human voices is learning how to unsee and unhear at the same time.[84] In its immanent machinery, it is a process of 'grounding' a nomadic (or subjectless) subject in order to pay tribute to the wilderness, to thematize the motifs into a configuration: into the 'figural'.[85]

Perhaps we can use Deleuze's 'concept of the Other Person' in *What is Philosophy*? to explain Wang Wei's absence/presence in this poem. Deleuze and Guattari point out:

> No longer being either subject of the field or object in the field, the other person will become the condition under which not only subject and object

> are redistributed but also figure and ground, margins and center, moving object and reference point, transitive and substantial, length and depth.[86]

Elaborating on this 'paradox of concepts', Gregg Lambert considers this Other Person as exemplary of what he calls 'non-philosophy' in art, science and philosophy, an in-betweenness as 'the condition of all perception, for others as well as for ourselves, but also the condition of passing from one world to another one, is at the same time the condition of the Other Person as the concrete expression of the possible as such'.[87] We can also note the difference between a Kantian sublime and its Chinese counterpart by the latter's negative–positive dialectic and its sticking to the kind of Deleuzian time-image by temporalizing spatial experience.[88]

The Chinese direct bodying forth of time which creates a 'fractured' kinesis, where, according to Deleuze, 'I is another (*Je est un autre*) has replaced Ego = Ego'.[89] Remember our elephant that became the shadowy image? *Ying xiang* 影象 has now transformed itself into the crystal-image, which is 'the genetic element of opsigns, something like an animated mirror-reflection'.[90]

With sound waves, we have the counter-motifs of light waves as presented to us in the second half of the poem 'Deer Enclosure'. The two kinds of wave interact in a conjunction of material flows, and their repeated reflection becomes the integral part of the figural with modulated tonalities. Perhaps this is a good place to explain further Deleuze's concept of event. An event, on top of that which provides us with duration which begets becoming, is 'a vibration with an infinity of harmonics or submultiples, such as an audible wave, a luminous wave, or even an increasingly smaller part of space over the course of an increasingly shorter duration';[91] it is also a nexus of 'prehensions' which include 'echoes, reflection, traces, prismatic deformations, perspective, thresholds, folds'.[92]

Having been 'foreshadowed' by the expansive emptiness as imaged in the first half of 'Deer Enclosure' as event, the light activates itself by 'highlighting' an absence of sensori-motor schema and reinforces 'a play of images in which virtual and actual are indiscernible because they co-exist in the real (and not just "in our head")'[93] as animated reflections. Remember our character *ying* 影? Here in the third line, the character *jing* 景 (landscape) is being animated by sunlight, thereby the etymological montage of *ying* which has the three slanting lines is now concretely presented by the dynamic trajectories of light waves. I would say that the second half of the poem thematizes the virtuality and intensity one finds in this light wave on matters, something like the Deleuzian 'gest of images' through the materializing of the slanting rays, bringing alive the ideogram *ying*, which in turn brings to the poet the 'ethics of joy' since he is 'enjoying a good encounter', a virtual becoming that is 'worthy of the event'.[94] There is, therefore, an active co-evolvement of the organic and the inorganic, the organic and its milieus, in their mutual determination within a circuit of intensity. An opening is cracked to the amorphous outside, to be followed by shapes emerging into shapes, and what happens inbetween would be the cyclical process 'between invisible forces and visible bodies'.[95]

The first half of Wang Wei's 'Deer Enclosure' presents the non-seeing by a human and hearing of human voices. It thus establishes a distance from the human world, but at the same time the poet is at a point of receiving a chaotic world of sensation by stepping 'off the path'. Here the situation where only human voice is overheard becomes a crystalline time-image where 'words are unnecessary, and prelinguistic signifiers open alternatives for engaging with the world'.[96] Stepping off the path of subjectivity embraces the famous body without organs in *A Thousand Plateaus*, where intensities of matter energy flows push the poet towards the edge of complexity.[97]

Then, in the second half of the poem, the reflection, and the reflection of the reflection, waver between distancing and zooming-in of light waves, revealing a cosmogenic movement of forces of/in the melodic landscape. The first character *fu* 復 (again) in the fourth line, by the way, stages the kind of direct presentation of time 'which takes the form of rendering characters as *components* of a space rather than the *centre* of a space. The space will then connote the temporal quality of permanence, or repetition or stasis.'[98] From the scientific point of view, 'colors we see must be located not in a pregiven world but rather in the perceived world brought forth from our structural coupling'.[99] This 'to-ing and fro-ing' inscribe the diagrammatic movements of Nature-thought on the plane, as Deleuze and Guattari have found in the Chinese poet.[100] Everything, every line, is traversed by the play of light, light and its coloured reflection, colour relation of tonality taking up the 'pathic communication' of a world where the human and the nonhuman become a nuanced entity. The haecceity of the moss is such that, on the pure surface of a continuous plane of merging its greenness with the golden colour of the setting sun, it is wavering in an oscillation of sounds, sensation of colours and lights – only the sensation is not being coloured but colouring.[101]

Thus the poem as a whole points to the differential differences, the flows of life energies in the space-time grounding of a mountain and woods. Right here the poet foregrounds communication through an absence, but he is everywhere in the landscape, every molecule of his moving into life-machine of heat, particles, organic bodies, and such is what one can best describe as an ecological ethics of becoming-imperceptible. One hears but does not listen; one looks afar but does not see. Wallace aptly describes it as 'Letting the mind remain at ease, one watches all manner of mental events arise and pass of their own accord, without intervention of any kind.'[102]

Now that we have established the Chinese version of natural sublimity in the light of Deleuze's cinematic movement-image and time-image, respectively, we can finally bring our theme of technovisuality, in its most archaic form, to bear on cultural re-enchantment, as we have promised. But before that, we still need to briefly familiarize ourselves with Deleuze's bioethics, in order to graft his geophilosophy onto how our ecological crises could possibly be coped with through events of cultural re-enchantment on a cosmic scale. Deleuze takes ethics – ecoethics for that matter – to be that which tells us 'not to be unworthy of what happens to us'.[103] This means that we should 'live up to the powers from which we are composed, to extend potentials or *life* to the *n*th power'; and insofar as 'life is a potential for imaging', then that potential is to open life 'to what is not already given'.[104] For MacCormack, Deleuze's ethics should be understood as 'qualitative' and, instead of obligation, it is about 'acknowledging all relations affect each other'.[105] Through the 'desiring machine', the Deleuzian transversal communication upholds the bioethics for humans to communicate with nonhumans, for every molecule (or force of the body) moves to communicate with other bodies, be they stone or animals.[106] Deleuze's move towards molecular indeterminacies (becoming- imperceptible) in an act of flows and lines, formed in both becomings and Chinese eco-aesthetics, can well be the very mechanistic blade which cuts into a kind of ecoethics going all the way, both downward into viruses and bacteria, and upward to the cosmic forces of the universe. As expounded in *Difference and Repetition*, Deleuze's point is that 'What is retained and preserved, therefore created, what consists, is only *that* *which increases the number of connections* at each level of division or composition.'[107]

Deleuze's is a biosophy of how life-force could be distributed on a plane of immanence, an ethics which goes beyond the controversies of the anthropocentric/ecocentric as well as the eco-feminist/deep ecology pairs. In a study of *Difference and Repetition*, James Williams sums up his discussion by recapitulating the Deleuzian ethics as a process of relational ontology. He succinctly confines Deleuze's ethical scope in a principle of 'not to explicate oneself too much with the other, not to explicate the other too much',[108] in order to maintain an intensive life in which 'It is inevitable that you will identify the other but you must seek to show how that identification is illusory'.[109] Daoist and Buddhist ecoethics would have agreed with such a call to stop trying to know too much or else things are inevitably destroyed; and I would claim that what Wang Wei has done in, say, 'Deer Enclosure' where the poet and mountain do not actually see but 'overhear' from off the path, would be to present a perceptual indeterminacy which is answered purely and quietly by the dramatized slanting (reflection and refraction) of sun-rays. Such a leaving open of affects is actually in accord with Deleuze's ethics; and Williams writes about the individual thinker who is 'moving beyond the sense of being burdened to a sense where humans, plants, rocks, and animals share a common charge in intensities and ideas and, hence, a common responsibility – not in the sense of a burden but in the sense of a common destiny'.[110]

We would all agree that, whenever we look at the vast reaches of the sky, the galaxies and stars, we generate within ourselves a certain enchantment and humility. But what is more important is, as Sean Cubitt tells us, in the face of these 'phenomena of terrible scale and bewildering strangeness, energies and contingencies whose immensity commands humility' that 'we have some kind of cosmic duty to nurture it (life, that is)'.[111] As the concept *tian ji* (Lathe of heaven) makes clear, modern technology can only derive from and be part of the primordial 'machine' of the cosmos before the coming of time; and 'What it is to be human is constructed from the relationship between nature and technology' and 'the meaning of nature is constructed out of the relationship between human and technology, and the technology from the relation between human and nature'.[112] For Cubitt, 'physis the stuff the world is made of, is already a communicating universe, composed as much of information, and therefore of differences that signify, as in the human and the technological'. Such a triadic mutuality prompts him to ask the question in the last sentence of his book: 'Could it be that nature is none other than mediation, and that the permutations in our conceptions of both are the histories of an integral communication to which we may yet aspire?'[113]

Nature as media reflects of course the becoming-technovisual, in which Wang Zhihuan's desire for a thousand-mile-eye can be rehabilitated within Deleuze's cinema-philosophy as a means of 'the production of the relationship generated through co-existing bodies, and the possible synergetic and catalytic effects of a shared topography'.[114] In turn, Wang Wei's 'sun's reflection reaches into the woods / Again shines upon the green moss' functions as an answer or response to the situation of his earlier 'not seeing only overhearing' of other bodies, a kind of tacit faith in haecceity of things. When we read in Deleuze that cinema helps us to 'restore our belief in the world', since we are 'in the world as if in a pure optical and sound situation',[115] we are reminded of the marvel of imaging the world and the imaging of life cycles, something we also find in Wang Wei's pure opsigns and sonsigns. The thousand-mile-eye, when taken to a higher level in modern technovisuality, becomes the camera which, as Vertov argued, can 'see what the human eye could not, like a telescope or microscope', and it sees 'through a dialectic *in* matter, by which "the whole merges with the infinite set of matter, and the interval merges with an eye in matter." '[116] The 'universe as cinema itself, a metacinema,'[117] Deleuze argues that Vertov's camera exhibits a universal variation 'which goes beyond the human limits of the sensory-motor schema towards a non-human world where movement equals matter [...]. It is here that the movement image attains the *sublime*.'[118] I would therefore argue that Wang Wei's 'sun's reflection (of reflection) reaches the woods / Again shines upon the green moss' acts as the kino-eye embodying 'consciousness in which nature and man (whole and interval) have become merged in a new material collective achieving the conscious of matter';[119] and such a consciousness would amount to either the Chinese sublime or the Buddhist heightened consciousness (*eittavarana*) at large.

In her *The Enchantment of Modern Life: Attachments, Crossings, and Ethics*, Jane Bennett lists a number of elements which contribute to our modern way of being enchanted. These include Deleuze's 'body without organs', 'becoming-animals', 'enchantment and repetition' and 'the technological wonder'. Regarding the last item, Bennett remarks that 'enchantment is not simply an experience to be received but something to be made, a technical or cultural effect.'[120] Following Deleuze and Guattari's dictum: 'connect, conjugate, continue', Bennett suggests that the way of enacting a body-without-organs is to 'conjugate your body as you would a verb',[121] something similar to the Chinese line where 'spring wind again greens the river shore'. Such a self-hybridization or crossing will bring wonders, and, echoing Donna Haraway's cyborg, Bennett's crossings extend to nonhuman animals, the wind, rocks, trees, plants, tools, machines.[122] Her ultimate point is that these inter and intra species crossings 'might help to induce the kind of magnanimous mood that seems to be crucial to the ethical demands of a sociality that is increasingly multicultural multispecied, and multitechnical'.[123] To this list of alerts for the sake of modern sociality, I would add ecoethics, the philosophical development that is Deleuze and Guattari's response to environmental crises since *Anti-Qedipus*. For Bennett, the word enchantment denotes of course certain marvellous chanting; and Wang Wei's poems analysed above could well be considered a kind of Buddhist chanting should one sing them out aloud. Also, the not-seeing but overhearing in an empty mountain touches on sound and voice before speech, a kind of sonority – a repetitive one – that holds a certain spell-binding effect of the 'enchanting power of chants'.[124] Alongside Deleuze's refrain and Wang Wei's 'Birds sounding from time to time', the orchestration acts as 'quivering dynamism of electron flows'[125] and brings us back to the forgotten marvel of our sonorous cosmos, the 'fuzzy aggregates' or 'forces, densities, intensities'.[126] Deleuze and Guattari would call our effort of edging back ourselves to this sonorous cosmos as 'becoming-molecular', the microscopic world, the 'atomization of the motif', going all the way to 'infinitely small units'.

Becoming-molecular and being cosmic through a thousand-mile-eye or through ascending to a higher floor in the Heron Tower (both images being technological mediation) both invite re-enchantment at every step of the way. If we follow Deleuze and Guattari's analogy that the body without organs is also a 'body without an image',[127] since 'the simulacrum is an image without resemblance',[128] we can then translate the Daoist *xiang-wǎng* or shadowy image as 'Elephant without an image'; and the retrieving of the Dark Pearl (truth) would mean that we surely feel re-enchanted through conjugating the body of the elephant as we would a verb, as in *xiang xiang* 象象 as we have mentioned. Also, the term *xiang wang* can be reversed as *wang xiang* 罔象 to mean 'shadowing forth of elephant/ image/ imaging/ imagining'; and we would be thrown into amazement every time we create a new elephant, every time we elephant/compare the myriad phenomena of the universe anew in a uniquely Chinese style of sublimity.[129] Here I am reminded of a series of books by Ervin Laszlo, with titles such as *Quantum Shift in the Global Brain* and *Science and the Reenchantment of the Cosmos*, in which ideas such as the amazing coherence of the universe, quantum entanglement, wave- function and non-locality, give the participatory observer, infinite ways of interpreting the world. We can also suggest that the Buddhist Akashic field is itself a model of panpsychism, something not unlike Higgs' zero-point energy field as the fabric of the universe. There is 'a perpetual dance of involution and evolution,[130] as well as a process or precession of 'convolution' where matter becomes conscious of itself. Such an anthropic principle[131] fits quite well with Chinese ecoethics which has a tacit faith in natural technology as the basic energy flows of the cosmos, something Laszlo calls 'planetary Ethics'.[132]

Notes

1 The word 'precess' is used by I. Livingston, 2006, in *Between Science and Literature: An Introduction to Autopoetics*, Urbana and Chicago: University of Illinois Press, to describe historical processes or 'events' as records of 'epistemic changes', 'spins' or 'boundary defrosting' between words and things, science and humanities. The way the author uses this biological concept of *autopoiesis* as self-organizing open systems to engage with the self-reflexivity of poetics in terms of its self-reference, performativity of language and return to resemblance, is supportive of my effort in bringing together Chinese ecopoetics and Deleuze's cinema through a precession of projection-reciprocation or feedback-loop dialectic throughout this chapter.

2 It is interesting to note, at the start of this chapter, that Deleuze's hermeneutics of becoming already uses 'montage' as a literary machine to describe the process of reading: 'For reading a text is never a scholarly exercise in search of what is signified, still less a highly textual exercise in search of a signifier. Rather it is a productive use of the literary machine, a montage of desiring-machines, a schizoid exercise that extracts from the text its revolutionary force.' See G. Deleuze and F. Guattari, 1977, *Anti-Oedipus*, Minneapolis: University of Minnesota Press, 106.

3 G. Deleuze and F. Guattari, 1987, *A Thousand Plateaus*, Minneapolis: University of Minnesota Press, 195

4 G. Deleuze, 1988, *Spinoza: Practical Philosophy*, San Francisco: City Lights Books, 124.

5 G. Deleuze, 1991, *Bergsonism*, New York: Zone Books, 107.

6 M. Kearnes, 2006, 'Chaos and Control: Nanotechnology and the Politics of Emergence' in J. Marks (ed.), *Deleuze and Science*, *Paragraph* 29:2, 60.

7 C. Colebrook, 2006, *Deleuze: A Guide for the Perplexed*, London and New York: Continuum, 10.

8 Deleuze and Guattari, *A Thousand Plateaus*, 426.

9 Colebrook, *Deleuze: A Guide for the Perplexed*, 10.

10 Deleuze and Guattari, *A Thousand Plateaus,* 238–9.

11 M. de Landa, 2002, *Intensive Science and Virtual Philosophy*, London and New York: Continuum, 160.

12 G. Deleuze, 1994, *Difference and Repetition*, New York: Columbia University Press, 117.

13 S. Eisenstein, 1929, 'The cinematic principle and the ideogram in film form' in *Film Form*, Orlando: Harcourt, Brace & Company (1949).

14 S. Zepke, 2005, *Art as Abstract Machine: Ontology and Aesthetics in Deleuze and Guattari*, New York and London: Routledge, 121.

15 The *Han Feizi* 《韓非子》 is the largest and most important of the treatises of the Legalist school (*fajia* 法家), written by Han Fei 韓非, philosopher and politician of the Warring States period 戰國 (500–221 BCE).

16 I am using Burton Watson's version here: B. Watson, trans. 1968, *The Complete Works of Chuang Tzu*, New York: Columbia University Press.

17 G. Deleuze, 1990, *The Logic of Sense*, New York: Columbia University Press, 262.

18 D. N. Rodowick, 1997, *Gilles Deleuze's Time Machine*, Durham and London: Duke University Press, 204. Incidentally, Rodowick's explanation here reinforces my point of drawing upon, say, quantum enigma and its many worlds interpretation as inspiration of cosmic re-enchantment towards the end of my paper.

19 His Holiness the Dalai Lama, 2005a, *The Universe in a Single Atom: The Convergence of Science and Spirituality*, New York: Morgan Road Books, 50. Nagariuna points out:

> Without detachment from vision there is no seer.
> Nor is there a seer detached from it.
> If there is no seer
> How can there be seeing or the seen?

Here J. L. Garfield annotates as follows: 'Perception is not accomplished by an independent entity known as vision. But that doesn't mean that things that are incapable of sight thereby perceive … On Nāgārjuna's analysis, we can't make sense of an autonomous subject of visual perception. For such a subject would by definition have its identity as a visual subject independent of perception.' J. L. Garfield, 1995, *The Fundamental Wisdom of the Middle Way: Nagarjuna's Mulamadhyamakakarika*, Oxford: Oxford University Press, 139.

20 J. W. Hayward and F. J. Varela, 1992, *Gentle Bridges: Conversation with the Dalai Lama on the Sciences of Mind*, Boston and London: Shambhala, 211.

21 H. Bergson, 1988, *Matter and Memory*, trans. N. M. Paul and W. S. Palmer, New York: Zone Books, 9.

22 There is similar structure between *ying* 影 and the character *cǎi* 彩, the latter's radical started out as a verb pointing to the act of gathering; now with the slants added it becomes 'colour' or 'colourful', loosely coinciding with the scientific finding as to how colours are created as a folded technicity of perception, particles and refraction of sunlight.

23 Colebrook, *Deleuze: A Guide for the Perplexed*, 11.

24 Incidentally, when explaining Deleuze's interval as irrational cuts, Rodowick evokes Deleuze's example of Marguerite Duras's *India Song* (1975) and writes: 'The opening shot of the film frames a red sun setting into clouds over a verdant delta. This is a direct image of time in its simplest manifestation: an autonomous shot describing a single event as a simple duration', Rodowick, *Gilles Deleuze's Time Machine*, 14.

25 M. Merleau-Ponty, 1962, *Phenomenology of Perception*, London and New Jersey: Routledge, 333. All translations are based on W. L. Yip's rendering of *Hiding* the *Universe* unless otherwise indicated. Here the two lines appear on p. 27. Subsequent references will be given in the text. W. L. Yip, trans. 1972, *Hiding the Universe: Poems by Wang Wei*, New York: Grossman.

26 S. B. Mallin, 1979, *Merleau-Ponty's Philosophy*, New Haven and London: Yale University Press, 37–8.

27 G. Deleuze, 1986, *Cinema 1: Movement-image*, Minneapolis: University of Minnesota Press, 14.

28 Ibid, 15.

29 R. Bogue, 2003a, *Deleuze: On Cinema*, New York and London: Routledge, 43.

30 H. Bergson, 1911, *Creative Evolution*, New York: Henry Holt, 22. Interestingly, Bergson in *Creative Evolution* has this to say about the sun and duration: 'Our sun radiates heat and light beyond the farthest planet. And, on the other hand, it moves in a certain fixed direction, drawing with it the planets and their satellites. The thread attaching it to the rest of the universe is doubtless very tenuous. Nevertheless it is along this thread that is transmitted down to the smallest particle of the world in which we live the duration immanent to the whole of the universe.' Ibid. 11.

31 Colebrook, *Deleuze: A Guide for the Perplexed*, 23.
32 Deleuze, *Cinema 1: Movement-image*, 58
33 G. Deleuze, 1989, *Cinema 2: The Time-image*, Minneapolis: University. of Minnesota Press, 27.
34 Deleuze, *Cinema 1: Movement-image*, 62.
35 Merleau-Ponty, *Phenomenology of Perception*, 330–1.
36 Deleuze, *Difference and Repetition*, 245.
37 F. Guattari, 1996, 'Subjectivities: For better and for worse' in G. Genosko (ed.), *The Guattari Reader*, Oxford: Blackwell, 198 in 193–203.
38 Deleuze, *Cinema 1: Movement-image*, 40.
39 Ibid, 64–5.
40 Bogue, *Deleuze: On Cinema*, 35.
41 Merleau-Ponty, *Phenomenology of Perception*, 423.
42 G. Flaxman (ed.), 2000, *The Brain is the Screen: Deleuze and the Philosophy of Cinema*, Minneapolis and London: University of Minnesota Press, Introduction, 35.
43 Flaxman, 'Cinema Year Zero' in *The Brain is the Screen,* 94.
44 Bergson, 1988, *Matter and Memory*, New York: Zone Books, 44.
45 Zepke, *Art as Abstract Machine,* 83.
46 Ibid, p. 101.
47 Deleuze, *Cinema 2: The Time-image*, 65.
48 Ibid. 271.
49 Deleuze and Guattari, *A Thousand Plateaus*, 263.
50 Yip, *Hiding the Universe: Poems by Wang Wei*, xi.
51 Ibid. 29.
52 Ibid. 101.
53 The translator Brian Massumi explains in his Notes to *A Thousand Plateaus* that 'In French, *milieu* means "surrounding", "medium" (as in chemistry) and "middle" (xvii).' 'Milieu is a rhizome with rhythms, born out of chaos' (Deleuze and Guattari, *A Thousand Plateaus*, 313). By definition, an event for Deleuze describes intensive interaction among forces. When Cliff Stagoll explains the concept, he happens to say: 'As the *product* of the synthesis of forces, events signify the internal dynamic of their interactions. As such, on Deleuze's interpretation an event is not a particular state or happening. In other words, an event is the potential immanent within a particular confluence of forces. Take as an example a tree's changing colour in the spring.' (C. Stagoll, 2005, 'Event' in A. Parr (ed.), *The Deleuze Dictionary*, New York: Columbia University Press, 87–8. For Deleuze's concept of 'predicate', see 1993, *The Fold: Leibniz and the Baroque*, Minneapolis: University of Minnesota Press, 52–3.
54 Deleuze and Guattari, *A Thousand Plateaus*, 280.
55 Colebrook, *Deleuze: A Guide for the Perplexed*, 31.

56 J. Marks, 2006, 'Introduction', *Deleuze and Science, Paragraph*, 29:2, 1–18, cited from p. 13.
57 Colebrook, *Deleuze: A Guide for the Perplexed*, 31.
58 Deleuze, *Bergsonism*, 185.
59 F. Zourabichvili, 2000, 'The eye of montage: Dziga Vertov and Bergsonian materialism' in G. Flaxman (ed.), *The Brain is the Screen*, 141–9.
60 Deleuze, *Cinema I: Movement-image*, 60.
61 Deleuze and Guattari, *What is Philosophy?* 210, Deleuze and Guattari give the reference in French: R. Ruyer, 1952, *Néo-finalisme*, Paris: Presses Universitaires de France. Other discussions on Ruyer in this respect include K. A. Pearson's 1999, *Germinal Life: The Difference and Repetition of Deleuze*, London: Routledge, 183; E. Alliez's 2004, *The Signature of the World, What is Deleuze and Guattari's Philosophy*, New York: Continuum, 63–4; R. Bogue's 2003b *Deleuze on Music, Painting, and the Arts*, New York: Routledge, 62–6, 172–4, 181–4; P. Bains' 2002 'Subjectless subjectivities' in B. Massumi (ed.), *A Shock to Thought: Expression after Deleuze and Guattai*, London and New York: Routledge, 101–116.
62 Bogue, *Deleuze on Music, Painting, and the Arts* 172–4.
63 Deleuze, *The Logic of Sense*, 21.
64 Ibid. 146–7.
65 Ibid. 169.
66 W. A. Shih 王安石 (1021~1086) 'Mooring at Guazhou' 泊 船 瓜 州
67 Deleuze, *Cinema 1: Movement-image*, 118.
68 G. Deleuze and C. Parnet, 1987, *Dialogues II*, London and New York: Continuum, 3. Etymologically speaking, the character *shi* is composed of the radical for 'sun' on the left, placed beside the radical for a human foot caught at the very moment of stopping and moving on. I would say that such a composite montage of time in Chinese culture could well be considered the time-image par excellence. Also, if you substitute the sun with *yan* 言 speech', you have 'poetry'; and the fact that temporality and art share certain genetic elements of rhythms and durations should give us more thoughts on Deleuze's time-image.
69 Deleuze and Guattari, *A Thousand Plateaus*, 261.
70 M. Bonta and J. Protevi, 2004, *Deleuze and Geophilosophy: A Guide and Glossary*, Edinburgh: Edinburgh University Press, 103.
71 Deleuze and Guattari, *A Thousand Plateaus*, 313.
72 Ibid. 318.
73 Ibid. 330.
74 For Deleuze, ethology is everything done by organic and inorganic life with their bodies: 'Concretely, if you define bodies and thoughts as capacities for affecting and being affected, many things change. You will define an animal, or a human being, not by its form, its organs, and its functions,

and not as a subject either; you will define it by the affects of which it is capable.' Deleuze, *Spinoza: Practical Philosophy*, 124.

75 S. Strogatz, 2003, SYNC: *The Emerging Science of Spontaneous Order*, New York: Hyperion, 3.

76 Deleuze, *Cinema 2: The Time-Image*, 13, 92 n. 251.

77 Deleuze, *Cinema 1: Movement-Image*, 88.

78 Deleuze, *Cinema 2: The Time-Image*, 192.

79 F. Schalow, 2006, *The Incarnality of Being: The Earth, Animals, and the Body in Heidegger's Thought*, Albany: State University of New York Press, 108.

80 Ibid. 94.

81 Deleuze and Guattari, *A Thousand Plateaus*, 15–16.

82 Ibid. 280.

83 Whereas one can take the Chinese 'Leaving it blank' as similar to Deleuze's idea of deterritorialization by 'freeing the line' (Deleuze and Guattari, *A Thousand Plateaus*, 295) or the 'effacement of the contour' (Deleuze, *The Fold*, 32) in Venetian paintings and the Baroque, one should note, nevertheless, that instead of an absolute non-doing of any brush stroke, the Western artists turn to making more use of colours so that, say, dark ground of obscurity takes the place of clear-cut lines in order to highlight the interplay of the deterritorialized matter-function in paintings. (Zepke, 2005, *Art as Abstract Machine,* 127–41).

84 Wang Wei's 'sounding of human voice' could be related to Livingston's precessing of words in different discursive ecologies. By quoting Virginia Woolf's idea of 'humming noise' which is 'not articulate, but musical', Livingston locates an 'interzone where meaning happens' in the 'defrosted boundaries between "the words themselves" and the "sort of humming noise" that is the sum of their many cross-amplifying and cancelling echoes' (Livingston, *Between Science and Literature*, 90–1).

85 Here I venture to appropriate D. N. Rodowick's configuration of 'the figural', even though he is using the concept to delineate what one sees, say, on a TV screen in the new media era. As 'becoming', Rodowick's 'figural' is: 'Ever permutable – a fractured, fracturing, or fractal space, ruled by time and difference – it knows nothing of the concept of identity.' D. N. Rodowick, 2001, *Reading the Figural, or, Philosophy after the New Media*, Durham, NC: Duke University Press, 46.

86 Deleuze and Gauttari, *What is Philosophy*? 18.

87 G. Lambert, 2002, *The Non-philosophy of Gilles Deleuze*, New York: Continuum, 34.

88 See my essays: 1986, 'Negative-Positive Dialectics of the Chinese Sublime' in C. Ying-hsiung (ed.), *The Chinese Text* Hong Kong: Chinese University Press, 119–58 and 1989, 'Temporalization of Spatial Experience in

Classical Landscape Poetry' in *Essays in Commemoration of the 30th Anniversary of United College*, Hong Kong: Chinese University of Hong Kong. K. W. Faulkner has a discussion of Kant's sublime in terms of 'synthesis of apprehension', and he compares it to Deleuze's 'intensive magnitude' in *Difference and Repetition*. When Faulkner points out that 'if we move around the object, looking at it from all sides, this synthesis remains subjective, requiring acts of synthesis over a greater period of time', he is to some extent describing what a Chinese landscape painter has been doing in temporalizing spatial experience. K. W. Faulkner, 2006, *Deleuze and the Three Syntheses of Time*, New York: Peter Lang, 14–17.

89 Deleuze, *Cinema 2: The Time-Image*, 133.

90 Bogue, *Deleuze: On Cinema*, 120.

91 Deleuze, *The Fold*, 77.

92 Ibid. 78.

93 Bogue, *Deleuze: On Cinema*, 121.

94 C.V. Boundas, 2005, 'Intensity' in A. Parr (ed.), *The Deleuze Dictionary*, New York: Columbia University Press, 131.

95 Bogue, *Deleuze: On Music, Painting, and the Arts*, 125.

96 C. J. Stivale, 2005, *Gilles Deleuze: Key Concepts*, Ithaca, NY: McGill-Queen's University Press,,153.

97 Deleuze and Guattari, *A Thousand Plateau*, 31, 33, 70 n. 507.

98 Due, *Deleuze*, Cambridge: Polity, 163.

99 F. J. Varela, E. Thompson and E. Rosch, 1991, *The Embodied Mind: Cognitive Science and Human Experience*, Cambridge, MA and London: MIT Press, 165.

100 Deleuze and Guattari, *What is Philosophy*? 91.

101 In *What is Philosophy*? Deleuze and Guattari write: 'the plant contemplates by contracting the elements from which it originates – light, carbon, and the salts – and it fills itself with colors and odors that in each case qualify its variety, its composition: it is sensation in itself. It is as if flowers smell themselves by smelling what composes them, first attempts of vision or of sense of smell, before being perceived or even smelled by an agent with a nervous system and a brain' (212). It is the claim of my analysis of Wang Wei's line here that it comes close to this sense of pure sensation in poetic art.

102 B. A. Wallace, 2007, *Contemplative Science: Where Buddhism and Neuroscience Converge*, New York: Columbia University Press, 145.

103 Deleuze, *The Logic of Sense*, 149.

104 Colebrook, *Deleuze: A Guide for the Perplexed*, 14 n. 40.

105 P. MacCormack, 2008, 'An ethics of spectatorship: Love, death and cinema' in I. Buchanan and P. MacCormack (eds), *Deleuze and the*

Schizoanalysis of Cinema, London and New York: Continuum, 133 in 130–42.

106 Deleuze and Guattari, *Anti-Oedipus*, 2 n. 8.

107 Deleuze, *Difference and Repetition*, 508.

108 Ibid, 261 n. 335.

109 J. Williams, 2003, *Gilles Deleuze's Difference and Repetition: A Critical Introduction and Guide*, Edinburgh: Edinburgh University Press, 209.

110 Ibid. 195. It might be fruitful to experiment with a 'compare and contrast' exercise with Wang Wei's 'Deer Enclosure' and Robert Frost's famous 'Stopping by Woods on a Snowy Evening'. In a chapter 'Poetic Interlude: Defrosting' of his book, Livingston executes an 'unwriting' of 'antipoem' on this poem by Frost, thereby defrosting the 'Western heroic self' which has been shouldering up a 'White man's Burden' (Livingston, *Between Science and Literature*, 93). In the same chapter, the author contrasts this with Chinese poetics: 'Chinese cosmology did not require the linchpin of geocentrism and thus was not shaken to its roots by Copernicus, while that great protagonist of Western lyrics, "I", has scarcely made an appearance in a couple of thousand years of Chinese lyric poetry' (91–2).

111 S. Cubitt, 2005, *EcoMedia (Contemporary Cinema 1)*, Amsterdam and New York: Rodopi, 133.

112 Ibid. 133.

113 Ibid. 145.

114 Stivale, *Gilles Deleuze: Key Concepts,* 14.

115 Deleuze, *Cinema 2: The Time-Image*, 172.

116 Deleuze, *Cinema 1: Movement-Image*, 61.

117 Ibid. 59.

118 Deleuze, *Cinema 2: The Time-Image*, 58. This dialectic in matter is discussed at length by S. Zepke in *Art as Abstract Machine*, 88–91.

119 Zepke, *Art as Abstract Machine*, 90.

120 J. Bennett, 2001, *The Enchantment of Modern Life: Attachments, Crossings, and Ethics*, Princeton, NJ, and Oxford: Princeton University Press, 51.

121 Ibid. 26.

122 Ibid. 29.

123 Ibid. 32.

124 Ibid. 154.

125 Ibid. 28.

126 Deleuze and Guattari, *A Thousand Plateaus*, 346–7.

127 Deleuze and Guattari, *Anti-Oedipus*, 8.

128 Deleuze, *The Logic of Sense*, 257.

129 The phrase 'imaging the universe' in my title works in the same way as Livingston's 'languaging the universe'. There Livingston's example is the

statement 'the sky is blue', which shows that the sky and its beholder are influenced – created as well as sustained – by each other, since both 'participated in discursive ecologies that are really entities fully involved in the physical universe' (Livingston, *Between Science and Literature*, 65). This example of blue sky, needless to say, applies just as forceful to my point of 'elephanting the universe anew' with and without an image at the same time.

130 E. Laszlo, 2006, *Science and the Reenchantment of the Cosmos: The Rise of the Integral Vision of Reality*, Rochester, VT: Inner Traditions, 110.

131 For 'Anthropic Principle' see J. N. Gardner's 2003, *Biocosm: The New Scientific Theory of Evolution: Intelligent Life is the Architect of the Universe*, Makawao: Inner Ocean, 10–11, 46–7; B. Rosenblum and F. Kuthner, 2006, *Quantum Enigma: Physics Encounters Consciousness*, Oxford: Oxford University Press, 199–201.

132 Laszlo, *Science and the Reenchantment of the Cosmos*, 63–75.

2

The World, Time

D. N. Rodowick

At the beginning of the Epilogue to his *Theory of Film*, Siegfried Kracauer asks: 'What is the good of film experience?'[1] The phrasing of the question clarifies what it means to bring ethics and cinema together as a philosophical problem. Kracauer does not want to know if a particular film or filmmaker is 'ethical', nor is the question the basis for making moral judgements of art-works and their makers. His asks, rather, how do we evaluate our *experience* of the movies, meaning in what ways do the movies offer themselves as a medium for an interrogation of ourselves, of our relationship to the world and to other beings? In other words, how do movies solicit and sustain the possibility of ethical thought?

Aesthetics and ethics do not make an obvious pairing, much less film and moral reasoning. In 1960, Kracauer is among the first to offer an explicitly ethical question to film theory. In so doing, he places the study of film along some of the most ancient lines of philosophical reasoning. From at least the fifth century BC, the activity of philosophy has been characterized by two fundamental questions: How do I know, and how shall I live? The latter is the most self-evidently ethical question. Yet how can the quality of one's thought be separated from the choice of a mode of existence? Both questions demand a reflexive examination of self, in its possibility of knowing itself and others, and in its openness to change or not. What links philosophy today to its most ancient origins are the intertwining projects of evaluating our styles of knowing, and examining our modes of existence and their possibilities of transformation. In this way, an ethics is distinct from the usual sense of morality. Morals refer ordinarily to a transcendental system of values to which we conform, or against which we are found lacking.

Ethics are an immanent set of reasoned choices. In ethical expression, we evaluate our current mode of existence, seeking to expand, change or abandon it in the effort to achieve another way of living and another form of community. Inspiring an individual to choose a mode of existence embodied in a community, real or imagined, philosophy thus entails the expression and justification of this existential choice and its representation of the world. Therefore, *philosophein* is, simultaneously, expression and existential choice – the medium and idiom of a life.

Gilles Deleuze never devoted a book exclusively to ethics. Yet the two philosophers with whom he felt the closest allegiances, Baruch Spinoza and Friedrich Nietzsche, are importantly connected to the history of moral reasoning, and his books and repeated references to these philosophers mark his frequent examination of ethical questions. Deleuze's most provocative comments on ethics, however, appear late in his work, specifically in the two books on cinema, *Cinema 1: The Movement-Image* and *Cinema 2: The Time-Image*.[2]

Here an interesting question detours our path. Why is film so important as the companion or exemplification for ethical self-examination? Indeed, the idea that art should inspire ethical inquiry marks the greatest distance between ourselves and the philosopher-citizens of Periclean Athens. At the same time, it is also one of the clearest signposts of philosophical modernity. In twentieth-century philosophy, especially in its Anglo-American and analytic incarnations, ethics has taken a back seat, indeed has been sent to the back of the bus by the more strident emphasis on logic and epistemology – an attitude forcefully summarized in Quine's insistence that the philosophy of science is philosophy enough.[3]

The turn to film as an important site of ethical interrogation is thus doubly curious. And if there is something that can be called 'film philosophy' today, moral reasoning persists as one of its most powerful, defining activities. Undoubtedly, this is due to the influence of Stanley Cavell as the contemporary philosopher most centrally concerned with the problem of ethics in film and philosophy, above all through his characterization of an Emersonian moral perfectionism. However, in Cavell's Emersonian ethics there are also curious and powerful echoes with Gilles Deleuze's Nietzschean and Bergsonian perspectives on cinema, wherein concepts of movement and time are related as the expression of belief in the world and its powers of transformation. This may appear to be an odd couple. But I am haunted by the idea of a dialogue, as if in a real conversation but between partners who seem only dimly aware of one another, where Deleuze's cinema books, published in 1983 and 1985, respond to Cavell's *The World Viewed* (1971) and *Pursuits of Happiness* (1981), and where *Contesting Tears* (1996) and *Cities of Words* (2004) echo some of the most provocative thinking in *The Movement-Image* and *The Time-Image.*

Both space and time are lacking here to develop all the implications of this missed philosophical friendship.[4] It is worth noting, though, that one important bridge between Deleuze and Cavell's thought on cinema and moral reasoning is their mutual interest in Nietzsche. Another is their original way of asking ethical questions in ontological contexts. Though Cavell uses the word frequently and Deleuze rarely, both evaluate ontology as a particular approach to Being. This is not the being or identity of film or what identifies film as art, but rather the ways of being that art provokes in us – or more deeply, how film and other forms of art express for us or return to us our past, current and future states of being. Also, in both philosophers, the ethical relation is inseparable from our relationship to thought. For how we think, and whether we sustain a relation to thought or not, is bound up with our choices of a mode of existence and our relations with others and to the world.

There is also an important contrast with Cavell. Part of the difficulty of Deleuze's thought has to do with his choice to ignore or circumvent the dilemmas of scepticism and its characterizations of the self in relation to being, the world and to others. These are central features of the philosophical culture most familiar to us, and it is disarming to consider seriously a thinker for whom the great difficulties of relating subject and object seem to have been completely dispelled or overcome. Indeed, throughout his career Deleuze turned consistently to philosophers for whom the division of the thinking subject from the world was ontologically irrelevant; hence, his recovery of a path alternative to Descartes leading from Spinoza and Nietzsche to Henri Bergson.

In Deleuze the fundamental ethical choice is to believe in this world and its powers of transformation. How does his avoidance or circumvention of the history of scepticism and Cartesian rationalism inform this question? Although Deleuze was not known for his love of philosophical systems, Alberto Gualandi has astutely recognized his commitment to two principles, which may be considered the basis of his ethics as well as his more general philosophy. The first is Spinoza's 'pure ontology', or doctrine of *the univocity of Being*. For Spinoza, there is no division between humanity and nature, but only one absolute and unique substance for all that exists – all attributes and identities are only different manners of being for this substance, or different modalities of its expressiveness. As Gualandi explains:

> the principle of univocal Being affirms the absolute *immanence* of thought in the world as it exists, as well as the categorical refusal of any form of thought *transcending* the Being of things in whatever form of the supersensible. For Deleuze as well as Spinoza, the intuition of the univocity of being is the highest intellectual expression of love for all that exists.[5]

This doctrine of a single expressive substance inspires a first ethical principle: the choice to believe in *this* world, the world in which we exist now, alive and changing, and not some transcendent or ideal world. This is also an affirmation of thought's relation to the world, as the movements of thought in relation to those of matter differ only in their ways of expressing a common being or substance.

The second principle is that of *Becoming*, wherein the univocity of Being is characterized by its relation to movement, time and change. Here substance is connected to force as self-differentiation, producing a universe of continual metamorphosis characterized by Bergson as 'creative evolution'. Becoming is the principle of time as force, and time is the expressive form of change: the fact that the universe never stops moving, changing and evolving, and that no static picture could ever be adequate to this flux of universal self-differentiation. In this, time is something like a metaphysical constant in Deleuze, characterized in *Kant's Critical Philosophy* as 'the form of that which is *not* eternal, the immutable form of change and movement'.[6] All that moves or changes is in time, but time itself never changes or moves. The highest expression of this force is not Kantian, however, but what Nietzsche called eternal recurrence.

Deleuze offers an original reading of the concept of eternal recurrence. In fact, it is the key element of his philosophy of difference, as well as his ethics, linking the univocity of Being and the force of Becoming. In *Nietzsche and Philosophy* Deleuze asks, 'What is the being of that which becomes, of that which neither starts nor finishes becoming? *Returning is the being of that which becomes*.'[7] What does Being speak of in one voice? It does not sing of identity, but rather of recurrence as change and differentiation, of a

> 'returning itself that constitutes being insofar as it is affirmed of becoming and of that which passes. It is not some one thing which returns but rather returning itself is the one thing which is affirmed of diversity or multiplicity. In other words, identity in the eternal return does not describe the nature of that which returns but, on the contrary, the fact of returning for that which differs'.

What returns eternally is not the identity of the same, but the force of difference or differentiation. What Being speaks of recurrently is difference from itself.

Welles, Nietzsche and the Powers of the False

The ethical stance in the cinema books is fundamentally Nietzschean. (The ontological passes through Spinoza and Bergson.) Deleuze characterizes a Nietzschean ethics as encompassing two related activities: interpretation and evaluation. 'To interpret', Deleuze wrote earlier, 'is to determine the force which gives sense to a thing. To evaluate is to determine the will to power which gives value to a thing'.[8] 'Interpretation' would relate here to Deleuze's theory of film semiotics, which is too complex to address here. Alternatively, evaluation is central to the ethical project of Deleuze's cinema books.

What philosophy must evaluate in any expression, including aesthetic expression, are its possibilities for life and experimentation in life. This is another important link between Nietzsche, Spinoza and Bergson in Deleuze's account. Both Spinoza and Nietzsche distinguish between morality and ethics. Morality involves sets of constraining rules that judge actions and intentions against transcendent or universal values. An ethics evaluates expression according to the immanent mode of existence or possibilities of life it implies. The ethical choice for Deleuze, then, is whether the powers of change are affirmed and harnessed in ways that value life and its openness to change, or whether we disparage life in *this* world in fealty to moral absolutes. Do we affirm life and remain open to its powers of continuous, qualitative self-transformation, or do we maintain an image of thought whose movements are stopped or frozen?

To evaluate is to ask: *What mode of existence is willed in a given expression?* One must go beyond the transcendent moral opposition of good and evil, but this does not mean relinquishing judgements of good and bad as ethical distinctions. Life should not be judged. But the will to power that informs or characterizes a mode of existence may be evaluated as good or bad, noble or base. From Nietzsche's vitalist perspective, all is a question of force, and ethics involves characterizing forces by evaluating the qualities of their will to power. For example, there are fatigued or exhausted forces that can be quantitatively powerful, but which no longer know how to transform themselves through the variations they can affect or receive. Deleuze finds this will to power often expressed in the films of Orson Welles – Nietzschean filmmaker *par excellence* – where characters such as Bannister in *Lady from Shanghai* or Hank Quinlan in *Touch of Evil* are the bodily expressions of a certain impotence: 'that is, the precise point where the "will to power" is nothing but a will-to-dominate, a being for death, which thirsts for its own death, as long as it can pass through others'.[9] Here, force finds a centre that coincides with death. These are characters who only know how to destroy or kill, before destroying themselves. This is the mode of existence of *ressentiment*, characteristic of the men of vengeance. And no matter how great the forces these characters exercise or represent, they are exhausted and incapable of transformation. This spirit of revenge is often paired in Welles' films with a blind will to truth as transcendent moral judgement. Thus Quinlan is paired with Vargas, or Iago with Othello. The latter are 'truthful men' who judge life in the name of higher values:

> They ... take themselves to be *higher men*; these are higher men who claim to judge life by their own standards, by their own authority. But is this not the same spirit of revenge in two forms: Vargas, the truthful man who invokes the laws for judging; but also his double, Quinlan, who gives himself the right to judge without law; Othello, the man of duty and virtue, but also his double, Iago, who takes revenge by nature and perversion? This is what Nietzsche called the stages of nihilism, the spirit of revenge embodied in various figures. Behind the truthful man, who judges life from the perspective of supposedly higher values, there is the sick man, 'the man sick with himself', who judges life from the perspective of his sickness, his degeneration and his exhaustion. And this is perhaps better than the truthful man, because a life of sickness is still life, it contrasts life with death, rather than contrasting it with 'higher values'... Nietzsche said: behind the truthful man, who judges life, there is the sick man, sick of life itself.... The first is an idiot and the second is a bastard. They are, however, complementary as two figures of nihilism, two figures of the will to power.[10]

Ethics, however, is not a question of passing judgement on these figures as if from some higher moral ground. Following Nietzsche, Deleuze (and Welles) want to do away with the system of judgement to evaluate, rather, modes of existence in their relation to life. '[It] is not a matter of judging life in the name of a higher authority', Deleuze writes, 'which would be the good, the true; it is a matter, on the contrary, of evaluating every being, every action and passion, even every value, in relation to the life which they involve. Affect as immanent evaluation, instead of judgement as transcendent value ... '[11]

Going 'beyond good and evil' does not mean renouncing ideas of good and bad, or in Nietzsche's parlance, noble and base. What is base is an exhausted, descendent and degenerating life, especially when it seeks to propagate itself. But the noble is expressed in a blossoming, ascendant life, capable of transforming itself in cooperation with the forces it encounters, composing with them an ever-growing power, 'always increasing the power to live, always opening new "possibilities"'.[12] There is no more 'truth' in one life than the other: there is only becoming, descendant or ascendant, and life's becoming is 'the power of the false', a noble will to power. 'False' here is not opposed to the 'true', but rather allied to an aesthetic or artistic will, the will to create. The base will to power is the degenerative becoming of an exhausted life with its destructive and dominating will. But the noble will to power is characterized by a 'virtue that gives'; it is an artistic will, the becoming of an ascendant life that creates new possibilities and experiments with new modes of existence. If becoming is the power of the false, then the good, the generous or the noble is what raises the false to its highest creative or transformative powers – a becoming-artist. If there is exhaustion in this aesthetic life, Deleuze writes that it is put in service to what is reborn from life through metamorphosis and creation:

> It makes of becoming a protean Being, rather than hastening it, from the height of a uniform and fixed identity, towards non-being. These are two states of life, opposed at the heart of an immanent becoming, and not an authority that would pose itself as superior to becoming in order to judge or dominate life, thus exhausting it. What Welles sees in Falstaff or Don Quixote is the 'goodness' of life in itself, a strange goodness that carries the living toward creation. It is in this sense that one can speak of an authentic or spontaneous Nietzscheanism in Welles.[13]

Choosing to Choose: Virtual Conjunctions and Any-spaces-whatever

The Nietzschean moral universe defines an ontology of descent and ascent, destruction and creation, a base will to power fuelled by *ressentiment* and the will to truth, and a creative or artistic will that affirms life and its powers of transformation while seeking out possibilities for enhancing these powers and this life. Between these two wills lies the deepest ethical problem: the problem of choosing a mode of existence defined by the possibility of choice.[14]

The problem of the choice of a mode of existence first occurs in the pages of *Cinema 1: the Movement-Image* devoted to 'lyrical abstraction', a style found principally in the films of Robert Bresson and Carl Theodor Dreyer. Deleuze is writing here, first, of the qualities and powers of affect in the image, especially in the treatment of light. This affection-image is distinguished from other types of cinematic movement-images through its virtuality or potentiality. In this, the affection-image is unlike action-images. The latter are caught up in chains of causality – or what Deleuze calls 'real connections' – and are always expressively related to succession, as well as sets of actions and reactions rebounding between objects and persons. The action-image is thus characterized as a sensori-motor whole, bound up in an organic representation that believes in the representability of the world for a perceiving subject, as well as the unity of subject and world. Related to C. S. Peirce's category of 'Firstness', or pure pre-signifying quality, affection-images present instead 'virtual conjunctions': 'There one finds pure qualities or singular potentialities – pure "possibles", as it were'.[15] These qualities are luminescent and affective. They are possibilities for meaning and emotion expressed not in a determined and meaning-laden space, but in an 'any-space-whatever' (*espace quelconque*). They are ready to act or to signify, but one does not yet know in what direction or with what meaning. They are the virtual expression of choices yet to be accomplished.

How does the expression of choice correspond to the compositional logic of lyrical abstraction? Deleuze contrasts this style to German Expressionism, whose approach to *chiaroscuro* defines a gothic world where the struggle of shadow and light submerges the contours of things in a non-organic life. Light and darkness collude here, prolonging the anticipation of a universal dread. But in lyrical abstraction, light and darkness alternate, thus expressing 'an alternative between a given state of things and a possibility or virtuality that overtakes them … . In effect, what is essentially spiritual to lyrical abstraction is to be in search of an alternative, rather than being caught up in a struggle.'[16]

What lyrical abstraction exemplifies in the construction of any-space-whatevers are scenarios of undetermined choice. Deleuze turns here to Pascal and Kierkegaard as emblematic of a new approach to ethics in modern philosophy, where moral dilemmas are less a matter of selecting from a limited set of alternatives – the lesser evil or the greater good – than the expression of the mode of existence of the one who chooses. The first case means persuading oneself of the absence of choice or to remain in ignorance of the power to choose, either because one believes in moral necessity (this is my duty, or this confirms to an ideal of the Good), or that the situation presents no viable alternatives, or that one is condemned by an inescapable drive or desire. What Deleuze calls 'spiritual determination', however, presents the possibility of choosing a way of life along with the philosophical reasoning that accompanies it. Here the essence of moral reasoning is awareness of the choice between choosing or not-choosing. Deleuze characterizes this awareness as an extreme moralism that opposes morality, and a faith that opposes religion, exemplified by Pascal's wager:

> If I am conscious of choosing, there are, therefore, already choices I can no longer make and modes of existence I can no longer pursue, which are all of those I followed in convincing myself that 'I had no choice.' Pascal's wager says nothing else: the alternation of terms is either the affirmation of the existence of God, its denial, or the suspension of doubt and uncertainty. But the spiritual alternative is something else – it is between the mode of existence of one who 'wagers' that God exists and the mode of existence of one who gambles on non-existence or who does not want to bet. According to Pascal, only the first is conscious of the possibility of choosing; the others are only able to choose in ignorance of the choices confronting them. In sum, choice as spiritual determination has no other object than itself: I choose to choose, and in this act I exclude every choice made in the mode of not having a choice.[17]

From Pascal to Bresson, and Kierkegaard to Dreyer, Deleuze identifies an ethical typology of characters whose moral choices typify different modes of existence that swing from belief in the inescapability of a moral path to those who choose the possibility of choice. Of the former, Deleuze characterizes three types of characters and modes of existence. First there are the 'white' men of moral absolutes, of God and Virtue – the perhaps tyrannical or hypocritical guardians of religious or moral order, as in the priest-judges of Dreyer's *Jeanne d'Arc*. There are then the grey men of uncertainty or vacillation, as in the protagonists of Dreyer's *Vampyr*, Bresson's *Lancelot du lac*, or *Pickpocket*. Third, there are creatures of evil and the blackness of drives: Hélène's vengefulness in *Les Dames du bois de Boulogne*; Gérard's wickedness in *Au hazard Balthazar*; the thievery of *Pickpocket* and Yvonne's crimes in *L'argent*. These are all instances of false choice or decisions made from denying that there is or may still be a choice.

Here, Deleuze's reading of lyrical abstraction is close to the ethical interpretation of Nietzche's eternal return. We are not caught by the absolute values of darkness and light, or even the indecisiveness of grey. Rather, the possibility of 'spiritual determination', indeed what Cavell might call moral perfectionism, is a choice not to be defined by what is chosen, 'but by the power choosing possesses of being able to start again at each instant, to restart itself, and to affirm itself of itself, by putting all the stakes back into play each time. And even if this choice means sacrificing the character, this is a sacrifice made in full knowledge that it will recur each time, and for all times.'[18]

This is an image figuring an authentic choice in and of consciousness of the power to choose. To each character and image there corresponds an affect. For the white, the dark and the grey, affects are actualized in an established order or disorder (moral absolutism, indecisiveness or tragic destiny). But authentic choice 'raises affect to its pure power or potential, as in Lancelot's courtly love, but also embodies or carries out this potential so powerfully as to release in it that which will not let itself be actualized, and which overwhelms its realization (eternal recurrence.'[19] (And there is yet a fifth type: the innocent embodied by the donkey in *Au hazard Balthazar*: the holy fool who is not in a state of choosing, and who cannot know the effect of humanity's choosing, or not choosing.)

The problem of choice is presented in the affection-image by a certain relationship to light, a fluctuation of light. It is an image that solicits thought and draws us to a space of moral reasoning. Expressionism thus conveys, for Deleuze, a space determined by the alternation of terms, each of which compels an inescapable choice, in fact, a non-choice. White-Black-Grey:

> white marks our duty or power; black, our impotence or thirst for evil; grey, our uncertainty, restlessness, or indifference.... [But] only one other implies that we choose to choose, or that we are conscience of choice.... We have reached a philosophical space [*espace spirituel*] where what we choose is no longer distinct from choice itself. Lyrical abstraction is defined by the adventure of light and white. But the episodes of this adventure mean, first, that the white that imprisons light alternates with the black that stops it, and then white is liberated in an alternative, which restores to us the white *and* the black. We have travelled, without moving, from one space to another, from a physical to a philosophical space of experimentation (or metaphysics).[20]

From Classic to Modern Cinema: The Crisis in Belief

This passage already anticipates the problems raised by modern cinema in *Cinema 2: The Time-Image*. The organic representation of the movement-image is based on connections that are 'rational' as well as real. The term 'rational' indicates a formal relation that assures the continuity of shots within each segment, the spatial contiguity of one segment to another, and the dialectical unity of parts within the whole of the film. But these rational connections also have an ethical dimension – they are expressive of a will to truth. They express belief in the possibility and coherence of a complete and truthful representation of the world in images, and of the world in relation to thought, that is extendible in a dialectical unity encompassing image, world and subject – hence Sergei Eisenstein's belief in the utopia of an intellectual cinema and of a direct relation between image and thought.

In Deleuze's account, however, modern cinema is inaugurated by a crisis in the action-image, and a corresponding crisis in belief. This crisis is profoundly related to the dilemma of scepticism, though Deleuze's conception of the history of cinema in relation to ontological and moral reasoning differs significantly from Cavell's. In its purest form, the movement-image – or what Deleuze calls the plane of immanence – defines a world where scepticism is absent or irrelevant. This is a world defined by Spinoza's pure ontology of one unique substance, or Bergson's world of universal change and variation based on the equivalence of matter and light, and memory and matter, in a world of open creation. But from this world there emerges the *cinematic* movement-image, which, in believing itself to have overcome scepticism in the form of an identity between image and thought, nonetheless perpetuates the division of subject and object as a problem. Thus the organic form of the cinematic movement-image believes in the representability of the world for a knowing subject, but in the form of a will to truth – a separation and rejoining of subject and object. Sergei Eisenstein's theories remain the most powerful visions of a cinematic movement-image that forges a dialectical unity of subject and world through cinematic representation – the utopia of a truthful representation founded on the laws of a 'non-indifferent nature'.[21] And indeed this is a 'white' theory where all is subsumed to the dialectics of nature, and choice is no longer a possibility.

It is important to emphasize here that the purest form of the cinematic movement-image image is rare. The logic of affection-images and the expressiveness of any-space-whatevers demonstrate that the action-image is, rather, in a continuous state of crisis or struggle with the essential movements of the world and of cinema, where time is defined not as space, but rather as force, the Open or the virtual – the eternally recurring potentiality for new creation in each passing present. Similarly, there is no clear historical break between the movement-image and the time-image, for the direct-image of time is an ever-renewable possibility recurring throughout the history of cinema, like an underground river that swells and recedes unpredictably, gushing up in springs or receding still and hidden beneath deserts.[22]

Therefore, the recurrence of Bresson and Dreyer in the second volume demonstrates a deep connection across the two cinema books. There is less a break between the modern and classic cinema, than a shift in the concept of belief, where the direct image of time restores or gives new expression to a potentiality always present, always renewable, within film's expressive movements. If the ethical stance of the cinematic movement-image is expressive of a will to truth, then that of the direct image of time is given in powers of the false that challenge the coherence and unity of organic representation. Indeed, for Deleuze, modern cinema emerges from a profound and global crisis of belief, experienced as a traumatic gulf between humanity and the world. With neither causality nor teleology directing the unfolding of images, nor a given totality in which they can be comprehended as a Whole, the powers of non-determined choice anticipated by affection-images are raised here to a new power. Consequently, there arises within the universe of modern cinema a new moral type defined by their sensitivity to 'pure optical and acoustical situations' and their susceptibility to 'wandering forms' (*la forme-balade*) – affective situations where characters stroll or stray without obvious goals, destinations or motivation. Best exemplified by Ingrid Bergman in Rossellini's great postwar trilogy – *Voyage in Italy*, *Europa 51*, and *Stromboli* – the protagonists of modern cinema wander and observe. They transmit sights rather than motivating movements and actions: 'the character becomes a kind of spectator. She may move, run or stir restlessly, but the situation in which she finds herself overflows her motor capacities on all sides, making her see and hear what no longer justifies a response or an action. She registers more than reacts. She surrenders to a vision, which she pursues or which pursues her, rather than engaging in an action'.[23]

Finally, this modern cinema is subject to a generalized paranoia, sensitive to conspiracy and suspicious of all forms of totality. In this, Deleuze writes, 'the pure optical and acoustical situation does not extend into action, any more than it is induced by an action. It makes us grasp, or it is supposed to make us grasp, something intolerable, unbearable. ... It is matter of something too powerful or too unjust, but sometimes also too beautiful, that henceforth exceeds our motor capacities.'[24] (In sum, the time-image produces characters and affective situations marked by a perceptual sensitivity to the intolerability of a world where faith and confidence in representation have disappeared, and where we are consumed by 'The idea of one single misery, interior and exterior, in the world and in consciousness ...'[25] Or, as Ingrid Bergman exclaims in *Europa 51*: 'something possible, otherwise I will suffocate'.

The Subtle Way Out

Both Cavell and Deleuze assert a special connection between cinema and the concept of belief. The movement-image as plane of immanence is the most direct expression of a link between being and the world, or matter becoming luminescent, and thought emerging in relation to the movements of the world. The *cinematic* movement-image and time-image, however, appear as two ethical directions across this plane of immanence: one a transformation of the world by humanity, or the Eisensteinian belief that one can construct an image that makes thought happen; the other is Antonin Artaud's intuition of an interior, deeper world 'before man' as it were, produced from a shock to thought or by thought's confrontation with what is unthinkable. This is a confrontation with a time which is not that of Being, identity or teleology, but rather an anticipatory time – of contingency, the purely conditional, the non-determined or not yet.

The dilemma of modern cinema is in many respects that of scepticism as Cavell describes it. But Cavell describes belief in the mode of credibility and a potential overcoming of scepticism. In contrast, a European pessimism pervades Deleuze's account. As in Kracauer's late theory, the confrontation with postwar destruction, genocide and the collapse of the grand narratives of ideology and utopia mark the decline of belief, expressed as a crisis in the action-image and the collapse of the sensori-motor schema. For Deleuze, modernity is experienced as a kind of traumatism. The break in the sensori-motor whole and the emergence of pure optical and acoustical situations:

> makes man a seer who finds himself struck by something intolerable in the world, and confronted by something unthinkable in thought. Between the two, thought undergoes a strange fossilization, which is as it were its powerlessness to function, to be, its dispossession of itself and the world. For it is not in the name of a better or truer world that thought captures the intolerable in this world, but, on the contrary, it is because this world is intolerable that it can no longer think a world or think itself. The intolerable is no longer a serious injustice, but the permanent state of daily banality. Man *is not himself* a world other than the one in which he experiences the intolerable and feels himself trapped.[26]

The problem then becomes: how to restore belief in a world of universal pessimism, where we have no more faith in images than we do in the world?

In the pure optical situation, the seer is alienated both within herself and from the world, but she also sees farther, better and deeper than she can react or think. This augmentation of the powers of sight and of sensitivity to the injustices of the world may give the appearance of passivity, or an impotence of thought before that which is intolerable to consider. But for Deleuze, the solution is not to quail before the thought that there is no alternative to this or any other situation. What Deleuze calls the 'im-powers of thought' demand a revaluation of our perceptual disjunction from the world that makes of it the possibility for a new faith, and a new thought. The problem of scepticism is here radically reconfigured. It is not that we are perceptually disjoined from the world, but rather that self, sight, and thought are divided from within and from one another by time, or by the force of time's passing. What is outside of thought that thought must confront as the unthought, is our existential and ethical relationship to time as an infinite reservoir of non-determined choice, which is also an ontology where life and thought are inseparable.

What Deleuze calls the 'subtle way out' of this dilemma has already been introduced through the concept of lyrical abstraction – to commit to a mode of existence in which one chooses out of faith in the link between world, thought and life. An arc must be drawn between the *Movement-Image* and the *Time-Image*, where new thought is generated by experiencing the powerlessness to think, just as new alternatives emerge in confrontation with the inability to choose:

> Which, then, is the subtle way out? To believe, not in a different world, but in a link between man and the world, in love or life, to believe in this as in the impossible, the unthinkable, which none the less cannot but be thought: 'something possible, otherwise I will suffocate'. It is this belief that makes the unthought the specific power of thought, through the absurd, by virtue of the absurd. Artaud never understood powerlessness to think as a simple inferiority which would strike us in relation to thought. It is part of thought, so that we should make our way of thinking from it, without claiming to be restoring an all-powerful thought. We should rather make use of this powerlessness to believe in life, and to discover the identity of thought and life.... '[27]

For Deleuze, the basic fact of modernity is that 'we longer believe in this world'. However, much is explained by emphasizing that 'we no longer believe in *this* world', that is, the world present to us, in which we are present, and which comprises the present time we occupy as a constant becoming:

> We no longer even believe in the events that happen to us, love or death, as if they hardly concern us. We do not make cinema; rather, the world looks to us like a bad film.... It is the link between man and the world that has been broken. Henceforth, this link must become an object of belief, as the impossible that must be given back in faith. Belief is no longer addressed to

> another world, or a transformed world. Man is in the world as if in a pure optical or acoustical situation. The reaction of which man is dispossessed can only be replaced by belief. Only belief in the world can reconnect man to what he sees and hears. Cinema must not film the world, but rather belief in this world, our only link. One often questions the nature of cinematographic illusion. To give us back belief in the world – this is the power of modern cinema (when it stops being shoddy). Christians or atheists, in our universal schizophrenia *we need reasons to believe in this world.*[28]

From Eisenstein to Artaud, the ethical problem for Deleuze is to understand that the traumatic unlinking of being from the world is yet more powerfully a leap towards faith in life, in *this* life or this world and its powers of self-transformation. The time-image's powers of the false do not show that the image is an illusion, nor do they replace a false perception with a true one. Rather, the powers of the false release the image from the form of identity and restore to it the potential for Becoming or eternal recurrence. From the cinematic movement-image to the time-image, from Pascal to Nietzsche, and in the cinema of Rossellini and Dreyer, a great shift occurs in philosophy, replacing the model of knowledge with that of belief as if in a conversion from piety to atheism, and moralism to morality – thus the turning points represented in the history of moral reasoning by Deleuze's pairing of Pascal and Hume, Kant and Fichte, or Kierkegaard and Nietzsche. One should emphasize that knowledge is based on faith no less than belief; namely, the will to truth and a belief in humanity's technological domination of nature. But even among the 'pious' philosophers here, belief no longer turns towards another, transcendent world, but is directed rather to *this* world, the one in which we exist. In Deleuze's account, what Kierkegaard or even Pascal assert in the concept of faith is something that returns to us humanity's link with the world and with life. Hence, belief only replaces knowledge when it elicits belief in this world and its future-oriented powers.

Deleuze's ethics, then, is a moral reasoning that wants to give back to us a belief capable of perpetuating life as movement, change, becoming – the eternal recurrence of difference. And rather than yearning for another transcendent or transformed world, we must believe in the body and the flesh, to believe in the substance of the world and the world as substance, returning to them all their one and unique voice:

> We must believe in the body as in the germ of life, a seed that splits the pavement, that is conserved and perpetuated in the holy shroud or mummy's wrappings, and which bears witness to life and to this very world such that it is. We need an ethic or a faith that makes idiots laugh, not a need to believe in something else, but a need to believe in this world, of which fools are a part.[29]

Belief must then be reconnected to the two principles of Deleuze's system. Scepticism is the sign of a thought disconnected from Life comprised of a single substance and a time of constant becoming. But Being and thought are in Life; they speak with a single voice and become in the same time, such that scepticism must be overcome with another will to power, which draws its energy from Life's potential for self-differentiation, and moralism overcome by choosing to believe in the ever-renewable possibility of beginning again – eternal recurrence.

Notes

1 S. Kracauer, 1960, *Theory of Film*, New York: Oxford University Press, 285.

2 *Cinema 1: The Movement-Image*, 1986, trans. H. Tomlinson and B. Habberjam, Minneapolis: University of Minnesota Press; and *Cinema 2: The Time-Image*, 1989, trans. H. Tomlinson and R. Galeta, Minneapolis: University of Minnesota Press. The original editions were published in Paris by Éditions de Minuit (1983 and 1985). I have modified most of the translations cited here. When this is the case, page numbers from the original French editions are cited in italics.

The ethical arguments of especially *Cinema 2* are taken up in interesting ways in Deleuze and Guattari's final published work, *What is Philosophy?* 1994, trans. H. Tomlinson and G. Burchell, New York: Columbia University Press. I comment on this relation in the concluding chapter of *Gilles Deleuze's Time Machine*, 1997, Durham: Duke University Press, 194–210.

3 W. V. Quine, 1953, 'Mr. Strawson on logical theory', *Mind*, New Series, 62:248, October, 433–51.

4 The relation between Deleuze and Cavell as the two most compelling voices in contemporary film philosophy is a central feature of my forthcoming book from Harvard University Press, *Elegy for Theory*, 2014.

5 A. Gualandi, 1998, *Deleuze*, Paris: Les Belles Lettres, 18–19; my translation, also A. Badiou's 1997 *Deleuze: La clameur de l'Être*, Paris: Hachette.

6 G. Deleuze, 1984, *Kant's Critical Philosophy*, trans. H. Tomlinson and B. Habberjam, Minneapolis: University of Minnesota Press, viii.

7 G. Deleuze, 1983, *Nietzsche and Philosophy*, trans. H. Tomlinson, New York: Columbia University Press, 48.
8 Ibid. 54.
9 Deleuze, *Time-Image*, 140–1, *183–4*.
10 Ibid. 140–1, *184*.
11 Ibid. 141, *184–5*.
12 Ibid.
13 Ibid. 142, *185–6*.
14 This problem is explored in depth in R. Bogue's 2010 'To choose to choose – to believe in this world' in D. N. Rodowick (ed.), *Afterimages of Gilles Deleuze's Film Philosophy*, Minneapolis: University of Minnesota, 115–32.
15 Deleuze, *Movement-Image*, 102, *145*.
16 Ibid. 112–13, *158–9*.
17 Ibid. 114, *161*.
18 Ibid. 115, *162*.
19 Ibid. 115–16, *163*.
20 Ibid. 117, *165*.
21 See S. Eisenstein, 1987, *Nonindifferent Nature: Film and the Structure of Things*, trans. H. Marshall, Cambridge, UK: Cambridge University Press.
22 On the historical relation between the cinematic movement and time-images, see my 2001 essay, 'A geneaology of time' in *Reading the Figural, or Philosophy after the New Media*, Durham, NC: Duke University Press, 170–202.
23 *Time-Image* 3, *9*
24 *Time-Image*, 18, *29*.
25 *Movement-Image*, 209.
26 *Time-Image*, 169–70, *220–1*.
27 Ibid.
28 Ibid. 171–2, *223*.
29 Ibid. 173, *225*.

3

Technologies of Enchantment: Figures of Wonder in Cyberfiction

Veronica Hollinger

The cyberfictions I will discuss here are stories about the networked worlds of technovisual media, digital communications and virtual-reality technologies. They provide some of the narrative shapes of our unnatural nature as human beings who are necessarily also technological beings, for whom technoscience has become a kind of second nature. 'What is at stake in technology,' Nick Mansfield writes in his study, *Subjectivity*, 'is not our inevitable doom if the machines get out of control ... but what it means to be in the world, the world's meaning for us and the horizons of possibility for human experience: what shall we feel, what might we become?'[1] Unconfined by the generic limitations of realism, science-fiction stories can literalize some of the complex metaphors of the subject suggested in contemporary theory, and can extend the project of critical estrangement from the abstractions of theory into the powerfully involving pleasures of genre fiction. From this perspective, it is science-fiction stories themselves that are the 'technologies of enchantment' of my title.

Techno-pastoral Re-enchantment

A poem written in 1967 by American counterculture writer Richard Brautigan looks forward to a newly re-enchanted world, a cheerful utopia in which nature and the machine are benevolently entwined, and in which the human subject is assured of a home:

I like to think (and
the sooner the better!)
of a cybernetic meadow
where mammals and computers
live together in mutually
programming harmony
like pure water
touching clear sky.

I like to think
(right now, please!)
of a cybernetic forest
filled with pines and electronics
where deer stroll peacefully
past computers
as if they were flowers
with spinning blossoms.

I like to think
(it has to be!)
of a cybernetic ecology
where we are free of our labors
and joined back to nature
returned to our mammal
brothers and sisters,
and all watched over
by machines of loving grace.[2]

Brautigan's *All Watched Over By Machines of Loving Grace* counters, at least in imagination, some features of what political theorist Jane Bennett calls the disenchantment of modernity. In her study *The Enchantment of Modern Life*, Bennett offers a kind of master-narrative of disenchantment distilled from the writings of such diverse thinkers as Rousseau, Marx and Weber. Arguably, for many people in Western technoculture, this is a much more convincing scenario than is Brautigan's techno-pastoral utopia:

> There was once a time when Nature was purposive, God was active in the details of human affairs, human and other creatures were defined by

> a preexisting web of relations, social life was characterized by face-to-face relations, and political order took the form of organic community. Then, this premodern world gave way to forces of scientific and instrumental rationality, secularism, individualism, and the bureaucratic state, all of which, combined, disenchant the world.[3]

Perhaps it is not so surprising that in many 'disenchantment' scenarios, technology figures as the material representation of the overwhelming forces of rationalization and routinization that are perceived to have, since the onset of Western Enlightenment, progressively deadened the world of nature and deprived us of our 'natural' home. Brautigan's poem is striking for the way in which it attempts to re-inscribe technology into the world of nature – computers like 'flowers with spinning blossoms' – and to imagine technology's providential role in freeing us from the exigencies of history.

'The Machine Stops': Trapped in the Scene of the Screen

> The whole life of those societies in which modern conditions of production prevail presents itself as an immense accumulation of spectacles. All that once was directly lived has become mere representation.[4]

This is the dire judgement that opens Guy Debord's *Society of the Spectacle*. It is a nice coincidence that Brautigan's counterculture vision and Debord's Marxist critique were both published in 1967, a relatively early moment in the cybernetic revolution. If Brautigan's dream of the technological future is about reconciliation with nature, Debord's nightmare is about the deadening effects of mass-media culture. This is clearly related to what Jean Baudrillard will later refer to as 'fascination' – a mesmerized passivity in the face of the hyperreality of the image, of the growing perfection of its simulations. While the experience of enchantment can be understood to imply the experience of presence, however understood, it is the function of the hyperreal to mask the fact of an absence – there is nothing that binds the simulation to the Real.[5] We might consider that, while enchantment can stimulate new and productive activity in the world, the effects of Baudrillardian fascination are passivity and paralysis, the very antithesis of political possibility.

One of the very earliest science-fictional stories to use technology as a figure for increasing social, political and cultural bureaucratization and homogenization was published just over a century ago. British writer E. M. Forster's 'The Machine Stops' (1909) is perhaps the first fully imagined dystopia in Anglo-American literature. The British tradition of 'scientific romance' that had its origins in the early novels of H. G. Wells and to which, arguably, Forster's story belongs, was always more suspicious of technoscientific progress than was the more expansive American tradition of gung-ho early pulp science fiction. Forster's story – the only one of its kind he ever wrote – is a prescient version of what has become a familiar critique of technoculture, and especially of the world-wide communications media that support (and often represent) the networks of transnational politics and economics.

'The Machine Stops' warns of the severe consequences of an increasing (Baudrillardian) fascination with ever more pervasive – and ever more invasive – technologies. These include:

(1) the loss of authentic communication and community (it was Forster who gave us one of the iconic modernist tenets: 'only connect');[6]
(2) the insignificance of the physical body, and the dismissal of desire and emotion;
(3) the erasure of the natural world, replaced by the cold sterility of 'the Machine';
(4) the alienation of the human subject from both the natural world and the second nature of technoculture.

'The Machine Stops' paints a harrowing portrait of human life trapped in 'the scene of the screen', to borrow a phrase from film theorist and phenomenologist Vivian Sobchack. Describing the experience of digital media two decades ago, Sobchack writes:

> Television, video cassettes, video tape recorder/players, video games, and personal computers all form an encompassing electronic representational system whose various forms 'interface' to constitute an alternative and absolute world that uniquely incorporates the spectator/user in a spatially decentered, weakly temporalized, and quasi-disembodied state.[7]

Although the system of global communications that Forster imagines is relatively primitive, his characters are trapped in just such 'an alternative and absolute world'. His attenuated future humans are described as white hairless slugs; they are abject, solitary and stunted, and utterly dependent upon 'the Machine', which has grown into a global network of total control. Even as Forster's future humans have lost the ability to understand how the Machine was constructed and maintained by their ancestors,[8] they have become ever more convinced of its transcendent nature. Eventually it demands that they worship it as a god. Forster's Machine is like the perverse dark side of Brautigan's 'machines of loving grace', given the awful price that human beings must pay in order to enjoy its blessings.

Forster's objections to the mediated nature of communication in his fictional dystopia are aesthetic as well as philosophical and political: it is bland, tasteless and alienating. It lacks the enchantment of authentic presence. As the narrator explains:

> the Machine did not transmit *nuances* of expression. It only gave a general idea of people – an idea that was good enough for all practical purposes.... The imponderable bloom, declared by a discredited philosophy to be the actual essence of intercourse, was rightly ignored by the Machine.... Something 'good enough' had long since been accepted by our race (emphasis in original).[9]

One of the characters issues a passionate protest at the distortion of 'natural' human relations:

> [The Machine] has robbed us of the sense of space and of the sense of touch, it has blurred every human relation and narrowed down love to a carnal act, it has paralysed our bodies and our wills, and now it compels us to worship it.... The Machine proceeds – but not to our goal.... [I]f it could work without us, it would let us die.[10]

As a story, 'The Machine Stops' dramatizes the disenchantment of the world under the soul-destroying regime of a vast technological system that reduces human beings to helpless nodes in its networks. As a cultural text, 'The Machine Stops' is an exercise in disenchantment as demystification. In true dystopian fashion, it warns its readers – who may also blindly worship the Machine – to consider the price of such willful blindness.

The story's final scene offers a glimpse of what has been lost – and reveals what might yet be found again. In an apocalyptic climax, the Machine finally collapses: 'the entire communication-system broke down, all over the world, and the world, as they understood it, ended'.[11] Before they join 'the nations of the dead', Forster's characters – and his readers also – are given a revelation of authentic nature as they are at last able to see, in the final words of the story, 'scraps of the untainted sky'.[12]

The Dialectic of Disenchantment and Re-enchantment

Science explains the world, but only Art can reconcile us to it.[13]

Here I want to take a brief tangent to consider the complex interplay of enchantment and disenchantment in science fiction.[14] As commonly understood, science fiction would seem to be an exemplary literature of disenchantment, devoted to the work of demystification. The science-fiction universe is unheeding of human beings and without inherent meaning. Science fiction's plots, at least in theory, rigorously adhere to the logic of cause and effect. There are no supernatural or transcendent elements in its fictional worlds, no magic, no events not susceptible to rational explanation. There are even jokes in the field about the number of science fiction stories written in which the climax goes something like: 'omigod, the all-powerful Oracle is really ... a computer!' Science fiction is 'the materialist genre par excellence'.[15]

But this is by no means the whole generic story, because of science fiction's 'oxymoronic fusion of the rational and the marvelous'.[16] Science fiction also appeals to the reader's 'sense of wonder'. In this view, the potential for (re)enchantment through story-telling is virtually hard-wired into the genre: early pulp magazines had titles such as *Amazing*, *Astounding* and *Thrilling Wonder Stories*, and even academics have not been immune to the genre's attractions: one of the field's most widely used reference works, now in its fifth edition, is Neil Barron's *Anatomy of Wonder*.[17] The editors of *The Cambridge Companion to Science Fiction* identify the 'sense of wonder' as 'the emotional heart of science fiction'.[18]

Darko Suvin has very influentially described science fiction as a 'literature of cognitive estrangement'.[19] Cognition points to the rational elements in its stories, to the logic of its universes – what we might consider its debts to realism. At the same time, the estrangement of the reader from the conventions and norms of the 'real world' gives the science fiction story the capacity to activate the reader's critical distance from those norms – thus its (Brechtian) potential as a political genre, its 'alienation' of the reader from things usually taken for granted. But estrangement also refers to the fact that science fiction can present the familiar things of the world in new and surprising configurations, inviting their reconsideration and fresh appreciation – evoking, in other words, the reader's sense of wonder. As Neil Easterbrook points out, this is the kind of estrangement usually associated with Russian Formalism; it is 'the revivified aesthetic experience generated by a literature that makes a tired, familiar world strange and wondrous again'.[20]

The cognition/estrangement binary is always open to deconstruction, of course, if only because intellectual reflection can itself be magical, and it is not always very easy to separate ideas and aesthetics: in Australian writer Greg Egan's *Schild's Ladder* (2001), two far-future post-human lovers, reunited after millennia, decide against renewing their sexual relationship: 'Nothing could have lived up to four thousand years of waiting. Except perhaps an original theorem.'[21]

Neuromancer: The Enchantments of Cyberspace

> Gibson's fiction returns, as to a tonic, to the question of how artists can represent the human condition in a social world saturated by cybernetic technologies.[22]

The dialectical play of enchantment and disenchantment is a key element in one of the most significant English-language novels of the late twentieth century, William Gibson's cyberpunk classic *Neuromancer* (1984). Here I want to take up Gibson's introduction of the idea of 'cyberspace' as an estrangement of the experience of technovisuality that appeals strongly to the reader's 'sense of wonder'. By the mid-1980s, warnings such as Forster's about the looming implosion of nature and (techno)culture were long out of date: that implosion was clearly well underway. It is the sense that the future is very close indeed, that it may already have arrived, that is so striking about *Neuromancer*. As David Bell notes in his 2007 study, *Cyberculture Theorists*, cyberspace still 'sounds like the future was supposed to be'.[23]

The recently published *Oxford Dictionary of Science Fiction*, rather enchantingly titled *Brave New Words*, defines cyberspace as:

> the entirety of the data stored in, and the communication that takes place within, a computer network, conceived of as having the properties of a physical realm; the environment of virtual reality.[24]

Here is the well known passage from *Neuromancer* which introduces cyberspace – juxtaposing cool 'scientific' description and irresistible visual propulsion:

> 'The matrix has its roots in primitive arcade games,' said the voice-over, 'in early graphics programs and military experimentation with cranial jacks.' On the Sony, a two-dimensional space war faded behind a forest of mathematically generated ferns, demonstrating the spatial possibilities of logarithmic spirals; cold blue military footage burned through, lab animals wired into test systems, helmets feeding into fire control circuits of tanks and war planes. 'Cyberspace. A consensual hallucination experienced daily by billions of legitimate operators, in every nation, by children being taught mathematical concepts.... A graphic representation of data abstracted from the banks of every computer in the human system. Unthinkable complexity. Lines of light ranged in the nonspace of the mind, clusters and constellations of data. Like city lights, receding .'[25]

Not for nothing does Csicsery-Ronay refer to Gibson's writing as effecting both 'a lyricism of estrangement and an allegory of the present'.[26]

Neuromancer was widely read as capturing the particular feel of 1980s and 1990s experiences of networked technovisuality, at the same time as it exuberantly evoked the future promise of 'the scene of the screen'. Gibson's cyberspace responds to virtually all of Forster's aesthetic objections to technological mediation. 'Jacking in' provides an immersive experience that is as immediate as can be imagined: it is completely absorbing and it overwhelms the senses – at least virtually – with speed and motion and *lightness*. It is everything that being a body – being *in* a body – is not. Gibson's cyberspace aesthetic has been compared to that of the Italian Futurists in its passion for movement, for the rush of adrenalin, for the thrill of disembodied flight.[27]

At the same time, *Neuromancer* is quintessentially a novel of disenchantment. It is worth noting the almost diametrically opposed treatment of the nature/culture binary in the worlds imagined by Brautigan and Gibson. In 'All Watched Over by Machines of Loving Grace', technological artifacts are naturalized, given their place in the 'cybernetic forest . . . where deer stroll peacefully / past computers / as if they were flowers / with spinning blossoms.'

The language of Gibson's text, on the other hand, draws everything into the framework of the technological; the world of nature is now captured in the metaphors of the artifactual, exemplified in the well-known first sentence of the novel: 'The sky above the port was the color of television, tuned to a dead channel.'[28] In contrast to the promise implied at the end of 'The Machine Stops', there is no 'untainted sky' in *Neuromancer*'s fictional world, except perhaps in the simulations of cyberspace.

Many readers have found in *Neuromancer* a dystopian vision as bleak as Forster's. Its action is set sometime after an apocalyptic three-week-long war and after a pandemic that has resulted in the extinction of most of the larger mammals. Its characters have little or no experience of the natural world, which is largely irrelevant to the story in any case; human agency is much diminished as well, as the human characters are manipulated by Wintermute, the vastly powerful artificial intelligence that literally drives the plot.

Gibson's protagonist, Case, is technology's creature, addicted to the rush of cyberspace, to the sensation of disembodied freedom from 'the meat . . . and all it wants'[29] – he is just 'wired' that way, as his lover tells him, once again collapsing nature into technoculture. At the beginning of the novel, when Case loses the ability to access cyberspace, it is as if he has been expelled from a virtual Garden of Eden: 'For Case, who'd lived for the bodiless exultation of cyberspace, it was the Fall . . . . The body was meat. Case fell into the prison of his own flesh.'[30]

When Case once again experiences cyberspace, it is a technologically induced moment of sublime wholeness:

> Disk beginning to rotate, faster, becoming a sphere of paler gray. Expanding –
>
> And flowed, flowered for him, fluid neon origami trick, the unfolding of his distance-less home, his country, transparent 3D chessboard extending to infinity. Inner eye opening to the stepped scarlet pyramid of the Eastern Seaboard Fission Authority burning beyond the green cubes of Mitsubishi

> Bank of America, and high and very far away he saw the spiral arms of military systems, forever beyond his reach.
>
> And somewhere he was laughing,... distant fingers caressing the deck, tears of release streaking his face.[31]

Passionately opposed to the *thingness* of the meat-body, Case experiences what one critic calls 'the information-network sublime'.[32] He has found his home in second nature.[33] Even so – and what is not always remembered about *Neuromancer* – the plot does not finally privilege the virtual over the actual: Case refuses the opportunity to remain in cyberspace, in spite of the AI's assurance that 'To live here is to live. There is no difference.'[34] He is not ready completely to abandon 'the meat and all it wants'.

The AI Wintermute also, in the end, utters the novel's most devastating denial of any possibility for genuine transformation in this worn-out near-future, in spite of the almost god-like powers it achieves in cyberspace. Case asks Wintermute: 'How are things different? You running the world now? You God?' To which the AI responds: 'Things aren't different. Things are things.'[35] *Neuromancer* is one of the great narratives of technoscientific disenchantment, both because of and in spite of the fearful attractions of cyberspace.

Building on this precursor, British science fiction writer Charles Stross, in his novel *Halting State* (2007), describes one character's experience of computer-gaming in a way that directly taps into the promise and the dread of Gibson's cyberspace; the passage also draws on Brautigan's poem as an intertext, to rather chilling effect. As players do today, Stross's character enters the game world through his avatar, and he uses a headset to communicate with other players. As he stares at his computer screen during the course of the game:

> The sky turns deep blue, the world freezes, and a progress bar marches slowly across it from horizon to horizon. Ethereal runes ... scrawl across the heavens, UPDATING REALITY, and for a moment your skin crawls with superstitious dread. *Someday we're all going to get brain implants and experience this directly. Someday* everyone *is going to live their lives out in places like this, vacant bodies tended by machines of loving grace while their minds go on before us into strange spaces where the meat cannot follow*. You can see it coming, slamming towards you out of the future ... (emphasis in original).[36]

Pattern Recognition: The Disenchantment of the Future

> I think we live in an incomprehensible moment, and what I'm actually trying to do is illuminate the moment – and make the moment accessible. I'm not even trying to explain the moment – I'm just trying to make it accessible.[37]

Gibson's seventh novel, *Pattern Recognition* – which appeared in 2003 – is unexpectedly set in the near past of 2002.[38] Its touchstone event is the fall of the World Trade Centre towers in New York on 11 September, 2001, and at the centre of its plot is a technovisual artifact – 'the footage' that could not be more different from 'cyberspace'. The 'footage' is a collection of film fragments that have been circulated anonymously on the internet. They seem to be from a mysterious work-in-progress, and they have become fetishized by an international community of devotees – 'footage-heads' – that includes Gibson's protagonist, Cayce.[39] In contrast to *Neuromancer*'s post-futurist passion for virtual reality's rush of disembodied mind through infinite space, the images of the footage suggest for Cayce a utopian fantasy of stillness. They lack sound, colour, movement and context. In the acceleration and noise of the post-modern present, their appeal – their claim to wonder – is precisely their silent minimalism.

Although set in the present, *Pattern Recognition* tells a story that Gibson has told before in his stories about the near-future – a story about how we find ourselves permeated by futurity in a present of constant change.

The 'typical' Gibson novel introduces the possibility of profound (technological) change into its fictional world and then breaks off as if unable to envisage what comes next; the event horizon looms too closely and puts paid to the futuristic imagination. At the end of *Neuromancer*, for example, this radical event is the unprecedented coming-to-consciousness of the cyberspatial 'deus ex machina', the Wintermute AI. At the end of his last science fiction novel, *All Tomorrow's Parties* (1999), inconceivable transformations are promised at the intersections of artificial intelligence and nanotechnology, but the novel ends before it can tell us what those transformations might be.[40]

In a 2003 interview, Gibson noted:

> There's something so obvious that it seems almost silly to point it out ... but we're living in a world that resembles nothing so much as dozens and

dozens of overlapping, really lurid science-fiction scenarios. Any attempt at literary naturalism in 2003 will bring the author into direct contact with material that 20 years ago would have been barely publishable as science fiction . . . .[41]

More directly than Gibson's science-fiction novels, *Pattern Recognition* self-consciously considers the difficulty of imagining viable futures. The most often quoted passage in the novel is spoken by Hubertus Bigend, the sinister businessman who represents the new world order of global corporate culture:

we have no idea, now, of who or what the inhabitants of our future might be. In that sense, we have no future. Not in the sense that our grandparents had a future, or thought they did. Fully imagined cultural futures were the luxury of another day, one in which 'now' was of some greater duration. For us, of course, things can change so abruptly, so violently, so profoundly, that futures like our grandparents' have insufficient 'now' to stand on.[42]

From this perspective, *Pattern Recognition* is about the disenchantment of futurity. It situates 9/11 as a kind of boundary event – on the other side of which we find ourselves confined to a future-present that promises only more of the same – that is, more of post-modern culture's perpetual difference.

Cayce is fascinated by the footage because it suggests to her a dreamworld unmarked by period or politics. Typical fragments show a young couple against a variety of unrecognizable but resonant backgrounds; the segments may or may not be the work of a single artist, and they may or may not be going to amount to a single and sustained narrative:

Light and shadow. Lovers' cheekbones in the prelude to embrace.

Cayce shivers. . . .

They are dressed as they have always been dressed, in clothing Cayce has posted on extensively, fascinated by its timelessness. . . . He might be a sailor, stepping onto a submarine in 1914, or a jazz musician entering a club in 1957. There is a lack of evidence, an absence of stylistic clues, that Cayce understands to be utterly masterful.[43]

Cayce is embedded in the transitoriness of the *now*, a moment that is virtually defined by the fact that it cannot remain itself. In contrast, the couple in the footage exist in a magical plane unmarked by history and they are situated by the text as the signifier of both authenticity and immediacy. *Now* has no present-ness, because it is so volatile; the images of the footage, because they are unmoored from the specificities of history and geography, represent for Cayce and other footage-heads a kind of stillness pervaded by presence.

Perhaps these images are a romantic *hommage* to an outdated ideology of the human subject as timeless and universal. Read this way, it makes sense that Cayce cannot access the experience of the footage in the way that Gibson's original Case had access to the enthralling realm of cyberspace. The footage shows her a world of impossible desire that she can only experience from the outside, as a spectator and never a participant. Like Baudrillardian simulacra, these images float free of the Real and represent, finally, the absence at the heart of image culture.[44]

Gibson's brilliance is his ability to dramatize, through Cayce's acute sensitivity to contemporary commodity culture, the psychic experience of the future-present in a way that thoroughly estranges it – Cayce's world of 2002 feels like science fiction:

> Looking up now into the manically animated forest of signs [in Tokyo], she sees the Coca-Cola logo pulsing on a huge screen, high up on a building, followed by the slogan 'NO REASON!' This vanishes, replaced by a news clip, dark-skinned men in bright robes. She blinks, imagining the towers burning there, framed amid image-flash and whirl.[45]

Fredric Jameson astutely notes that, for Cayce, the 'utter lack of style' of the footage 'is an ontological relief.... The footage is an epoch of rest, an escape from the noisy commodities' which increasingly fill up the post-modern world of global capitalism.[46] Not surprisingly, Hubertus Bigend is also fascinated by the footage, which for him represents the ultimate product: 'My passion,' he tells Cayce, 'is marketing, advertising, media strategy, and when I first discovered the footage, that is what responded in me.'[47] In part, the plot hinges on whether or not Bigend will succeed in transforming the footage from mysterious artwork to popular commodity. In fact, the footage turns out to be without any inherent significance at all.

If cyberspace sounds 'like the future was supposed to be', the footage suggests a surprising retreat from that future. Cayce spends much of the novel travelling, and she suffers from almost constant jet lag: 'her mortal soul is leagues behind her'.[48] She is unable to catch up with herself, unable to rest, unable to feel at home anywhere. Gibson's 'happy ending' is to show us Cayce at last sleeping peacefully. No revelation, no transformation – nothing but Gibson's attempt to 'make the moment accessible'.

Air and the Singularity: The Re-enchantment of the Future

All that is solid melts into air.[49]

It has become a serious challenge for contemporary cyberfiction to imagine futures that are both open and accessible, and to tell stories about how subjects who are more or less like ourselves can get there from here – to address what Nick Mansfield calls 'the horizons of possibility for human experience'.[50] This difficulty is perhaps most evident in 'Singularity fiction', a particular kind of far-future fiction associated with authors such as Iain M. Banks, Cory Doctorow, Greg Egan, Justina Robson and Charles Stross; Singularity fiction is one of science fiction's most intriguing responses to the breathless pace of technoscientific change. It appeals strongly to the reader's sense of wonder, detailing the complexities of a vast natural universe and imagining the post-human subjects who might be at home in it – often these are postbiological entities, virtually immortal, finally unrestrained by the limitations of the body. But, arguably, their futures are no longer human futures.

As originally proposed in 1993 by mathematician and science fiction writer Vernor Vinge, the Singularity is a radically transformative event that will likely occur within the next 20 years or so, as an inevitable consequence of ever-accelerating technoscientific development. Vinge believes it will be the sudden coming-to-consciousness of a genuine artificial super-intelligence. In contrast, self-styled 'Singularitarian' Ray Kurzweil envisages a more gradual transformation, 'the culmination of the merger of our biological thinking and existence with our technology, resulting in a world that is still human but that transcends our biological roots'.[51] What all its proponents agree on, however, is that the 'coming technological Singularity' will so radically alter the course of human history that logical extrapolation into the future from the present is rendered more or less impossible.[52] In Vinge's words:

> We will soon create intelligences greater than our own. When this happens, human history will have reached a kind of singularity, an intellectual transition as impenetrable as the knotted space-time at the center of a black hole, and the world will pass far beyond our understanding.[53]

This has not prevented some writers from leap-frogging over the wall of the Singularity – to tell stories about the many conceivable weirdnesses of the post-Singularity future. Greg Egan's novels, for example, construct a speculative trajectory of increasingly complex environments and increasingly alien post-human and artificial intelligences for whom virtuality is as natural as embodiment. His novel, *Incandescence* (2008), takes place more than one million years from now, and some of its characters are thousands of years old:

> [Rakesh] had lived embodied for his first thousand years ... but the return to the flesh was still disorienting. This body, like the one he'd been born with, was efficient and flexible, with very modest material needs, so being subject to the laws of physics would not be much of an inconvenience. Nevertheless, it felt odd to be on such intimate terms with the world again, without a single layer of simulation, mediation, or obfuscation. It was like being naked for the first time in a century.[54]

Singularity fiction is some of the most imaginative and exuberant fiction being written today – one critic describes Egan's stories as 'profoundly liberating'[55] – but it cannot have much to say about the possibilities for responsible and effective action in the social and political present or near future of post-modern late-capitalism; anything like 'post-modern late-capitalism' will have long since disappeared, along with the rest of human history. Csicsery-Ronay refers to the Vingean Singularity as 'the quintessential myth of contemporary technoculture'[56] – it has also been called, less kindly, 'the rapture of the nerds'.[57]

As a contrast to far-future Singularity fiction, I want to introduce Canadian-British writer Geoff Ryman's wonderful 2004 novel, *Air (or, Have Not Have)*. Although it climaxes with the arrival of a recognizable technological Singularity, *Air* unfolds on a resolutely human scale and its political and ethical commitments are very clear. Several years ago Ryman half-seriously instigated what has become known as 'the Mundane Movement', a kind of demystification project for science fiction writers that starts from the assumption that 'the most likely future is one in which we only have ourselves and this planet'.[58] For Ryman, too many science-fiction stories are 'not really about the future':

> SF, especially mainstream commercial SF, copies the past onto the future to make it comfortingly entertaining.... Perhaps that's because so many people now fear the future ...[59]

Ryman's *Air* is set in the very near future of 2020; its central character is Chung Mae, an illiterate peasant-farmer who lives in an isolated mountain village in the fictional nation of Karzistan. Just as the first sentence of *Neuromancer* sets the cyberpunk scene – 'The sky above the port was the color of television, tuned to a dead channel' – so does the first sentence of *Air* set the scene for its story of radical transformation: 'Mae lived in the last village in the world to go online.'[60]

Like the rest of the world, Mae's community has only one year to prepare for the coming of Air. This is a virtual information and communication system that will literally invade every human mind on the planet when it comes online. Its name – 'Air' – suggests ubiquity and ease of use ('as easy as breathing'); at the same time it signifies very directly the implosion of nature and technoculture that is one of the key motifs of cyberfiction. Everyone, willing or not, will be directly connected in Air. Everyone will have access, instantly and without hardware, to all the world's information. 'The scene of the screen' will become everyone's lived reality. Air is a first-world initiative, organized under the auspices of the United Nations. Global access will, it is argued, eradicate the political, economic and cultural conflicts that have divided the world into 'haves' and 'have-nots'. It is a given, of course, that no one has bothered to inquire of the 'have-nots' whether it is their wish to be catapulted into the West's technoscientific future. As Mae complains, 'I'm sure the people who do this think they do a good thing. They worry about us, like we were children.... But how dare they call us have-nots?'[61]

It would be easy to sentimentalize Mae's story as yet another disenchantment scenario, to understand her community as a kind of 'premodern' utopia on the verge of dissolution under the onslaught of

Western technoscience – a version, in other words, of Forster's 'The Machine Stops'. To recall Jane Bennett's description of the enchanted world before its fall from grace, 'human and other creatures were defined by a preexisting web of relations, social life was characterized by face-to-face relations, and political order took the form of organic community'.[62] But if there are no machines of loving grace in this imagined world, neither is there the absolute hegemony of technology that Forster feared. Rather, the novel is about learning to work with and through technology, to understand it and take responsibility for it, to come to the best possible terms with its inevitabilities, to begin to understand humanity's co-evolution with 'the Machine'. In this way, Ryman's novel refuses the idea of the Singularity as inevitably deterministic, supporting instead a vision of human participation in shaping the post-Singularity future.

As a figure for the increasingly pervasive cultural and economic imperialism of global media, Air threatens the lives of Ryman's characters with both annihilation and transformation. The novel plots the tensions between, on the one hand, the small community's anxieties about what in their very traditional lives will necessarily be lost to routine and bureaucracy once Air has connected the entire world, and, on the other, their very sensible desire for the enrichment in their lives promised by that new connection to second nature:

> 'The world out there has grown bigger. There are two worlds. There is the one you can see, and another world people have made up, and it is bigger than the real one. They call it "Info".'
>
> And Mae felt lust.
>
> Lust to be part of that world, lust to know how it worked, lust to know how the television worked, and how the Net and how the Air would give all that wings.... I will learn, she promised herself.[63]

Like Gibson's cyberspace, Ryman's *Air* is a powerfully evocative figure for the technoscientific future.[64] As the whole world prepares for Air, Mae comes to see the increasing discontinuity between her community, which inhabits the past, and so much of the rest of the world, which is already living in the future. For Mae, the future becomes a magical place of potential belonging:

> She would be among the ones who won in this life, through work and virtue. Air was new, Air was strong, Air would bear her up. She felt the long root go back and she knew now. She was rooted in the world but the world was rooted in Air.[65]

The resolution of Ryman's novel is a dramatic re-enchantment of futurity. *Air* ends just as the global virtual network is about to come online, but unlike Gibson's fiction, the future now holds the promise of potentially positive radical transformation as the consequence of the coming technological Singularity (to recall Vinge's title). On the one hand, as Stephen Dougherty notes, 'Air is a relentless force that sucks up everything in its path – rites, practices, traditions, alterity, heterogeneity – and dissolves it down to a ready matrix of biomass for Western techno-consumer culture'. Dougherty also points out, however, that 'the narrative arc moves from demonization of technology to its sacralization'. The political concerns for the 'have-nots' of globalization that have provided so much of its narrative drive are transformed, finally, into the dream of a vast post-human network that will be Air's radiant outcome. Just before the coming of Air, Mae shares with her family and friends the realization, at once tragic and filled with promise, that '[w]e are the last... human beings. After tonight, everywhere, we will be different.'[66] *Air*'s last sentence is as resonant as its first: 'all of them... turned and walked together into the future'.[67]

Notes

1 N. Mansfield, 2000, *Subjectivity: Theories of the Self from Freud to Haraway*, New York: New York University Press, 158. For Mansfield, 'every issue in modern and postmodern life is inevitably filtered through the terms that are the landmarks of the debate about the subject: humanity, individual will and agency, power, culture and experience' 149.

2 R. Brautigan, 1968, 'All watched over by machines of loving grace' in *The Pill Versus the Springhill Mine Disaster*, New York: Delta, 1.

3 J. Bennett, 2001, *The Enchantment of Modern Life: Attachments, Crossings, and Ethics*, Princeton, NJ, and Oxford: Princeton University Press, 7. As Bennett outlines it, 'disenchantment is sometimes decried as the destruction of a golden age when the world was a home, sometimes celebrated as the end of a dark age and the dawn of a world of human freedom and rational agency, and sometimes presented as a mixed blessing. But, in each of these cases, it is agreed that disenchantment describes the contemporary condition' 33.

4 G. Debord, 1968, *Society of the Spectacle*, Detroit: Black and Red (1977), 12.
5 'To dissimulate is to feign not to have what one has. To simulate is to feign to have what one hasn't. One implies a presence, the other an absence', J. Baudrillard, 1983, *Simulations*, trans. P. Foss, P. Patton and P. Beitchman, New York: Semiotext(e), 5.
6 E. M. Forster, 1910, Epigraph, *Howards End*, London: Edward Arnold.
7 V. Sobchack, 1994, 'The scene of the screen' in *Materialities of Communication*, eds H. U. Gumbrecht and K. L. Pfeiffer Stanford: Stanford University Press, 83–106. Referring to technoscientific dreams of abandoning the body for digital or other more efficient material platforms, Sobchack writes: 'Devaluing the physically lived body and the concrete materiality of the world, electronic presence suggests that we are all in danger of becoming merely ghosts in the machine' 106.
8 This is a not uncommon theme in science fiction scenarios about human devolution.
9 E. M. Forster, 1909, 'The machine stops' in *Science Fiction: The Science Fiction Research Association Anthology*, eds P. S. Warrick, C. G. Waugh and M. H. Greenberg, New York: Harper Row (1988), 42. As in many disenchantment scenarios, intellectual life and genuine experimentation are also sacrificed to the Machine. A famous lecturer insists to his audience:

> Beware of first-hand ideas! ...They are but the physical impressions produced by love and fear, and on this gross foundation who could erect a philosophy? Let your ideas be second-hand, and if possible tenth-hand, for then they will be far removed from that disturbing element – direct observation 57.

10 Forster, 'The machine stops', 54.
11 Ibid, 61.
12 This phrase provides the title of T. Moylan's study, 2000, *Scraps of the Untainted Sky: Science Fiction, Utopia, Dystopia*, Boulder, CO: Westview Press. Moylan argues that it is 'the systemic logic of the Machine that gradually alienates its own creators from themselves, turning them from inventive agents to reified cogs in its own expanding mechanism' 117. He sees in Forster's critique of mass-mediated culture similarities to the critiques of Frankfurt School theorists such as Theodor Adorno, 116.
13 S. Lem, 2005, 'King Globares and the sages' (1965), G. Westfahl, *Science Fiction Quotations: From the Inner Mind to the Outer Limits*, New Haven: Yale University Press, 25.
14 This is one of the ways in which we can appreciate science fiction not only as a narrative genre appropriate to technoculture, but also as a way of thinking that I. Csicsery-Ronay, Jnr, 2008, calls 'science-fictionality' – 'a mode of response that frames and tests experiences as if they were aspects of a work

of science fiction', *The Seven Beauties of Science Fiction*, Middletown, CT: Wesleyan University Press, 2.

15 S. Spiegel, 2008, 'Things made strange: on the concept of "Estrangement" in science fiction theory', *Science Fiction Studies*, 35:3, November, 373.

16 I. Csicsery-Ronay, Jnr, 2005, 'Science/fiction criticism' in D. Seed (ed.), *A Companion to Science Fiction*, Oxford: Blackwell, 43.

17 N. Barron (ed.), 2004, *Anatomy of Wonder*, 5th edn, Westport, CT: Libraries Unlimited.

18 F. Mendlesohn, 2003, 'Introduction: reading science fiction' in E. James and F. Mendlesohn (eds), *The Cambridge Companion to Science Fiction*, Cambridge, UK: Cambridge University Press, 3.

19 D. Suvin, 1979, *Metamorphoses of Science Fiction: On the Poetics and History of a Literary Genre*, New Haven: Yale University Press, 7–8. See Spiegel's 'Things made Strange' for a good critical discussion of Suvin's construction of science fiction as an estranged genre.

20 N. Easterbrook, 2005, 'Estrangement' in G. Westfahl (ed.), *The Greenwood Encyclopedia of Science Fiction and Fantasy: Themes, Works, and Wonders*, Vol. 1. Westport, CT: Greenwood Press, 253.

21 G. Egan, 2001, *Schild's Ladder*, London: Gollancz (2003), 322.

22 I. Csicsery-Ronay, Jnr, 1992, 'The sentimental futurist: cybernetics and art in William Gibson's *Neuromancer*', *Critique: Studies in Contemporary Fiction* 33:3, Spring, 221.

23 D. Bell, 2007, *Cyberculture Theorists: Manuel Castells and Donna Haraway*, London: Routledge, 2.

24 J. Prucher (ed.), 2007, *Brave New Words: The Oxford Dictionary of Science Fiction*, Oxford: Oxford University Press, 31.

25 W. Gibson, 1984, *Neuromancer*, New York: Ace, 51.

26 Csicsery-Ronay, Jnr, 'The sentimental futurist', 221.

27 In *Subjectivity*, Mansfield writes of the Futurist aesthetic: 'Speed ... functions as a kind of sublime violence that brings an unparalleled thrill, but also a sense of human renewal, a renewal that will shatter the physical and sentimental limits of our subjectivity in order to make a wholly new experience of the world possible' (150).

28 Gibson, *Neuromancer*, 3.

29 Ibid, 9.

30 Ibid, 6. As a figure for the body, 'meat' is here a kind of ultimate reification. British author J. Robson re-privileges the term in her 2005 far-future novel *Natural History*, New York: Bantam: in a world of easy and perfect postbiological simulation, the flesh retains its own enchantment: 'All the marvelous forms of living meat *are* memories.... [W]e are walking, talking, screaming and running articulations of an almighty living mnemonic' (108; emphasis in original).

31 Gibson, *Neuromancer*, 52.

32 S. E. Jones, 2006, *Against Technology: From the Luddites to Neo-Luddism*, New York: Routledge, 203.

33 Gibson has come in for sharp criticism from many politically-engaged critics – especially feminist critics – for his apparent readiness to give in to power fantasies of abandoning the body for virtual reality (and the promises of its futuristic pleasures). But it is more useful, I think, to separate the author from his character and to appreciate how, in S. Vint's 2007 words, 'Gibson's [*Neuromancer*] articulates a particular type of subjectivity that is interested in repressing the body, and it suggests why this stance would be desirable', *Bodies of Tomorrow: Technology, Subjectivity, Science Fiction*, Toronto: University of Toronto Press, 109.

34 Gibson, *Neuromancer*, 258.

35 Ibid, 270.

36 C. Stross, 2008, *Halting State*, New York: Ace 96. *Halting State* also includes a sentence that I read as an oblique metatextual *homage* to *Neuromancer*'s often quoted opening sentence: 'There's a faint popping noise, and the entire wall of the incident room shifts to the colour of the night sky above a Japanese city', 180.

37 W. Gibson, N. Easterbrook, 2008b, 'Review of *No Maps for These Territories* DVD', *Science Fiction Film and Television* 1:1, Spring, 160.

38 This section expands on my 2006 comments about *Pattern Recognition* in 'Stories about the future: From patterns of expectation to pattern recognition.' *Science Fiction Studies*, 33:3, November, 452–72.

39 Her name is pronounced the same as *Neuromancer*'s Case. Gibson has insisted that this is a coincidence, but the very title of his novel – *Pattern Recognition* – invites readerly scepticism.

40 This formal structure aligns Gibson's novels with the Singularity fiction I discuss below.

41 S. Poole, 2003, 'Tomorrow's man' interview with William Gibson, The *Guardian* 3 May. www.theguardian.com/books/2003/may/03/sciencefictionfantasyandhorror.william gibson' accessed 30 October 2013.

42 W. Gibson, 2003, *Pattern Recognition*, New York: Putnam's, 57.

43 Gibson, *Pattern Recognition*, 23.

44 In *Simulations*, Baudrillard writes of the metaphysical despair which 'came from the idea that the images concealed nothing at all, and that in fact they were not images, such as the original model would have made them, but actually *perfect simulacra forever radiant with their own fascination*' (my emphasis). He continues: 'it is dangerous to unmask images, since they dissimulate the fact that there is nothing behind them', 9.

45 Gibson, *Pattern Recognition*, 125.

46 F. Jameson, 2005, 'Fear and loathing in globalization' in *Archaeologies of the Future: The Desire Called Utopia and Other Science Fictions*, London: Verso, 391.
47 Gibson, *Pattern Recognition*, 65.
48 Gibson, *Pattern Recognition*, 1.
49 K. Marx, M. Berman, 1982, *All That is Solid Melts into Air: The Experience of Modernity*. 2nd edn, New York: Bantam, 21.
50 Mansfield, 158.
51 R. Kurzweil, 2006, *The Singularity is Near: When Humans Transcend Biology*, New York: Penguin (2005), 9.
52 In *The Seven Beauties of Science Fiction*, Csicsery-Ronay describes the Singularity as 'a sudden leap by the technosphere into self-interested self-consciousness, sealed off from the human world that created its conditions of possibility' (110). The Singularity, in this view, is nothing if not apocalyptic in its consequences. I am indebted to Norman Ford for pointing out that television's various *Star Trek* series also envisage a kind of post-Singularity future, albeit a less radical one than the literary futures of writers such as Egan and Stross. *Star Trek*'s version is more modest and user-friendly, a galactic post-scarcity utopia with a human(ist) face.
53 V. Vinge, 1993, 'The Coming Technological Singularity'. www.faculty.english.vt.edu/Collier/4874/pdfs/vinge_1993.pdf' accessed 30 November 2013.
54 G. Egan, 2008, *Incandescence*, San Francisco, CA: Night Shade, 39. The vast power of Egan's post-human intelligences makes its own existential demands: 'When the means existed to transform yourself, instantly and effortlessly, into anything at all, the only way to maintain an identity was to draw your own boundaries. But once you'd lost the urge to keep on asking whether or not you'd drawn them in the right place, you might as well have been born *Homo sapiens*, with no real choices at all' (*Schild's Ladder*, 7).
55 R. Blackford, 2005, 'Greg Egan' In D. Seed (ed.), *A Companion to Science Fiction*. Oxford: Blackwell, 450.
56 Csicsery-Ronay, Jnr, *The Seven Beauties of Science Fiction*, 262.
57 Ibid. The potential of the Singularity to function as a powerful figure is evident in the fact that the chapter in *Pattern Recognition* most focused on the fall of the World Trade Centre towers is titled 'Singularity'. Gibson's metaphorical evocation of the Singularity suggests the extreme cultural and political impact of 9/11; in *Pattern Recognition* it is the radically transformative event that breaks the link between present and future and that renders 'fully imagined cultural futures', to recall Bigend's words, 'the luxury of another day' 57.
58 G. Ryman, 2007a, 'The Mundane Manifesto', *New York Review of Science Fiction* 226, June, 4.

59 G. Ryman, 2007b, 'Take the third star on the left and on til morning!' *New York Review of Science Fiction* 226, June, 1, 5.

60 G. Ryman, 2004, *Air (or, Have Not Have)*, New York: St. Martin's Griffin, 2.

61 Ryman, *Air (or Have Not Have)*, 19. Given today's Cloud computing, as well as the recent launch of the MacBook Air laptop, Ryman's novel has proven impressively prescient, not least in its concern for the uneven distribution of global futurity. In this context, see J. L. Qui's 2009 study, *Working-Class Network Society: Communication Technology and the Information Have-Less in Urban China*, Cambridge, MA: MIT Press.

62 Bennett, *The Enchantment of Modern Life: Attachments, Crossings, and Ethics*, 7.

63 G. Ryman, *Air (or, Have Not Have)*, 99. Mae and her fellow villagers already live in a network of complex relations in their small community, and *Air* is especially astute in tracing the careful negotiations of ethnic, religious and social lines of force. See N. Easterbrook's 2008a 'Giving an account of oneself: ethics, alterity, *Air*', *Extrapolation* 49:2, 240–60, for an excellent reading of the novel as an (ethical) 'allegory of the time' (244).

64 'Air' takes on an intriguing resonance in light of Marx's statement in the *Communist Manifesto* about what it means to be modern: 'All fixed, fast-frozen relations, with their train of ancient and venerable prejudices and opinions, are swept away, all new-formed ones become antiquated before they can ossify. All that is solid melts into air ... ' (Berman, *All That Is Solid*, 21).

65 Ryman, *Air (or Have Not Have)*, 70.

66 Ryman, *Air (or Have Not Have)*, 384. This is in radical contrast to the Wintermute AI's devastating pronouncement, 'Things aren't different. Things are things' (Gibson, *Neuromancer*, 270).

67 Ryman, *Air (or Have Not Have)*, 390.

4

The Birth of Wonder in the Database Economy

Sean Cubitt

> the train down in the city
> was once a snowy hill[1]

Wonder is a virtue, which is to say that it is something to aspire to, rather than something given. Indeed, far from being the natural state of human beings coming face to face with the world, in a phrase Max Weber (1946) borrowed from the poet Schiller, we advance, as secular and industrialized people, into 'the disenchantment of the world'. To achieve wonder requires the apprenticeship that Wordsworth described in *The Prelude* and that Rimbaud described as a long, immense and disciplined deregulation of all the senses.

We speak indeed of the world being full of wonders, of wonderful things, that is, things deserving of wonder; but wonder itself is a quality of the human (and perhaps animal) sensorium, and one that is too easily lost. We are limited creatures: we have to protect ourselves against the endless shocks of perception, not least in the modern city. To do so we acquire habits, and habit is the enemy of wonder. In what follows, I hope to indicate both how habitual frames, especially those sponsored by communications media, insulate us against wonder; how those same media, turned to aesthetic purpose, might let us once again experience enchantment; and why this might be something more and better than the kind of sensory overload that is the hallmark of twenty-first-century consumerism.

The idea that the world has lost its enchantment comes to us Europeans from the Romantics, that first generation to confront and express the triumph of the bourgeoisie. Among them, the poet Wordsworth perhaps most clearly of all of them speaks of the fading of glamour, the end of childhood's pantheism, even as he embraced his own disillusionment, 'just for a ribbon to hang on his coat' as the young Browning expressed it, by accepting Victoria's laureateship. We have to beware nostalgia. Wordsworth's peasantry, like Yeats' a hundred years later, were poor and ignorant, their Hobbesian lives nasty, brutish and short. They lived lives in which knowledge, and in many respects the magic that inhabited the world, was already delegated elsewhere. It is that delegation that characterizes the history of disenchantment.

It is pleasant to imagine a mythic world where a primitive communism of knowledge prevailed; where all knowledge was equally esteemed, and where all could share in it. Such a time is mythic in both senses. It belongs to the world of Lévi-Strauss' *pensée sauvage*, and it is, for us who live in the industrialized, informatic cities of the twenty-first century, a legend of what might have been. Even if, in pre-history, there was such a primitive communism of knowledge to enchant the world and human actions in it, we must be deeply cautious in proposing that we might reconstruct it. If we see the current state of information as a return to an ancient democracy of knowledges, we risk discovering, as we approach the awakening figure, that it is not an Adamic whole, but a Frankenstein's monster, built from all the right parts, but each of them dead. Such is Marx's vision of vampyre capitalism,[2] and his image of the general intellect ossified, as 'dead labour', placed in antagonistic relation to the alienated living. Such is the outcome of the thesis that, in Western history and the history of empires, the characteristic form of both economics and politics has been the delegation of knowing, and by extension of consciousness, to elites.

It is suggestive to distinguish three moments in the modern history of knowledge. The medievals still inhabited the epoch of secrecy, an ancient mode of knowledge formation. Secrecy guards arcane, hermetic, hieratic, knowledge in closed groups: priests, hierophants, maguses, shrouded in Latin, hieroglyphics and mysteries. It appears in guild monopolies over knowledge, for example of dyes, revealing which was a capital offence in many cities in Medieval and Renaissance Europe. Secrecy operates by magic: by the logic of *post hoc ergo propter hoc*,[3] the collocation and contemporaneity of symbols and events. Its world is animate but alien and fundamentally unknowable, save to those who guard knowledge from the ignorant. Thus its effectivity was at least as much (inter)subjective as it was objective.

The age of science that succeeded it was governed by mathematicization and by the taxonomic but nonetheless democratizing impulse of enlightenment science. That democratization was however subject to parcelling out guardianship through specialisms, expertise and professionalization. Its logic was causal – 'know this in order to achieve that' – and it structured the world as object and resource. Its invention of the encyclopedia bears witness to the pious hope that the project of knowledge was completable.

In the age of information, which we began to enter during the twentieth century, knowledge becomes statistical, probabilistic data, to be managed and commodified. The atoms of knowledge are no longer facts (which implies implicit meaning attaching to the known item, an iconic or referential relation to the world) and are instead the objects of the management of data flows, regardless of their content or referentiality. Abandoning the concept of World, it substitutes for the world the mass of data about it. Such symbolic representations can be both amassed and owned. They can be organized into performative statements, on the model of software code. They are operationalized in pervasive systems of expression from urban planning to internet protocols. All packets of information become equivalent: commodities whose use-value (magical power, referential/causative efficacity) has been subsumed into their exchange value. The amassing of such data is of more importance than the data themselves, such that distribution of information matters more than its production or consumption. All three epochs share in the alienation – of subject from world, of subject from object, and now of subject from subject. This alienation increases, the more deeply our thinking appears to us as the external agency of the media that encode it.

We enter today into a database economy, one in which Deleuze's (1997)[4] control society merges with Galloway's (2004)[5] thesis of the protocological, a world in which we no longer internalize discipline, or obey the biopolitical strategies of population management, but in which we are no longer free to act dangerously because the systemic production of regulated systems – from traffic management to crowd movements, and from cellnet to Disneyworld – constrain us to act according to the precepts of the system. In such an economy, ideas are tradable entities, scientific knowledge is commercialized and hoarded, the person is a data-image, personal information can be traded for services and discounted goods, and space itself is commodified in geographical information systems.

Perhaps most significantly, creativity is now harnessed across networks through content-sharing, unpaid content production, the gift economy in software (commercialized through companies like Ubuntu and platforms like Internet Explorer), and the sequestration of scientific knowledge production in an e-journals sector whose pricing has exceeded inflation by 200 to 300 per cent since the mid-1990s.

The database economy integrates the protocological mode of power-knowledge with the extension of the commodity form to include data and creativity. In such a condition, our understandings of agency, of materiality and of sociality are once more in question. Already in the 1920s, Karl Krauss observed 'Nowadays, events no longer occur: the clichés operate spontaneously'. Today, as Badiou notes,[6] nothing worthy of the name 'event' escapes the actuarial management of time, space, people and places, cash and knowledge: nothing, he says, but love, scientific discoveries, art and revolution. The case is easily made that the first three have been accommodated into the grand strategies of the database economy, and the revolution is indefinitely postponed.

Such is the apocalyptic vision. It is essential to identify the worst case, since the worst case has a horrible habit of coming to pass. Admittedly, this scenario only accommodates those portions of the world that have not been deemed supernumerary to the requirements of capital. Industrialization has moved from the factories to the extraction industries – mining, agribusiness, fisheries, in the latter case to the point of extinction. Those left out of even these now rusty sectors are excluded from the new economy as well, and left to rot, or to make their perilous ways to the immiserated service industries – catering, cleaning and sex – of wealthy cities. The alternative to the commodification of knowledge is to be deprived of it. While still dependent on material industries and distribution, the emergent mode of information capitalism increasingly leaves in the gutter those who do not choose to shop in its malls.

Eco[7] distinguishes apocalyptic from integrated intellectuals, those for whom everything is about to collapse from those for whom everything is fine. That is not the case here: the supposed 'triumph' of liberal capitalism is no more an end of history than it is a solution to global poverty. Since the 'sub-prime mortgage crisis' (magnificent euphemism) in 2008, the invisible hand of the market has shown itself entirely capable of slitting its own wrist. Moreover, a captive state system is perfectly happy delivering, as John Pilger neatly expresses it, socialism for the rich when the market demonstrates its fallibility. The database economy is, like every previous expression and expansion of capital, an attempt to answer the tendency to crisis by finding new zones to expand in to. Realising that the environment, which we once believed to be infinite in its generativity, is polluted and depleted to a fatal degree, capital moves into the domain of ideas and creativity with the same faith in their endless resistance to degradation and over-extraction. Integration into such a system is really not an option, not as long as its failure to provide even basic subsistence and peaceful existence for the majority of the world's population is so clear. What then is the alternative to apocalypse?

First, if I am correct in conceptualizing the database economy as an *emergent* hegemony, it is important to understand the significance of the currently dominant hegemony, and the residual forms that lie in layers beneath it. Among these residues are not only the remnants of earlier formations but also, if the thesis of 'residual media' is correct, also a history of dead-ends and roads not taken.[8] Such dead-ends might include not only eight-track cassettes and magic lanterns but social forms like European fascism, which eked out a miserable afterlife in the Iberian Peninsula until the death of Franco in 1975. It should also include a history of temporary autonomous zones[9] and other moments of popular uprising and self-rule.

A second undermining derives from the same thesis of hegemonic process in history: the unlikely event of a complete and universal achievement of the database economy. The failure of ubiquitous surveillance in city centres to secure disciplined behaviour among violent drunks or suicide bombers demonstrates that no system is entire unto itself.

A third undermining comes from the Foucauldian thesis that power of necessity generates resistance, and equally from the Freudian thesis of the return of the repressed. The ubiquity of the database as the delegated home of consciousness produces as its repressed the database unconscious, the untamed phenomena of the embodied crowd, whose movements may be controlled at a statistical level, but whose multiple, changing *experience* of its own existence resists the formulae of control.

A fourth undermining concerns the affordances of the very technologies which enable the database economy to function. As G. A. Cohen argued,[10] Marx's concept of capitalist history not only ascribed to it permanent revolution in the means of production but also the thesis that the means so revolutionized constantly outrun the mode of production which generates them. As Adrian Mackenzie concludes in his study of software:

> flattening of distinctions between production and consumption, between technology and culture, between abstract and concrete is not completed effortlessly, consistently or even fully. New structures 'adequate to global space' and organizations of 'production on a new scale' are unstable. The absorption of mediation is uneven, partial – and contested.[11]

There are further challenges to the emergence of this new hegemony. It requires for its completion a global system capable of regulation, but there is no such regulation. In its place we have what can be described as the actually-existing transnational public sphere, a planet-spanning knotwork of bilateral and multilateral agreements, free trade zones, most-favoured nation statuses, WTO directives, Washington consensus obligations and, critically for the database economy, a huge argument between cartels, corporations, independent producers, expert bodies, nation-states and NGOs over the future of technology governance. That this is indeed a public sphere (and not therefore a hierarchical pyramid) is clear from David C. Clark's 1992 slogan, adopted with passion by the Internet Engineering Task Force: 'We don't believe in presidents, kings or voting; we believe in rough consensus and running code'.[12]

This spaghetti bowl of competing sectors, effectively controlling internet and mobile use through the formats they employ, raises afresh the issue of agency. Technical formations (internet protocol, platforms, applications, codecs) and business models of the past structure and constrain action in the present, and so shape what can be meant by the term agency. On the one hand, agency depends on affordances established by earlier generations, such as the end-to-end design of packet-switched networks,[13] and on the other, on the multiple and changing memberships and goals of global players.[14]

At a more modest scale, but still with an eye to the multitude of end-users who are increasingly also the producers of network communication, the database economy faces the phenomenological and affective experience of users at all levels. A risk here is that such a phenomenology latches onto positivist nostalgia for a blameless world of objects, captured in William Carlos Williams' phrase 'No ideas but in things'.[15] The phenomenology in question is that of emergence as a product of mass behaviours in both physical and digital crowds, not of leadership. Indeed, leadership is the precise opposite of emergence. Finally, resistance emerges in interstitial spaces between zones of control, but also between layers of emergent, dominant and residual hegemonies. Disaggregated from the formalizing functions of the database economy, a different mode of transnational public sphere emerges in such between-spaces and between-times. Such places and times are public to the extent that they find themselves between hermetic systems. They are analogous to those places that the logic of production and control did not create:

> beneath the fabricating and universal writing of technology, opaque and stubborn places remain ... A piling up of heterogenous places. Each one, like a deteriorating page of a book, refers to a different mode of territorial unity, of socioeconomic distribution, of political conflicts and of identifying symbolism ... made up of pieces that are not contemporary and still linked to totalities that have fallen into ruins.[16]

de Certeau's reading parallels Gramsci's, but his heterogenous places must be understood to exist in a system which also recognizes their existence, and which seeks both to prevail over them through checks and balances, and to derive from them the innovations which its own functionalism can no longer produce. To an extent these autonomous zones are bounded spaces and times, granted the permission to exist, first, to produce the illusion that freedom exists, and second, to generate the unforeseen in a system whose rule is foresight and planning. Thus the crowd as emergent phenomenon is a generative force, not merely the object of rule. Yet it is just as capable of mob violence as it is of carnival, and the two can emerge indecently close to one another, as in the joyful expressions of race hatred in carnivals of racist violence across Europe in recent years. Here too older fragments of past totalities, not to say totalitarianisms, reemerge in palimpsests, the *longue durée* of an imaginary oppression stretching back to the wars against the Romans.

'The dead hand of the past weighs on the mind of the living like a nightmare' then, but nonetheless, we make our own history, even if we cannot choose the conditions under which we make it. Neither the emergent hegemony of the database economy, nor the struggle to build alternatives to it, are creations *ex nihilo*. The hegemonic process builds by extension, the alter-hegemonic process by unpacking the weight of history, trying to decipher in the density of the actual the lost capacities, the unfulfilled promises, the dead-ends that can be resuscitated for the uses of the living. In what follows I hope to indicate a little of how re-enchantment might be possible as an alter-hegemonic process at work in popular culture and in the art world. The risk is real, that the principle of hope might be merely utopian, in the weak sense of a sentimental desire for something to cheer us up in the darkness. That risk is worth taking, because without such hope there is no point in going on.

My first example runs the greater risk, because it is the kind of scene which attracts the word 'enchanting' from audiences, critics and reviewers; indeed it looks very much as though it was included in Peter Jackson's version of *King Kong* precisely for that purpose. The scene occurs in Chapter 45 of the DVD, at about the 2:31:50 mark: Kong carries Ann Darrow (Naomi Watts) to the lake in Central Park, where they slide on the ice. The scene comprises 25 shots in about a minute and a half, an average shot-length (ASL) of 3.6 seconds, which is a very languid pace compared both to the ASL of most Hollywood features this century, and to the pace of editing in the rest of the film. Not one shot is locked off: the sequence spins consistently in the same direction, and the crane and Steadicam work are extremely smooth until the idyll is broken by the arrival of the first artillery assault. Kong's initial clumsiness on the ice mimics Ann's pratfalls in the earlier sequence when she charms Kong with her vaudeville skills. The mood is romantic, tender, scored to strings by James Newton Howard with strong affiliations to the work of Max Steiner, composer for the 1933 original. How does this enchantment work? Partially because the tale itself is enchanted, a version of the Beauty and the Beast fairytale; partly because of the status of the Cooper and Schoedsack movie as a cultural icon;[17] partly because the performances by both Andy Serkis and Naomi Watts are delicate, in marked contrast to the action and horror sequences elsewhere in the film. Certainly the love between species is handled with deep tact and realism, built on the Bazinian principles of long takes and deep focus.

What is striking in the context of enchantment is not so much *how* as *what* is enchanted here. It is, quite remarkably, the technology. What is Kong made of? Among the elements composing the screen creature are Andy Serkis, motion-capture technologies dating back to Etienne-Jules Marey and the Helmholtz theory of the human body as thermodynamic engine,[18] Alvy Ray Smith's dictum that 'reality begins at 50 million polygons per second', the history traced by William Ivins[19] of representations of the typical and the particular in print culture, evolving into the debates over the propriety of using photographs in Darwin's *Expression of Emotion in Humans and Animals*, the history of movies, vaudeville, and figure skating ... Kong is in short a construction made out of the likely and unlikely, the recalled and the forgotten, assembled into a moving, breathing and affective agent in the world of the cinema spectator. The true enchantment moves beyond merely releasing the potential buried in these and all the other histories that flood into Kong, the ancestral 'dead labour' brought back to life. It arises in the interface between that achievement and the articulation of a triad composing woman, ape and technology in an achieved moment of dynamic grace, pathos and humour in a dispersed and already tragic equilibrium.

In much of the literature on the disenchanted world, it is technology which is held to stand between us and the lost magic of an innocent and childlike experience. Heidegger's expression of this constitutive loss has been especially influential, yet even Heidegger concedes that:

> the frenziedness of technology may entrench itself everywhere to such an extent that someday, throughout everything technological, the essence of technology may come to presence in the coming-to-pass of truth.[20]

Earlier in the essay, Heidegger has argued that 'man' is not yet present, not yet revealed in the truth of Being. Man is what has not come to presence (31), so we can decipher the lines just cited as suggesting that, in its ubiquity, technology may eventually reveal as its essence the Being of the human which otherwise it 'enframes', blocking the revelation of Being in man and the world. This will come about, he says, as a result of the re-engagement of *poesis* and *techne*, severed since the Ancient Greeks.

Although phrased as rhetorical questions, Heidegger seems to conclude that the synthesis of art and technology is the critical move that will unfreeze the process of revealing. This is a heavy burden to place on art. But it does give us one way of understanding the enchantment of the sequence from *King Kong*: that it opens a vista on an autonomous technology capable, not just of dialogue, but of laughter, invention and love. What Heidegger has missed is the species-specific nature of his argument (even more than its gender-specificity). The articulation will only occur if it includes *physis* as well as *techne*. Moreover, Heidegger's 'man' is an individual. Something else misses its mark as a result of this premise.

Robert Cahen's *L'étreinte* (*The Embrace*, 2003), a single-screen video projection, fades up from black to a series of landscape shots of wooded valleys shrouded in blowing mist, two of them briefly allowing a little autumnal colour into the piece, which is otherwise monochrome. Three electronically treated breaths, along with a beep like that of medical monitoring devices, some sounds that might be either close-miked breathing or wind noise or both, and a noise like the scraping of metal sheets lie over the scene. Crossfade to the image of a hand clutching a sheet, perhaps, and then very distinctly, to the accompaniment of an indrawn breath, a pigeon beats its wings in slow motion, on the downbeat flooding the screen with darkness.

We enter the embrace itself. It is hard to see what the figures are doing, but it seems to be love-making. We do not know and do not need to know if Cahen shot this footage, or whether it was found. The bodies are anonymous to us. The treatment of the images in post-production makes us constantly question whether what we see is skin, or flesh, muscle and bone; and whether the darkness is hair or simple darkness. Areas of the screen become distinct from time to time: a mouth or a hand tense, in rapture or pain we do not know. The lovers, if that is what they are, are *locked* in the embrace. They have no other existence for us. At certain moments it seems as if the textures of the opening landscape have been matted in to the image. The pigeon in flight reappears, its beak open as if it were calling. Three more sounds enter the audio lexicon: a granular noise as of fine sand, small domestic noises, and a sound like the cracking of ice or wood.

It is hard to tell, after a while, whether the footage is moving or merely changing: whether the tape includes a record of motion, or whether all the movement comes from its treatment in post-production. Near its end, the human forms interlace with an image of grass blown in the wind, or perhaps of reeds waving in a stream. That image fades up, then back to mix with another image of what might be a hand, which fades to leave the grasses, which themselves fade to black, as the score resolves to beeps underlain by the rustling of remaindered sounds. We are probably no wiser when we end than when we came in (although for the technically or aesthetically minded, Cahen has achieved an astonishingly lustrous black in the piece).

Who is involved in the embrace? In this embrace, there is no clarity over who is involved: one couple? Or two, or more? We might be sure for a moment that a face is female, but then unsure whether it is the right way up, or whether it is a face at all: whether a particular black form is a lip or an eyebrow. But we do feel that it is an embrace, and that means two: two who are not one, because one cannot embrace itself, and because an embrace is if anything a pursuit of an unreachable unity. What else? There was a camera present, and that is already a third. There may have been an operator, and if so, that operator, even if it was the same person who signed the tape, is not the same person: not there, in the presence of the others. The one who signs is a fifth, and he is not alone, working with an editor, a special effects technician and a sound artist. There are, too, the landscapes and the bird. How they fit into or frame the embrace is a matter of interpretation, but there they are, integral to it, if only as termini between which the embrace occurs. And then there is the one who watches the work. This embrace is quite a crowd, albeit a crowd which, if we are to believe our eyes, is not bound by any ordinary epidermis.

With only a hint of or at colour, *L'étreinte* is a surface in motion, masses of shadow and saturated light. The embrace is also a landscape, that is, a landscape imaged on a surface; as it also shares the biological world of the bird. A landscape filled with mist, a bird flying through the mist, calling. And all of these are embraced in a technical procedure which establishes them in the same surface, strips them of their colour, abstracts them, places them in proximity to the sounds of human breath, something akin to Kong's soft grunts and chuckles. Breathing, Barthes points out,[21] comes from the intimate interior of the body: amplification is the equivalent of close-ups, allowing us into the immediate personal space which usually we reserve for children and lovers. Like Kong's fur, this surface is intensely tactile.

In this, the sequence from *King Kong* and Cahen's video are alike: they employ advanced technologies to synthesize a meeting of the baffling triad of human, natural and technological in a single unsettled terrain. The difference is that Jackson narrativizes the unsettling, with the interruption of the army into the love scene, where Cahen's scene is already tense, unsettled from within. Pieties about the naturalness of sex have no place here: the intense difficulty of the embrace, its challenge, evokes Lacan's dictum: the sexual relation is impossible. Two people are never reducible to union. Neither partner is a stable entity either: the multiplicities multiply around the impossibility of resolution. The impossibility of sexual union, and the demand that we return to it over and again, is the evidence not just of desire but of the temporality of existence: that it is incomplete is its glory as well as its tragedy.

Existence in time is the theme of Daniel Crooks' works, which stretch the affordances of FinalCut Pro, Apple's edit software, to produce multiplane single-screen works whose temporalities analyse the interstices within movement. If in some sense Cahen's work looks to the infinity of real time, opening up the experiential moment inside the relationship – which is not one but doubled, multiplexed – to its own extension in time, Crooks looks into the intensities within unanalysed and all but unexperienced time in the vague spaces we traverse in urban geographies. *Pan No 6 (of steps and clocks)* (2007) unravels over its nine minutes of running time a single pan shot at a busy Melbourne intersection. It is a landscape of traversals and waiting, of one of Augé's non-spaces analysed in terms not of empty space – this space is extraordinarily full – but of empty time.

Fragments of the ambient sound of the street bubble to the surface of a soundscape otherwise composed of drones and pulses whose machinic rhythms, timbres and pitches seem to respond to abstract qualities of the image: the quantity of black, the speed of change. In the image, obviously human figures distend into sculpture, only to coalesce into recognizable figures whose only strangeness is that they walk backwards. Motion becomes liquefaction and fugue, in the senses of both the compositional mode of formal extrapolation and the medical sense of a loss of time. The figures populating the landscape retain their characters – an older man in a flat white cap pulls his wife along, a young man welcomes his arriving friend with the backpack with an arm around the shoulder. Little intimacies in public places which, however, seem deserted in the almost architectural spaces produced by the lateral organization of the widescreen format and the extension of more distant events into parallel lines across the screen. Their proximities and distances, even to the sensation of brilliant sunlight, organize the space of viewing as a temporal experience.

Here too the movement is towards a synthetic enchantment. We cannot go back to nature, or to the mythic past. Nor can we afford to pass the task of knowing on to our databases, for it is they that have depopulated public space, made it an empty quarter where strangers pass like caravans that have somewhere else to get to, or are embarrassed to find themselves just waiting.

Crooks' work contradicts Wittgenstein. It seems to say that what is essential in any given situation is what is not the case. There is first of all what cannot be made into a statement. In this exposed landscape of times where the spaces between events extend indefinitely, there is nothing that can be extrapolated. The biopolitical management of traffic flows and pedestrian movements is unhinged by the act of waiting, or of crossing these spaces in haphazard motions. If public space today is governed by a database consciousness, what Crooks shows is the database unconscious: the embodied and deeply physical experiences of waiting, strolling, greeting a loved one. Statements can only abstract from the complexity of relationships and from their perpetual change But the second sense of 'what is not the case' that rises from *Pan No 6* is the sense of the distended present, and more especially of what in the present moment is no longer or not yet.

These three enchanting examples of work from the last few years reflect a shift of interest from epistemology (representation, simulation) towards ontology. What is, is a result of what preceded it, but that which has come into existence excludes whatever in its past did not eventuate. That order of the past, the past as it is unfulfilled in the present, is essential to the present for the same reason that what is not yet the case is essential: because both open up the inessential nature of what *is* the case. Like the roster of histories buried in the techniques for animating Kong, the uneventuating past persists in the present as the roads not taken, resources for the present's unique property, which is that it is alone the moment in which it is possible to act. The making of art, and of cultural artefacts, of ideas, of relationships, are such actions. If they are to occur, the inessentiality of the present has to be laid bare. Only then will we be able to escape the eternal present and confront it in its potentiality, what it has yet to become. The not-yet is essential, because it empties the present of plenitude, and because it is in the future, not the present, that actions have their consequences.

This ontology implies an epistemology: *knowledge* – that element of human traffic which can be made secret, professionalized and owned, that forms the essential givenness of data in the database economy – is constituted in discourses which present what is the case, that is the inessential, abstracted and removed from the capacity for action. '*Truth*', for want of a better word, concerns the essential, that which is otherwise than what is the case, both preceding and proceeding from the present. The business of these three works is to disengage truth from knowledge, and in that to make possible, thinkable and actionable, the idea of change.

That there is in this no individual human agent is by now clear. Crooks' disconnected crowd, his expansion of the space between into parallel, unmeeting rivers of time, expands on the loneliness and incapacity of the subject as we have traditionally conceived it, as reflexive with Descartes, as transcendental with Kant, and as psychological with Freud. Nor is the new agency purely human. Crooks' visions are unthinkable without his tools, just as *King Kong* is unthinkable without the ape. It has been clear since Aristotle that individuals are not capable of politics, even if they can live a good life. In the *polis*, it is not the actors but the network that has agency, a network that is the virtual essence of the situation, one which incorporates all our Others: human, natural and technological. This enchantment is not one of eudaemonistic relaxation and delinking. It belongs to the active synthesis of the three phyla: human, natural and technological. In the new networks, in these emergent forms, including forms of popular culture, we see the richness of a future we may yet find ourselves capable of constructing, and the reasons why we might want to construct it.

Notes

1 G. Snyder, 1971, *The Back Country*, London: Fulcrum Press, 51.
2 K. Marx, 1973, *Grundrisse*, trans. M. Nicolaus, London, Penguin/New Left Books, 690–711.
3 After this, therefore because of this.
4 G. Deleuze, 1992, 'Postscript on the societies of control', *October* 59, Winter, 3–7.
5 A. R. Galloway, 2004, *Protocol: How Control Exists After Decentralization*, Cambridge, MA; MIT Press.
6 A. Badiou, 1999, *Manifesto for Philosophy*, trans. N. Madarsz, Albany: State University of New York Press.
7 U. Eco, 1994, *Apocalypse Postponed*, R. Lumley (ed.), Bloomington: Indiana University Press.

8 C. R. Acland (ed.), 2007, *Residual Media*, Minneapolis: University of Minnesota Press.
9 H. Bey, 1991, *T.A.Z.: The Temporary Autonomous Zone, Ontological Anarchism, Poetic Terrorism*, New York: Autonomedia.
10 G. A. Cohen, *1978, Karl Marx's Theory of History: A Defence*, Princeton NJ: Princeton University Press.
11 A. Mackenzie, 2006, *Cutting Code: Software and Sociality*, New York: Peter Lang, 184.
12 A. M. Froomkin, 2003, 'Habermas@Discourse.net: Toward a critical theory of cyberspace', *Harvard Law Review* 116, January, 751–873.
13 J. Zittrain, 2008, *The Future of the Internet and How to Stop it,* London: Allen Lane.
14 P. Chakravartty and K. Sarikakis, 2006, *Media Policy and Globalization*, Edinburgh: Edinburgh University Press.
15 W. C. Williams, 1946, *Paterson* (Book 1). New York: New Directions (1963).
16 M. de Certeau, 1984, *The Practice of Everyday Life*, Berkeley: University of California Press, 201.
17 C. Erb, 1998, *Tracking King Kong: A Hollywood Icon in World Culture*, Detroit: Wayne State University Press.
18 A. Rabinbach, 1990, *The Human Motor: Energy, Fatigue and the Origins of Modernity,* New York: Basic Books; Berkeley: University of California Press.
19 W. M. Ivins, Jnr, 1953, *Prints and Visual Communication*, Cambridge, MA: MIT Press.
20 M. Heidegger, 1977, 'The question concerning technology' in *The Question Concerning Technology and Other Essays*, trans. W. Lovitt, New York: Harper & Row, 3–35.
21 R. Barthes, 1977, 'The grain of the voice' in *Image-Music-Text: Selected Essays*, trans. S. Heath (ed.), London: Fontana.

Section 2

Perceiving

5

The Performative Archive: New Conceptions of the Archive in Contemporary Theory, Art and New Media Practices

Eivind Røssaak

> The archive cannot be described in its totality, and in its presence it is unavoidable.[1]

This chapter will sketch an outline of a theory of the 'performative archive' in contemporary art and exhibition practices. I will use newer insights from philosophy, art and media theory.

The practice of gathering and displaying audio-visual material which may have a private and/or public, historical and/or contemporary character has become a widespread tendency, both among amateurs on the internet and among internationally acclaimed artists, such as Gerhard Richter.[2] How should these practices be understood? I will suggest that many of these alternative collections within art and new media practices could be called 'performative archives'. They are collections that *do* something, not with words, but with things, ideas or images that may embody an argument, a sensation or a conception of society and history. They are in a way structured like 'performative utterances' in J. L. Austin's sense of the term.[3] Jacques Derrida's deconstruction of Austin's distinction between the performative and the constative was instrumental in instigating what has been called a performative turn within the humanities and social sciences.[4] Many disciplines and areas of research have studied the performative or constructive aspects of identities, nationalities, gender, the arts, disciplines and sciences more generally. This chapter will assess the current proliferation of alternative archives and archival philosophy, and will claim that a performative turn in relation to archives, as a critique and challenge to archiving, has been going on throughout the twentieth century, and is increasing with the ubiquity of new media. This proliferation is in urgent need of new distinctions, and we need to be aware of the fact that the difference between, say, a performative and a non-performative or classical archive is no longer self-evident. This is key, because the performative archive seems to be part of a deconstructive operation, in the sense that it reveals a certain blindness or loss with regard to the so-called legitimate archive or collections, and, as a consequence, will point to a hidden aspect of the performative and the construed that already exists in the bureaucratic or state-driven archive. Indeed, the performative was and still is an essential part of the ritual of any state formation.

While the classical archive claims its authority through some principle of neutrality – such as chronology (since time ostensibly stands outside of human control) – the performative archive tends to suggest quite openly an alliance to another principle, often ambiguous, biased or even subjective. The adherence to the archival as medium is most often put forward through the use of a series or some principle of collection. The performative may have to do with a playful or ambiguous relation to the principle of selection. It may mime the principle of 'neutrality', but most often to question or ridicule it. The ordering principle may be thematic or genealogical, that is, the material may be delimited thematically or according to a given origin. In the latter case, it may concern material that pertains to a specific event, an institution or a person.

Very often the latter principle is used, because it displaces the focus from the neutral to the idiosyncratic, and brings about a new relational force between the objects. This is obvious in most archival artistic experiments and exhibitions, as we will see. However, a certain archival mode has also been instituted on personal websites and blogs on the internet. The 'list' is in focus: it could be my favourite movies, books or games, 'everything I do', my photos, my e-mails, my text messages, my friends, hobbies, and so on. On social websites such as Facebook, the principle of the personal or the idiosyncratic has become industry and is perhaps no longer subversive in relation to the principles of the classical archives. Nevertheless, the rise of such new social websites and modes of communication has placed the archival into the centre of a new kind of social construction and interaction. Furthermore, many established archives and libraries have embraced the performative as an integrated aspect of the way they display and invite their audience to interact with their collection. What we need is a critical rethinking and reconceptualization of the potential of the archive and the archival, the differences they make and the differences between them. What can traditional archives learn from aesthetic experiments? What can different theoretical perspectives reveal about the contemporary archival impulse?[5]

While archival science is an older discipline, the more general approach to notions of the archive, memory and media is a tendency or, at best, an emerging field of study. Derrida launched the term 'archivology' in this connection.[6] It has not been organized as an independent discipline with a theory, method and single object of study. Nevertheless, it is possible to draw a tentative trajectory through philosophy, art and media studies where certain concerns are shared. At least three approaches relevant to an assessment of the performative archive can be delineated. They can be differentiated according to their main focus. Broadly speaking there are three interrelated *foci*: power relations, the aesthetic and technology. They will be treated accordingly.

Power Relations

To understand the way an archive may regulate knowledge and govern the way we are, it is necessary to find a theory which can address the archive as an empirical entity, as a collection of some sort, and, on the other hand, the way this entity regulates an order. The French philosopher Michel Foucault's archaeology of knowledge has this theoretical structure. To Foucault, power is everywhere, diffused and embodied in discourse, knowledge and regimes of truth. His notion of the archive is crucial in this connection, and has been very influential in the humanities, and especially where there is a particular take on power relations, as in post-colonial studies, but also in a different way, as we will see, in aesthetics and certain strands of media archaeology.

In Foucault's writings there are, as Wolfgang Ernst has shown,[7] two fundamental conceptualizations of the archive: The *archives*, in plural, and the *archive* in singular. The first one is the traditional concept of the archive as a storage place for acts and files, collections of some sort; in French, these collections always come in plural – governmental archives, state archives, medical archives, economical archives, statistical archives, and so on. According to Foucault, it was one of his ethical imperatives to try to animate the often 'dead' and forgotten information of these archives, to find the lives behind the numbers, to have them speak, to have them tell their stories, as is witnessed in one of his late essays with the wonderful title: 'The lives of infamous men' (1977).[8]

The other concept of the archive at play in his work is the archive as a 'historical a priori', as an order of the sayable at any given time. It is not the sum of all the sentences and texts written and published in our books and newspapers at a given time; books or individuals 'do not communicate solely by the logical procession of propositions that they advance', but by what Foucault calls 'the form of positivity of their discourse' and these forms define 'a field in which formal identities, thematic continuities, translations of concepts, and polemical interchanges may be deployed'.[9] The archive is 'the group of rules that characterize a discursive practice' (128). The archive should, in other words, not be sought in what is said, but rather in *what is not said in what is said*, that is, the archive determines what Foucault calls 'the enunciative possibilities and impossibilities': 'The archive is the first law of what can be said, the system that governs the appearance of statements as unique events' (129). 'The archive cannot be described in its totality, and in its presence it is unavoidable' (130). The archive is that which is 'outside, ourselves, delimits us'. Foucault poetically calls it 'the border of time that surrounds our presence' (130). In other words, the archive is both a dimension of possibility, which conditions our lives, and at the same time, an entity that is unreachable and imperceptible. Foucault developed his archaeology of knowledge as a method for analysing this archive. Judith Butler has highlighted a performative aspect of Foucault's critique. She describes performativity as 'that reiterative power of discourse to produce the phenomena that it regulates and constrains'.[10] In other words, any archive, both in the specific and in the general sense of the term, would be the result of a certain performativity, even if this aspect would be hidden.

Technology

During the 1980s, the German historian of literature and media, Friedrich Kittler, wrote two remarkable studies extending Foucault's archaeology of knowledge to also include the role of new media technologies.[11] Kittler's method has been called media archaeology. He thinks Foucault's discourse analysis disregards the role of new media technology: 'Discourse analysis cannot be applied to sound archives or towers of film rolls,' Kittler writes.[12] He claims that the new technological media of film and the gramophone must change our conceptions of storage and communication. The archive will never be the same. The transition from writing to modern technological media is actually a transition between two incommensurable regimes of storage. He uses Jacques Lacan's methodological distinction between the real and the symbolic to explain this transition. While the regime of writing is based on the symbolic, where communication is limited to what is conceivable through alphabetization, new technological media stores and communicates reality differently. It is primarily the gramophone, sound-recordings, that to Kittler marks the transition to a reign of the real. 'Writing, a technology of symbolic encoding, was subverted by new technologies of storing physical effects in the shape of light and sound waves ... Two of Edison's developments – the phonograph and the kinetoscope – broke the monopoly of writing.'[13] This inaugurates what Kittler calls a new *aufschreibesysteme,* literally a new 'system for inscription' or a new 'discourse network' as it has somewhat unfortunately been translated into in English. We move from Goethe's *aufschreibesysteme* of 1800 (where letters are traces of the soul) to Edison's *aufschreibesysteme* of 1900 (where signals have become inscriptions of the real).[14]

While writing tended to be regarded as a natural extension of man and his soul, new media introduces the machine, both as a metaphor for man and as something at times superior to man as far as vision, precision, storage and memory is concerned. Kittler radicalizes McLuhan's idea of media as extensions of man, and writes in a way which rather echoes Foucault and his critical intuition into how means and modes of communication not only extends what is human, but more importantly, from their perspective, assists and nurtures new modes of regulating, controlling and analysing human beings as machines. To Kittler, the inventions from around the 1880s, film, gramophone and the typewriter, differentiate and implicitly modernize functions such as the eye, the ear and 'the soul', and render them 'improvable':

> Once the technological differentiation of optics, acoustics and writing exploded Gutenberg's writing monopoly around 1880, the *fabrication* of

> so-called Man became possible. His essence escapes into apparatuses. Machines take over the functions of the central nervous system, and no longer, as in times past, merely those of muscles. And with this differentiation … a clear division occurs between matter and information, the real and the symbolic. When it comes to inventing phonography and cinema, the age-old dreams of humankind are no longer sufficient. The physiology of eyes, ears and brains have to become objects of scientific research … So-called Man is split up into physiology and information technology.[15]

Foucault's and Kittler's ideas have in recent years led to many new and insightful works on the experimental relationship between media and man. The recording of traces of man for medical and disciplinary purposes were carried out most intensively in the latter half of the nineteenth century. Étienne-Jules Marey's mapping of the responsive mechanisms of the nervous system is remarkable. He used mechanical registering apparatuses, such as the myograph, attached to the muscles of animals and humans to register instinctual motor-sensory reaction mechanisms in our body indistinguishable to the human eye. These apparatuses produced precise mechanical graphic patterns of our nervous system. Jean-Martin Charcot carried out similar investigations of the mentally ill, using hypnosis to induce states of hysteria which were minutely photographed and registered. Indeed, he was the first to scientifically prove that hysteria was not a fiction but a condition. Eadweard Muybridge perfected the speed of still photography to capture human and animal locomotion never before seen by the living eye. The technological way of recording and storing the body produced a medical and scientific archive of the body, both the external and the internal body.[16] Wolfgang Ernst and Sven Spieker are among the first scholars to address these questions systematically from the perspective of the transformation of the archive. Spieker answers the question – What separates the eighteenth-century archive from its nineteenth-century successor? – by claiming that, whereas the eighteenth-century archive was an archive of symbolic representations, its successor became an archive of 'what eludes symbolic representation': 'In short, its trust in the possibility of registering contingent time in the form of discrete traces (records), the hope that the present moment – contingency itself – might become subject to measurement and registration.'[17] It became an archive of the new sciences heralded by pioneers such as Marey and Anschütz.

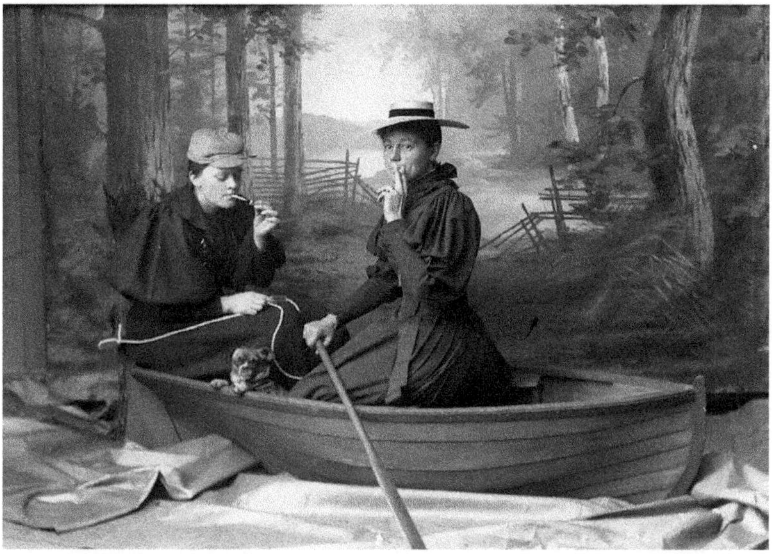

Figure 5.1. Marie Høegh and Bolette Berg, c.1904. (Preus Museum, Horten)

The nineteenth-century archive has been subject to many studies and exhibitions related to film and photography. In 2008 the National Library of Norway in Oslo held an exhibition called '80 million pictures'. The figure '80 million pictures' represents the number of photographs believed to exist in public archives in Norway today. Four hundred and fifty of these photographs were displayed in this exhibition. The role of the new medium of photography in the construction of Norway, both as an identity and a territory, was investigated. The images were collected from archives of prisons, hospitals and universities unknown to the general public. Together these archives constituted a secret genesis of a nation, a kind of cartography of the minds, faces and landscapes of Norway. The evidentiary force of the new medium of photography was used in police surveillance, medical research, phrenology, physiognomy, and in the colonial practice of measuring the territory.

Some of the most interesting counter-cultural performative archives from the early days of Norwegian photography stem from two women on the south-east coast of Norway. Since the art of photography was a young art, women in this profession could from the beginning work alongside men. Marie Høegh and Bolette Berg were two such women

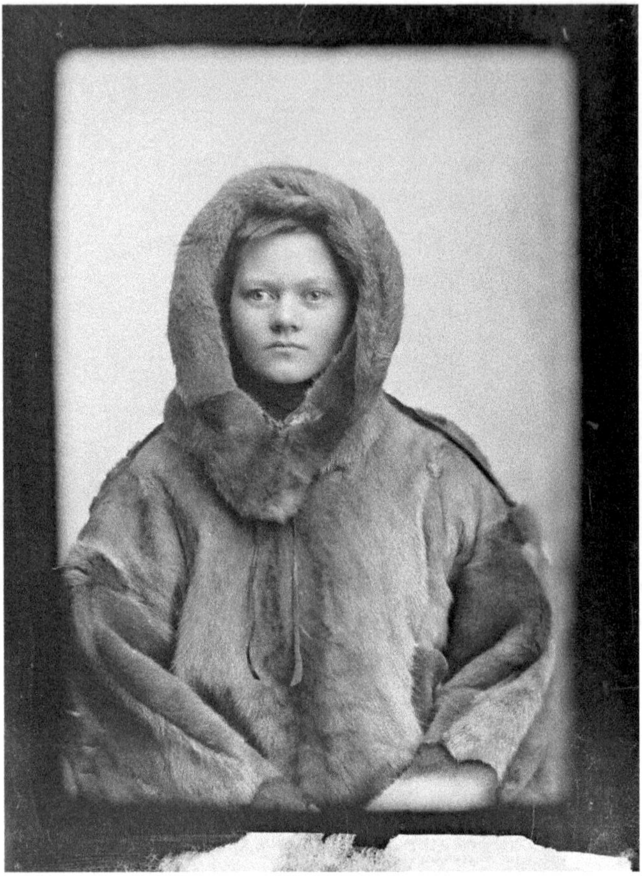

Figure 5.2. Marie Høegh and Bolette Berg, c.1904. (Preus Museum, Horten)

who worked during the turn of the last century. Their pictures from 1904 were found hidden until 1996 when they were discovered in a basket in a loft of their studio. Here they cross-dress as men and transvestites, and some of the photos comment directly, sarcastically and in a somewhat carnivalesque manner on current political events, such as Fridtjof Nansen's return from the world-renowned trip to the North Pole. This series of travesties taken by female photographers predates later artistic work such as Cindy Sherman's *Untitled Film stills* by 70 years. Findings like these demonstrate that new technological media were used subversively from the very beginning, but for political or other reasons, remained a secret for a long time.

Aesthetics

Many film and media artists throughout the twentieth century have been engaged in a research into the potential and uses of their preferred medium. The thousands of short films by the Lumière Brothers constitute an archive of everyday life during the turn of the last century in its own right. This archive registers life as it was. With the practice of found footage film among artists of the early and late avant-garde, we can begin to talk of a new performative archive tradition. Russian constructivists and the surrealists were pioneers. They both created new visions of the world, using montage as their preferred style. For a long time Lenin blessed the use of new media such as film for political purposes. The pioneering Dziga Vertov developed a film style where he recycled footage from newsreels for propaganda purposes. Films like *The Man with a Movie-Camera* is a collage of news footage in combination with new footage and a very complex editing style. In New York the surrealist Joseph Cornell used found footage from feature films, science films, trick films, fairy tales and especially footage from the circus and the Tivoli which he mixed to create some of the most wonderful and enigmatic universes.

William C. Wees' *Recycled Images: The Art and Politics of Found Footage Films* is among the most comprehensive film historical investigations into film as a performative archive.[18] To him, there are three main categories of found footage film: (1) found films which are not re-edited (like Ken Jacobs' *Perfect film*); (2) found films which are re-edited (like Joseph Cornell's *Rose Hobart* or Bruce Conner's *Report*); and (3) found films which are otherwise altered, that is, for example scratched or chemically altered (like Peter Weibel's *Scratched films*). These categories could be extended further after the digital computer, and websites such as YouTube would be an important place to investigate. Also films simulating the archival would be important, such as Abigail Child's *Mayhem*. While Wees focuses exclusively on found footage films, some more recent studies, like those of Hal Foster[19] and Charles Merewether[20] (2006), talk about a more general archival turn in contemporary art. Especially the art historians and art critics associated with the New York-based journal *October* have for a long time been interested in these issues in a more theoretical, even Foucauldian fashion. Several essays in the journal from the 1980s have explicitly referred to an archival mode in art. Three important essays from *October* referring explicitly to an archival turn in contemporary art are: Craig Owens, 'The Allegorical Impulse I-II',[21] Benjamin Buchloh, 'The Anomic Archive' (1999), and Hal Foster, 'An Archival Impulse' (2004). All three talk about how newer archival art establish a counter-history or a counter-memory. Their approach is Foucauldian in the way they imply how an alternative archive or collection may highlight a certain regularity which can subsequently illuminate the existence of a history or a desire which we did not know existed, or which we were not aware of. The stories the *October* writers tell in this regard usually start out from the avant-garde and photomontage, in particular. Indeed, it was photomontage which in the 1920s represented a shift toward an archival critique. The surrealists and the Dadaists tended to undermine the immediate indexical and mnemonic functions of photography and the photographic collections through sometimes shocking montages. Sven Spieker summarizes:

> Rather than endorsing the nineteenth-century confidence in the registration of time, however, members of the twentieth-century avant-gardes critiqued and ultimately dismantled that confidence, first, by pointing out that the contingency and chance may affect the archive's operations literally at every level (Marcel Duchamp); second, by compiling collections of moments of rupture that elude the archive (early Surrealism); and third, by challenging the Newtonian underpinnings of the archive's topography and its optical correlatives by way of film (El Lissitzsky, Sergei Eisenstein).[22]

In his classic essay 'The Allegorical Impulse: Toward a Theory of Post-modernism I–II' (1980), Craig Owens presents a dense and wide reaching preparation for handling some of the main strategies at play in contemporary post-modern art, where the artist no longer primarily sought originality and uniqueness in expression, but rather a kind of appropriation and recirculation of the already existing. How can these sometimes obscure accumulations of remnants and fragments be understood? Owens uses the term allegory. He presents Robert Rauschenberg as one of his main contemporary examples. Rauschenberg develops the old photomontage into what he calls 'combined paintings'. Rauschenberg even entitled some of them 'allegories'. He collects fragments and relics from his life and contemporary media and combines them, often without any obvious or coherent meaning; they are rather 'without meaning and in need of decipherment, like a rebus without an answer', Owens asserts. Owens discusses a host of artists using this procedure in different media as a kind of oblique technique of quotation: Laurie Anderson, Robert Smithson, Sherrie Levine, Robert Longo and Cindy Sherman.

The term 'allegory' comes from *allos* which means 'other' and *agoreuei* which means 'to speak'. The allegorical procedure has to do with making something speak again, somewhere else and at another time. Things are cut off from their habitual or original situation and fragmented and recontextualized in another. Thus, there is a cult of the ruin, the fragmented, the remains, traces, in these allegorical efforts, according to Owens. Series of objects are collected or accumulated following a seemingly arbitrary order. The paratactical or paradigmatic, not the syntagmatic arrangement, predominates. Thus, the disconnected becomes reconnected and synthesized in aesthetic border-crossings and hybridizations. An atomizing and a 'disjunctive principle lies at the heart of allegory'. This creates an unpredictable excess which replaces the meaning the object had in its original setting. Owens quotes Walter Benjamin, who himself was a notorious collector of fragments and quotations during the 1930s and 1940s. Benjamin's early dissertation on the German tragic drama is to a large extent still one of the most unique and original readings of the allegorical. It is especially the enigmatic and double coding of words and images in the allegory that fascinates Benjamin. He believed that the allegorical transforms things into a kind of secret writing, into a script to be deciphered – even redeemed. For Benjamin, *inter*pretation is dis*inter*ment, Owens writes (84).

The Atlas

Benjamin Buchloh's 'Gerhard Richter's *Atlas*: The Anomic Archive' (1999) deals with one of the most unclassifiable archival projects in contemporary art: Gerhard Richter's *Atlas*. The anachronistic term *atlas* was defined from the end of the sixteenth century as a book format that compiles and organizes geographical and astronomical knowledge. In the nineteenth century it has been used to identify any tabular display of systematized knowledge, especially positivist systems of knowledge. Richter's use of the term may refer to these traditions more or less ironically, but more importantly it may also refer to the art historian Aby Warburg's *Mnemosyne Atlas* from the 1920s. Warburg's *Atlas* could be said to represent an anti-positivist atlas which tried to reproduce experientially the movements of art history through the century. While Warburg's *Atlas* consists of an organized display of photographs and reproductions from the history of art, Richter's *Atlas* is more oriented toward a contemporary situation.

From 1962 to 2006, Richter filled 788 sheets of paper with more than 10,000 images ordered by the formal procedure of accumulating found or intentionally produced photographs. The procedure is 'strangely enigmatic', Buchloh writes. While the work of Bernhard and Hilla Becher and Christian Boltanski displays an astonishing homogeneity and continuity, Richter's demonstrates a remarkable heterogeneity and discontinuity. Richter started out in 1962 collecting private photographs of family and relatives, an activity not uncommon for an artist who just emigrated from East Germany to West Germany. Then suddenly, around 1963, the homogeneity of the family album-series is interrupted, first, by the Western mass cultural genres of the illustrated journals, and later, by images from the concentration camps and then, in the more recent sheets, by photos of his models and landscapes used in his more recent paintings. According to Buchloh, Richter is difficult to handle because he follows two attitudes, the historical and the aesthetic. Buchloh openly prefers the historical attitude, seemingly because of its scepticism about commercialism and pop culture. According to Buchloh, the historical attitude displays, through a wide range of media images, newspaper-clippings and commercials, the banality of media images as a condition of the repression or forgetting of a historical memory. For Buchloh, this attitude turns Richter's *Atlas* into 'an anomic archive' (an archive of forgetfulness, i.e. *anomic* refers to 'a form of aphasia characterized by inability to recall the names of objects', *Oxford English Dictionary*). The aesthetic attitude, on the other hand, is its counterpart. It demonstrates a fascination for the liberating and libidinal banality of an amateur photograph, a newspaper image or the splendidly seductive commercial image. Richter's first encounter with the Western mass cultural genres of the illustrated journal seems to reveal a fascination for a proliferation of images heretofore unknown to him during his life in the former East Germany. Richter says: 'The most banal amateur photograph is more beautiful than the most beautiful painting by Cézanne.' Buchloh thinks this is a joke, and prefers to relate Richter to Siegfried Kracauer's dictum: 'The flood of photos [in contemporary mass-media] sweeps away the dams of memory.'

While the historical avant-garde's photomontage often demonstrated a belief in the emancipatory dimension of the photograph, where the serial structuring of visual information in the photo-collage implicitly adheres to an open form and a potential, even utopian infinity, Richter seems, according to Buchloh, to consider photography and its various practices (primarily in the mass media) as a system of ideological domination, more precisely, as one of the instruments with which collective anomie, amnesia and repression are socially inscribed and accepted. The strange juxtapositions in *Atlas* of media images and family images demonstrate two forms of cultural construction to Buchloh: the construction of a public identity, on the one hand, and the construction of a private identity, on the other. 'Memory is thus constituted of as an archaeology of pictorial and photographic registers, each of which partakes in a different photographic formation, and each of which generates its proper psychic register of responses,' Buchloh writes.

In 'An Archival Impulse', Hal Foster presents contemporary art strategies and installations as counter-archives or alternative archives. He uses the term 'archival impulse' to describe a new and distinct tendency in contemporary art: 'archival artists seek to make historical information, often lost or displaced, physically present. To this end they work on the found image, object, and text, and favor the installation format as they do so' (4). Some practitioners, such as Douglas Gordon, gravitate toward what Foster call 'time ready-mades', that is, visual narratives that are sampled in image-projections, as in his odd installations of films by Alfred Hitchcock, Martin Scorsese and others. 'These sources are familiar, drawn from the archives of mass culture, to ensure a legibility that can then be disturbed or *detourné*; but they can also be obscure, retrieved in a gesture of alternative knowledge or counter-memory' (ibid.). Works by Tacita Dean and Thomas Hirschhorn's *Monuments* are of the latter kind. After having seen the cultic manifestations of spontaneous public shrines after the death of Princess Diana, Hirschhorn decided to create monuments for thinkers devoted to radical transgressions. He created cultic monuments, ritualistic, phandom-like installations filled with books, photos and notes on philosophers and artists, where the visitor can take part and leave something behind. These monuments were set up in unexpected suburbs, as at *Documenta* in 2002 in Kassel, Germany, where the *Bataille Monument* was placed way outside town in a Turkish neighbourhood. Hirschhorn made at least three such monuments: *The Bataille Monument, The Deleuze Monument* and *The Artaud Monument*.

Experiments in New Media

We have, in other words, a growing collection of writings on the archival impulse in contemporary art, but few of these art critical essays make connections to newer forms of digital archives. As the performative archive goes digital, several aspects of the archive needs rethinking. Foucault's general archive, the ordering structures of the visible and sayable, takes on a new apparition. Many have pointed to the relationship between the word archive and 'arkhe', the latter meaning command, and its relationship to computer language (codes and algorithms).[23] The Foucauldian notion of a general archive may perhaps in the future be aligned to nonhuman agents operating through algorithms, commanding and regulating orders of the sayable and the visible. And as the computer's storage capacity increases, ideas of total storage pose new practical and theoretical challenges. Furthermore, procedures for tracing the provenance of a document become increasingly difficult as copies and fakes proliferate, and manipulation can be done on the fly. Cultural habits change. With the maturing of Web 2.0 into a functional infrastructure, large populations move more of their everyday activities to online environments. This leads to new kinds of interactive and collaborative practice, but also to a programmed and controlled sociality. These challenges may be boiled down to three strategies that are unique to digital media: manipulation, interactivity and the idea of total storage. Interestingly, all three strategies are equally effective in regard to both liberation and repression. Manipulation works effectively both within propaganda and within artistic practices. Interactivity has become a double edged sword on the internet: it creates new forms of communication, but it has also become a way of draining every individual of his or her personal desires for new forms of marketing and profiling. Finally, the idea of total storage must be the ultimate Panopticon. I will focus primarily on how these strategies may work to set up new kinds of performative archives within contemporary art.

Manipulation

The Norwegian artist Vibeke Tandberg is among the most interesting early artists addressing the problem of new media in terms of image manipulation.[24] In 1996 she exhibited 27 photos from what looks like a private photo-album. The series is called *Living Together,* and it shows two girls (sisters, friends or lovers?) in what looks like a long and mostly joyful summer-vacation. On closer inspection, the two girls look like twins or more uncannily, one of them is a clone; we soon realize that it may be the same girl who has been artificially incorporated into the same image twice. Tandberg used Adobe Photoshop to digitally interpolate a copy of herself in self-portraits. Some of the photos address the classical self-portrait and some a quasi-religious iconography, like washing bare feet. This defamiliarization of the classics is done within the framework of the all too familiar private photo-album. Furthermore, these images are in the feminist tradition of the staging of the self from Cindy Sherman to Sophie Calle, but while they use masks and literature for their theatre of the self, Tandberg uses digital manipulation. She utilizes both the analog *and* the digital qualities of modern photography, that is, she uses in the same image, qualities defining both the classical photographical index *and* the new manipulative techniques of the post-photographic era'.[25] In the middle of the most innocent of archives, a private photo-album, she installs with urgency and a striking sensitivity the shock of the cyborg. Thus, she treats the problem of identity, life and 'visual truth' after the digital revolution by creating an archive which is both analog and digital.

Interactivity

In recent years more and more artists have started experimenting with interactive technologies, which fundamentally transform the art viewer into a participant – even at times a creative participant. Still the largest interactive art shows take place outside the Parnassus of contemporary art. One of the most important scenes for interactive art today is the annual Ars Electronica Festival in Linz, Austria. Two of the most celebrated works in 2008 were devoted to interactive music. In *Reactable* by the Spanish artist-group led by Sergi Jordà, the computer interface is externalized and visualized as a sensitive table where players can activate sounds and rhythms in a large database by moving cubes in different constellations. The sound-combinations seem endless. The artist Björk had Jordà build her a version of the *Reactable* which she used to remix some of her songs during live performances.

Teri Rueb's celebrated *Core Sample* is a complex installation which interacts with the environment via satellite technology. She uses GPS-navigation, a computer database and a headset to create an interactive sound-atmosphere for people strolling in a marked territory (actually an artificial island created by rubbish and debris from the city of Boston). The movements within the physical landscape are registered by the GPS-system which sends feedback to a computer which sequentially activates different sounds including statements on environmental issues, randomly chosen from a database according to the movements of the promenading listener. More than 250 sounds and messages are stored in the database. Both Jordà and Rueb's installations produce an intense kinesthetic and synaesthetic experience for their user. The installations work as a complex interface between an individual and an archive: the archive is here transformed into a collection of alterable data. These kinds of art works take the principle of the avant-garde montage one step further, in the sense that here it is no longer the artist who creates the montage, but the viewer as participant who alters the montage according to algorithms that are activated through the participation. They become performative archives *par excellence.*

Total Recording

Lev Manovich explains in a short essay how new media partake in the dream of total storage. So far the history of representations has been based on the principle of selection, but now, new media can actually re-present and store everything:

> Since the beginning of the 1990s, working within the paradigms of Computer Augmented Reality, Ubiquitous Computing and Software Agents at places such as MIT Media Lab and Xerox Park, computer scientists have advanced the notion of a computer as an unobtrusive but omnipresent device which automatically records and indexes all personal communications and other user's activities.[26]

According to Manovich, this 'unique opportunity' may lead to a shift from 'sampling to total recording'. Everything can be recorded and stored. But who wants to and has the time to watch the total recording of a person's life? Well, nobody, but this is no problem, says Manovich, because new storage media can become active; a software programme can go through thousands of hours of surveillance video and prepare a selection of events that would be interesting for you. Is this utopia or the absolute nightmare? [27] Artists such as Harun Farocki have demonstrated through moving image installations such as *Fussball* and a series of works called *Eye/ Machine I-III*, how new media as a kind of artificial intelligence gradually have been implemented in our societies for surveillance and management purposes. These issues often transgress a border zone, difficult to reach or grasp, in between bodies and bits, relying on biology and informatics.

It shouldn't come as a surprise that an investigation into the problem of archives ends up with the challenge of total storage. The dream of total storage is inherent to the very foundation of the idea of the archive.[28] The archives of the earliest city-states were always the place where the people, finances, objects and animals of the city were subject to cataloguing, inventory and administration by letters and by numbers. As we enter the high-tech world of surveillance cameras and electronic identity cards, the border between archiving and controlling has become more fragile than ever. What is needed is a comprehensive and thorough study of the transformations and politics of storage and recording. The archives of the future will not be like the archives of the past, that is for sure, but what kind of archives do we want, and what can artists, scholars and creative programmers do to address these questions in ways that tend to the urgency of these problems and challenges? The performative archive is not a solution to this challenge, but part of an ongoing investigation into the problem.

Notes

1 M. Foucault, 1989, *The Archaeology of Knowledge*, London: Routledge (1969), 130.

2 B. Buchloh, 1999, 'Gerhard Richter's *The Atlas*. The anomic archive', *October* 88, Spring, 117–45.

3 J. L. Austin, 1962, *How to do Things with Words*, Cambridge MA: Harvard University Press.

4 J. Derrida, 1982, *Margins of Philosophy*, trans. with introduction by A. Bass, Chicago: University of Chicago Press (French edn 1972).

5 The question what can archives learn from media archaeology, aesthetic and artistic strategies? was the question posed in my 2010 edited collection, *The Archive in Motion* Oslo: Novus Press. This issue will therefore not be treated here.

6 J. Derrida, 1995, *Archive Fever: A Freudian Impression,* Chicago: University of Chicago Press, 34.

7 W. Ernst, 2002, *Das Rumoren der Archive. Ordnung aus Unordnung*, Berlin: Merve.
8 M. Foucault, 1977a, 'La vie des hommes infâmes' in *Les cahiers du chemin,* 12–29.
9 M. Foucault, *Archaeology of Knowledge*, 126–128.
10 J. Butler, 1993, *Bodies that Matter: On the Discursive Limits of 'Sex'*, London: Routledge, 2.
11 F. Kittler, 1985, *Discourse Networks 1800/1900*, Stanford, CA: Stanford University Press (1990). and *Gramophone, Film, Typewriter* [1986]. Stanford, CA. Stanford University Press (1999).
12 Kittler, *Gramophone, Film, Typewriter,* 5.
13 Ibid. xxv.
14 Kittler, 1999, *Discourse Networks 1800/1900.*
15 Ibid. 16
16 See A. Sekula, 1986, 'The body and the archive', *October* 39, Winter, 3–64.
17 S. Spieker, 2008, *The Big Archive: Art from Bureaucracy*, Cambridge, MA: MIT Press, 5.
18 W. C. Wees, 1993, *Recycled Images: The Art and Politics of Found Footage Films*, New York: Anthology Film Archives.
19 H. Foster, 2004, 'An archival impulse', *October* 110, Autumn, 3–22.
20 C. Merewether (ed.), 2006, *The Archive*, Cambridge, MA: MIT Press.
21 C. Owens, 1980, 'The allegorical impulse: Toward a theory of postmodernism. I–II', *October* 12, 13, Spring and Summer.
22 Spieker, 2008, *The Big Archive,* 6–7.
23 See Derrida, 1995; also, aspects of Foucault's ideas on the archive in relation to the computer are discussed more fully in the books and essays by W. Ernst see especially his *Medium Foucault*, 2000.
24 A more complete survey of Vibeke Tandberg's work in new media is available in E. Røssaak, 2005, *Selviakttakelse: En tendens i kunst og litteratur,* Oslo and Bergen: Norsk kulturråd.
25 W. J. Mitchell, 1992, *The Reconfigured Eye. Visual Truth in the Post-Photographic Era*, Cambridge, MA: MIT Press.
26 L. Manovich, 2003, 'Metadating the image' in A. Adriaansens (ed.), *Making Art of Databases*, Rotterdam: V2 Publishing, 23.
27 The handling of big data is thematized on many levels nowadays – not only in connection with state surveillance, search algorithms or social media. The Belgian experimental archival group, Constant, uses what it calls software agents to classify and analyse the huge life-archive left after the Finnish artist Erkki Kurenniemi (www.kurenniemi.activearchives.org/logbook), and the movie *The Final Cut* (2004) taps into the idea of editing and selling life-stories. Also, several Digital Humanities projects explore new ways of reading big data.

28 The idea of total storage is in many ways contradictory to the idea of an archive, as basically a mechanism of selection and qualified erasure. New media recording devices tend to record randomly and by chance, while the archive was basically depositing items according to a agreed-upon protocol. To put it differently, media and archives operate according to different technical protocols. Furthermore, the idea of storing 'everything' will always have to compromise on certain known or unknown elements of what could possibly constitute 'everything'. This also involves the much larger question: What is life, What constitutes life, What is the 'everything' of life?

6

Visualizing the Universe: Mandala and Buddhist Cosmology as Technovisual Embodiment

Amy Chan Kit-Sze

> It is a wisdom or a religion – it does not much matter which.[1]

> art: (i)s the production of situations, of rituals, which allow us to access states beyond the everyday and beyond habitual subjectivity.[2]

Introduction

The concept of the mandala is very complex and it can be found in Buddhism, Hinduism and Christianity, as well as Jung's psychology. This chapter mainly focuses on the mandalas in Tibetan Buddhism (especially Tantric Buddhism). In Tantric Buddhism, it is believed that, by visualizing oneself as a deity living in the centre of the universe, the long way to attain Buddhahood will be much shortened. Moreover, by visualizing the universe in the mandala, one can 'purify the polluted environment and bring prosperity to the world'.[3] In Tibetan Buddhism, a mandala is described as 'a paradigm of cosmic involution and evolution'.[4]

While visualization is a major process in this Tantric ritual, the construction process of the mandala relies highly on technicity. Unlike other artworks, construction of a mandala must follow the tradition strictly. There are 725 basic mandalas in total.[5] All mandalas must follow one of these basic forms and no variation is allowed. Moreover, all the squares and concentric circles in the mandala (for example, Fig. 6.1) have to be carefully measured according to classical Indian instructions.[6] The dimensions are based on Indian architecture which, in turn, is a reflection of the cosmos according to Buddhist cosmology. I will go through the process of the construction of mandala by highlighting its technicity later.

The pouring of the coloured sand using a cone-shaped metal funnel, or *chak-pur*, looks simple, but again, the process is technical and time-consuming. First, the lamas have to go through many years' vigorous training in drawing, praying and meditation before they are allowed to participate in the construction of a mandala. Second, it usually takes a long time to finish it. For example, a seven-foot square mandala will take 20 lamas in shifts two weeks to complete. They have to chant while they are pouring the sand. Third, the sand is usually made of precious stones or minerals. According to Barry Bryant, nowadays the sand is made from ground white stones or marbles dyed with opaque water colours. There are five basic colours – white, black, blue, yellow and green. Each of the last four colours has three shades – dark, medium and light.[7]

The focus of this chapter is on the enchanting power of the mandala through a visualization process of its technical display of contours and lines. Although no technovisual devices – such as camcorder, digital camera or computer – are used in the construction of the mandala, we understand 'techno' in a broad sense here, denoting technical, systematic, mechanical arts and craftsmanship,[8] so it can be said that the mandala transforms the universe in a technovisual fashion.

In the first section of this chapter, I will explain briefly the creation and structure of mandalas. In the second section, I will discuss the ways in which mandalas visualize the Buddhist cosmology of time and space. In the final part, I will attempt to read the mandalas alongside Deleuzian philosophy, in particular his philosophy of visual images. When Deleuze and Guattari discuss the concept of thinking in *What is Philosophy?,* they write that '[t]hinking here implies a projection of the transcendent on the plane of immanence.'[9] Moreover, they argue that, 'the prephilosophical shows that a creation of concepts or a philosophical formation was not the inevitable destination of the plane of immanence itself but that it could unfold in wisdoms and religions …'[10]

In fact, my discussion later will illustrate that Deleuze and Guattari do mention the Chinese hexagrams and Hindu mandalas as examples of figures that populate the plane of immanence. In light of Deleuze and Guattari's concept of thinking, I propose in this chapter that the mandala shows us an image that is a brain which re-enchants the universe. To borrow Trungpa's words: 'When the mandala experience begins to occur, we see the true world, 100 per cent, without distortion, without conceptualizing it.'[11]

What is a Mandala?

The Sanskrit word 'mandala' literally means 'circle'. The Tibetan word for mandala is *kyilkhor*, which means 'centre and surrounding environment'. Simple as it seems, a mandala as a visualization of Buddhist tantra is far more complicated than a 'circle'. According to Robert Thurman, the mandala idea originated long before Buddhism. In the earliest Indo-European religion, '*mandala* is the term for a chapter, a collection of mantras or verse hymns chanted in Vedic ceremonies, perhaps coming from the sense of *round*, as in a round of songs'.[12] And from the early days, 'mandala had the generative meaning of a circle as a universal symbol for womb, for breast, for the nurturing source of life'.[13] In his introduction to the Dalai Lama's *Kalachakra Tantra: Rite of Initiation*, Jeffrey Hopkins explains that ' "mandala" refers to *birth-places*' and '[o]ur world is conceived as residing on mandalas or spheres of wind, water, and so forth ... "mandala" refers to the four elements that are the *foundation*'.[14]

Denise Patry Leidy says that '[m]andalas are often described as cosmoplans in both the external sense, as diagrams of a cosmos; and in the internal sense, as guides to the psycho-physical practices of an adherent ... mandalas represent manifestations of a specific divinity *in* the cosmos and *as* the cosmos'[15] (emphasis in the original). This echoes Carl Jung's study on the mandala. After creating a mandala each morning during his stay in Switzerland (1918–1919), he recognizes the significance of mandalas and concludes that the mandala is representing both the self and world. According to Jung, mandalas can be found in many cultures, but the 'best and most significant mandalas are found in the sphere of Tibetan Buddhism'.[16]

Giuseppe Tucci remarks in his book *The Theory and Practice of the Mandala* that, 'It [mandala] is, above all, a map of the cosmos. It is the whole universe in its essential plan, in its process of emanation and of reabsorption'.[17] This process of 'emanation and of reabsorption' finds a distinct resonance in the Deleuzian territorialization, deterritorialization and reterritorialization concepts. Interestingly, Deleuze and Guattari also mention mandalas in their book *What is Philosophy?* when they discuss how to think through figures:

> Thinking here implies a projection of the transcendent on the plane of immanence. Transcendence may be entirely 'empty' in itself, yet it becomes full to the extent that it descends and crosses different hierarchized levels that are projected together on a region of the plane, that is to say, on an aspect corresponding to an infinite movement. In this respect, it is the same when transcendence invades the absolute or monotheism replaces unity: the transcendent God would remain empty, or at least *absconditus*, if it were not projected on a plane of immanence of creation where it traces the stages of its theophany. In both cases, imperial unity or spiritual empire, the transcendence that is projected on the plane of immanence paves it or populates it with Figures. It is a wisdom or a religion – it does not much matter which. It is only from this point of view that Chinese hexagrams, Hindu mandalas, Jewish sephiroth, Islamic 'imaginals' and Christian icons can be considered together: thinking through figures.... The mandala is a projection on a surface that establishes correspondence between divine, cosmic, political, architectural and organic levels as so many values of one and the same transcendence. That is why the figure has a reference, one that is plurivocal and circular by nature .... the figure is essentially paradigmatic, projective, hierarchical and referential ...[18]

Had Deleuze and Guattari further studied the mandala, they would have discovered this 'figure' holds a great significance to their concept of time, and I will return to this later.

Matthieu Ricard writes in his 'Introduction to the Purpose and Symbolism of the Mandala in Tibetan Buddhism' that 'mandalas are objects of meditation with a specific purpose: to transform our ordinary perception of the world into a pure perception of the buddha nature which permeates all phenomena'.[19] Meditation upon a mandala is not merely a daydreaming musing through the chantings, but a process of visualization. In this process, '[o]ne sees oneself as the main deity, which is considered not as a "god" or as a separate entity, but as the manifestation of one's own wisdom, nature. The outer world is seen as a buddha-field and the other beings therein as male and female deities'.[20]

In Tibetan Buddhism, ' "[m]andala" also refers to an *inestimable mansion that is the residence* of deities, as well as to the resident deities ... it can refer to the *combination of divine residence and residents*'[21] (emphasis in the original). The most commonly known mandalas are made of coloured sand, depicted in two-dimensional form, showing the three-dimensional palace of the deity and its surrounding environment. The sand mandala is a visual representation of a tantra, its purpose being to acquaint the student with the tantra and the deity. One of the most famous mandalas practiced by Tibetan Buddhists is the *Kalachakra Tantra. Kalachakra* is a Sanskrit word which means 'the wheel of time'. The Kalachakra deity represents omniscience, since time is not seen as linear; past, present and future and the flow of all events are present at the same time in the wheel of time.

Ritual of Creating a Mandala

The creation of a mandala is an extensive process and usually takes 12 to 14 days. In the preparation stage, the vajra master first has to generate himself as the embodiment of the central deity and make offerings to the deities. He then begins the construction of the sand mandala by defining the major axes and four base lines with chalk strings. The threads mark the main outlines of the square mandala and the outer, concentric circle. After reciting the mantra of all the deities which take abode in the mandala, the vajra master can apply the first sand on the mandala as foundation. Then, the monks (usually four of them but this depends on the size of the mandala) continue the process of sand painting in ten directions.[22] No matter how large the mandala is, the monks always start at the centre and progress outward. After the mandala is completed, it will be blessed by the vajra master.[23]

While the monks are applying coloured sand to the mandala, the students are being prepared to enter the mandala. The preparation process, which is usually called 'enhancement', involves 40 steps. The students are instructed to use visualization to become acquainted with the mandala. Before they are allowed to enter the mandala when it is completed, they have to cleanse their bodies and compose themselves for spiritual rebirth. At the initial stage of entering the mandala, the students are blindfolded, as it is considered inappropriate for them to see the mandala at this early stage. The vajra master leads them to circumambulate the mandala and instructs them to visualize themselves as the Buddhas of the four entrance gates to the mandala.[24] 'A complex visualization is led by the vajra master, in which deities are dissolved into blessings within the students, to the accompaniment of cymbals, bells, drums and incense.'[25] In the generation stage, the students are allowed to see the mandala. Besides visualizing themselves as the central deity, the students also visualize every minute detail of the mandala while being led through the seven initiations – the water initiation, the crown initiation, the silk ribbon initiation, the vajra and bell initiation, the conduct initiation, the name initiation and the permission initiation.[26]

Upon the completion of the initiation ritual, the mandala is dismantled to symbolize impermanence. After chanting and praying to all the deities to ask them to leave the mandala, the vajra master cuts the major lines of the mandala with the point of a vajra. All the sand is swept up and put in a vase which is carried very carefully in a procession to a nearby lake, river or sea.[27] The sand is poured into the water and the whole ritual is thus concluded.[28]

Structure of a Mandala

Creating a mandala is not a free creation of art, as every detail must follow the tradition. Each mandala has a central deity: Vajravarachi (The Diamond Female Yogi), Jnanadakini (Intuitive Wisdom Angel), Chakrasamvara, Amitabha, Hevajra (Laughing Diamond-Thunderbolt), and so on.

One of the most popular mandalas is the 'Wheel of Life' or the 'Wheel of Life and Death' (Fig. 6.1). According to Vesna A. Wallace in *The Inner Kālacakratantra*, the wheel of time 'designates the dynamic and nondual nature of a single reality that manifests primarily in two ways – the conventional (*samvrti*) and the ultimate (*paramartha*)'.[29] The conventional reality itself is further divided into internal and external aspects. In the external aspect, 'the term "the wheel of time" refers to the passage of days, month and years in the cycle of time. The *Vimalaprabhā*[30] defines time (*kāla*) as a circle of 12 solar mansions or zodiacs (*rāśi-cakra*). The unit day-and-night (*aho-rātra*) is also called "time"'.[31] Internally, the wheel of time designates a circulation of 'twenty-one thousand and six hundred pairs of inhalations and exhalations, which take place in the course of a day-and-night called "time".'[32] Wallace further explains that 'the Kalacakra tradition views time as the sole cause of the origination and cessation of all living beings'[33] as it is believed that 'human being comes into existence, dies, and is born again due to the flow of the wind of *prāṇa* through the twelve internal zodiacs'.[34]

This mandala (Fig. 6.1) embodies all times, directions and geography. In the middle of the mandala is the Monster of Impermanence which holds the wheel of life. The innermost circle is divided into nine parts, and each part has a Sanskrit seed syllable inside which represents the seasons in the Tibetan calendar. Then, there are eight lotus leaves and

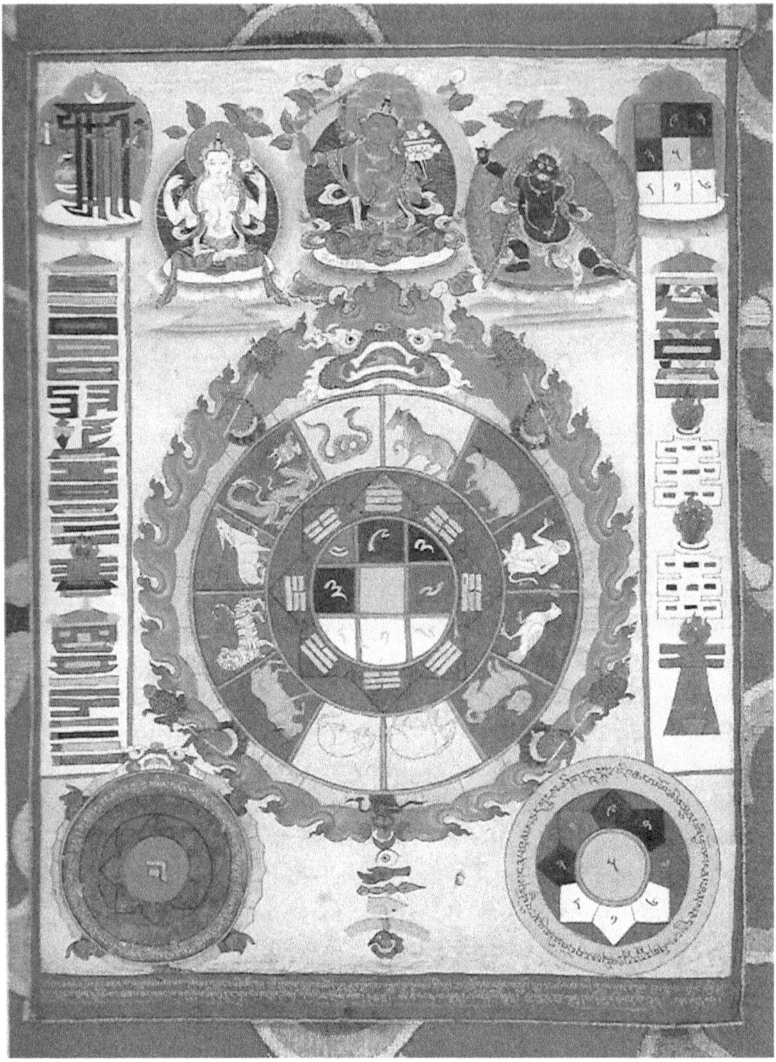

Figure 6.1. Wheel of Life and Death (吉布 & 楊典, 2006, 頁 19).

each has a trigram on it which stands for fire, earth, lake, heaven, water, mountain, thunder and wind. The circle that surrounds the lotus leaves has 12 animals in it which represent the earthly branches. Combined with the five heavenly stems, these twelve animals will make up a sexagenary cycle which lasts for 60 years. The Monster of Impermanence rotates the wheel of life and death, reminding people that seasons come and go and so does life.

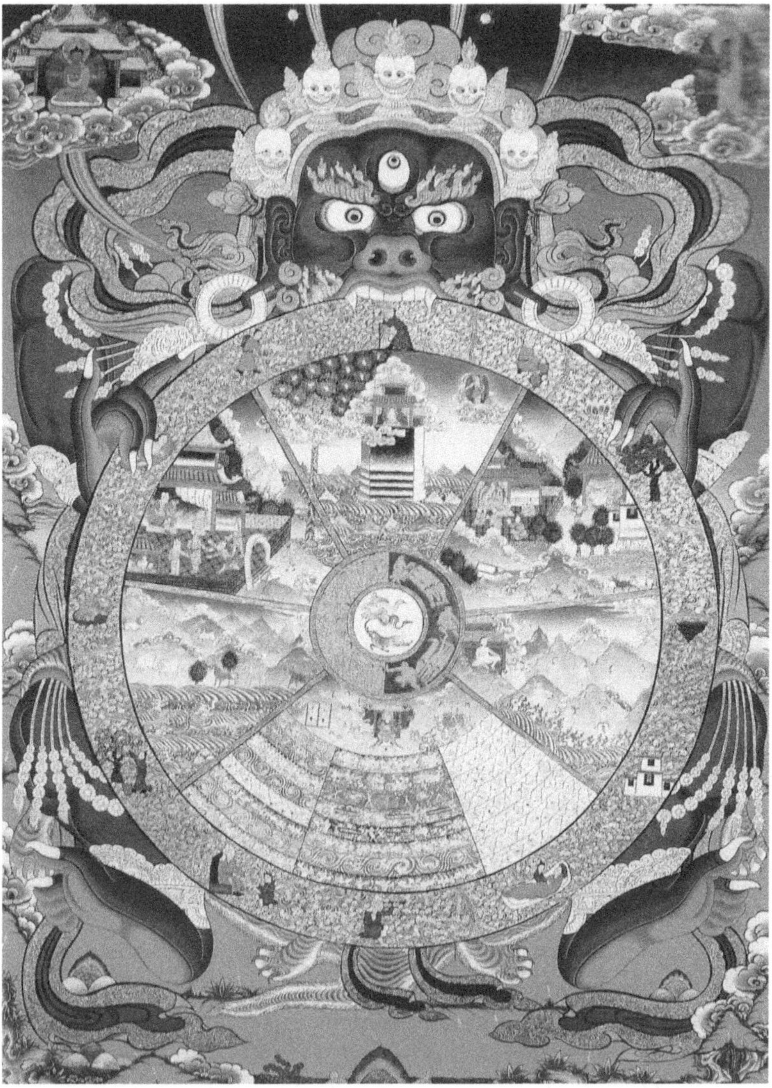

Figure 6.2. Monster of Impermanence (Tibet Window, 2008).

On the four corners of the mandala, there are four simplified mandalas. The top left one represents time and space, the universe and everything in the world made up by the ten directions – East, South, West, North, South-East, South-West, North-East, North-West, below and above – and year, month and day.

Figure 6.2 is another manifestation of the Monster of Impermanence. This mandala illustrates the essence of Buddhist teachings, the

Four Noble Truths. According to the Dalai Lama, the Four Noble Truths are the truth of suffering, the truth of the cause of suffering, the truth of the cessation of suffering, and the truth of the path to the cessation of suffering.[35] The Wheel of Life describes the cause of suffering and its effects. The outermost circle describes the 12 interdependent causes and their effects, for example, ignorance, the five senses, desire, sensual entanglement, and so on. The next circle is the Symbolic Six Worlds: the temporal paradise, the world of humans, the world of animals, the world of Titans, the world of the hungry ghosts, and the cold and hot hells. Depending on one's karma, one will be reborn in one of these six realms after death until one achieves nirvana. The ring that surrounds the three poisons in the centre is made up of the dark path and the white path. Anyone who falls into the temptation of the three poisons will follow the dark path leading to the cold and hot hells and bad rebirth. The white path, on the other hand, leads to good karma and final liberation from *samsara*.

The most important and notable mandala probably is the Kalachakra Mandala based on the *Kalachakra Tantra*.

Structure of Kalachakra Mandala

The Kalachakra sand mandala is a two-dimensional representation of the palace of the deity Kalachakra (Fig. 6.3). The centre of the mandala is the top of the five-storey palace, and it is surrounded by four squares, which represent the other four storeys of the palace. The Kalachakra resides on the top storey of the palace, and the other four floors are Mandala of Enlightened Wisdom, Mandala of Enlightened Mind, Mandala of Enlightened Speech and the Mandala of Enlightened Body. The palace is divided into four quadrants, each with walls, gates and a centre. Four colours are used to represent the four directions and four elements: black, in the East, is associated with wind; red, in the South, is associated with fire; in the West is the element of earth in a yellow colour; and white, which represents water, is in the North.

The five squares are surrounded by six circles. The most inner circle is yellow earth, which is filled with an unbroken chain of green swastikas, representing the earth's stability. In the North-East direction is a rising full moon and in the South-West a setting sun. The next circle is the white water, containing the blue waves and two chariots pulled by mythical animals. The white water is surrounded by the pink-red fire and

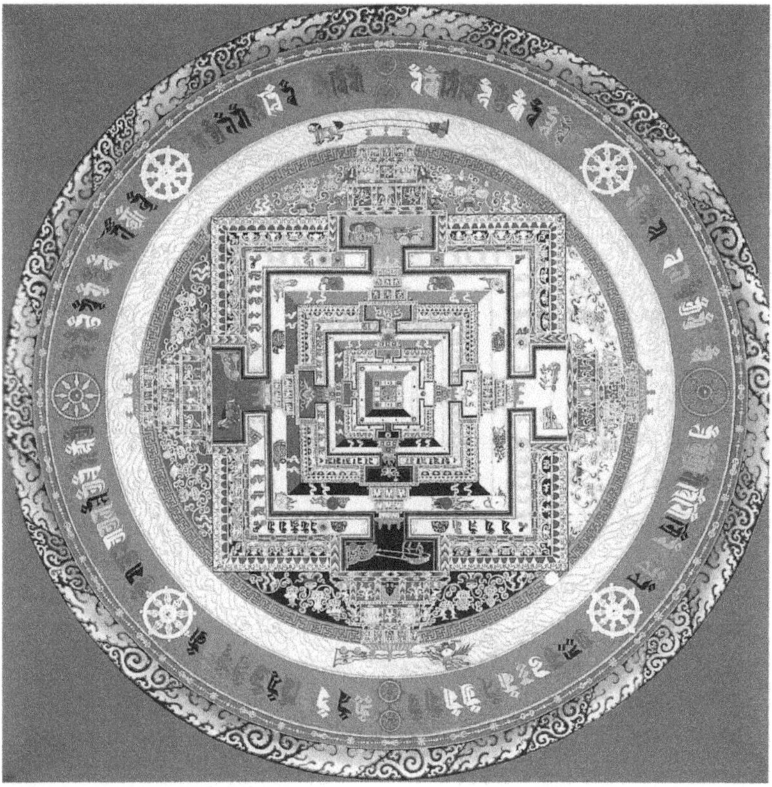

Figure 6.3. Kalachakra Mandala (Mandala, 2008).

the grey wind, which together forms the cemetery grounds. There are also 88 Sanskrit seed syllables representing the protective deities within these two circles. These Sanskrit seed syllables can also be found in the Mandala of Enlightened Body to represent the offering goddesses. Next comes the green colour representing space. There is a fence of golden vajras symbolizing protection of the practitioner from harm. The outermost circle is brightly coloured lights, known as the 'great protective circle',[36] representing a mountain of fire which protects the mandala. The lights are in four colours – blue, green, red and yellow – representing 'the rays of the Buddha's five wisdoms in the form of a rainbow'.[37,]

According to Jung, 'the 'squaring of the circle' is one of the many archetypal motifs which form basic patterns of our dreams and fantasies'.[38] He calls this shape an 'archetype of wholeness'.[39] In fact, this 'squaring of the circle' shape has a deeper significance in Chinese culture. The earliest record of this saying is found in a book called *Zhou-bisuanjing* (《周髀算經》) written in the Han Dynasty, circa 100BCE. It is written that 'Square belongs to the earth. Circle belongs to the sky. The sky is a circle and the earth is a square' (方屬地，圓屬天，天圓地方。)（卷上之一）. We have seen this clearly in the structure of Kalachakra mandalas in which the circle represents the cosmos and the square the earth.

Visualizing the Mandala

Upon the completion of the sand mandala, students are led to enter the mandala and begin the meditation under the guidance of the vajra master. As mentioned earlier, the meditation on a mandala is mainly a visualization. Robert Thurman explains the process of visualization in a concrete and vivid way:

> By using body mandalas to visualize tiny deities in every pore, the yogin loses the discrete sense of the coarse body and feels every atom of every part of his body and senses as a buddha-deity. The visualization explodes beyond the organizing capacities of the ordinary imagination and the practitioner perceives himself as a jewel-like subtle body, a vajra body, composed of nerve-channels, neural wind-energies, and endocrine drops (*rtsa rlung thig-le*).[40]

Barry Bryant says that by 'contemplating a mandala one can gain deep insight or inner peace....This mandala also serves to purify the polluted environment and bring prosperity to the world.'[41] This may sound very puzzling to people who have never participated in the ritual. How can a visualization of a painting bring such an enormous transformation, not only to the participant or the yogin, but also to all the people in the world? If we believe that the purpose of mandala is 'to assist meditation and concentration',[42] then it is unlikely that visualizing a mandala can bring re-enchantment to the cosmos. According to Tucci:

> [A mandala] is, above all, a map of the cosmos ... The universe not only in its inert spatial expanse, but as temporal revolution and both as a vital process which develops from an essential Principle and rotates round a central axis, Mount Sumeru, the axis of the world on which the sky rests and which sinks its roots into the mysterious substratum ... it also implies, by magical transposition, the world itself, so that when the magician or mystic stands in

> the centre he identifies himself with the forces that govern the universe and collects their thaumaturgical power within himself.[43]

When such meditation is successful, the practitioners develop a clear appearance of themselves as the deity, 'all ordinary appearances of bodies made of flesh, blood, and bone and houses made of wood and so forth vanish from the mental consciousness (not the sense consciousnesses) such that all that appears is divine'.[44] It is also the moment of spiritual awakening: 'At the time of the transformation of the individual's body into the transcendent body of Kalachakra, the constituents of the phenomenal body manifest as the constituents of spiritual awakening'.[45]

To illustrate how visualization of mandala could bring about cosmic re-enchantment, the Kalachakra is perhaps the best example. To meditate upon a Kalachakra mandala, one becomes the deity Kalachakra. Kalachakra 'is a compassionate appearance of a wisdom consciousness realizing the emptiness of inherent existence. The nature of the glorious Kalachakra is, therefore, great bliss, since a supramundane deity is someone who has brought to full development the capacity of the most subtle, innate, blissful consciousness to realize emptiness.'[46] I have introduced the Four Noble Truths earlier, which is the essence of Buddhist teaching. And to understand the Four Noble Truths, we have to realize that the world is void. The higher the level of empowerment, the clearer one realizes emptiness. So, the 'thaumaturgical power' Tucci refers to is in fact the power to perceive the cosmos as empty, as well as one's own self. The attainment of enlightenment and liberation from *samsara* could be accelerated by this fundamental change in our perception of reality, of the cosmos, of ourselves.

If all this sound too unscientific to modern people, I suggest we turn to the scientific world for support. A series of experiments carried out by an Italian physician tested the coherence between the human mind and the universe. His experiments show that as 'people enter an altered state of consciousness – in deep meditation or prayer – the electrical activity of the left and right frontal hemispheres of their brain becomes synchronized'.[47] Lopez also informs us that, over the past 25 years, researchers in the field of cognitive science have begun to measure the effects of Buddhist meditation in terms of physiology and neurology. Lopez points out that the ultimate aim of Buddhist meditation 'is not self help but a radical reorientation toward the world ...'[48] This further explains why the Tantric teachings believe that we can achieve peace or improve the world by meditating upon mandalas.

The recent development of science, especially in the field of quantum physics, finds its resonance in the cosmology of religions. In his *Science and the Re-enchantment of the Cosmos*, Ervin Laszlo points out that the concept of quantum vacuum 'rediscovers' the idea of Akashic Field in Hindu cosmology. '[T]he vacuum is the most fundamental field of the universe. It "glues" quarks, stabilizes atoms and solar systems, and created mass as well as the forces of inertia and gravitation. It connects all things with all other things.'[49] Besides, this vacuum is also 'nature's collective memory'[50] and it stores 'trans-universe information.'[51] According to the Big Bang and Big Crunch theories, the universe 'undergoes an endless sequence of cosmic epochs, each of which begins with a "Bang" and ends in a "Crunch".'[52] Every time the universe expands after the Crunch, it does not start from zero. The vacuum 'records the evolution of each universe, it enables the successive universes to build on the experience of their predecessors.'[53] Laszlo claims that this concept 'clarifies the mystery of why our universe is so finely tuned to the evolution of life: it was not the first universe to be born in the Metaverse'.[54]

In Budddhist cosmology, there is also more than one universe. Each universe has to go through the cycle of four periods: the *kalpa* of Dissolution, the *kalpa* of Nothingness, the *kalpa* of Creation, and the *kalpa* of Duration of Created World.[55] These four *kalpas* make up one great *kalpa* and 64 great *kalpas* constitute a cycle. Furthermore, in each of the four *kalpas*, there are 20 intermediate *kalpas,* which are in turn made up by 20 small *kalpas*. There is insufficient space to go into the details here,[56] but the fundamental idea is that the universe is not in a steady state, and there is actually a cycle of destruction and re-formation.

The impermanence of the world and the universe, the continuous flow of time and life-forms, and the continuous flow of karma are manifested in the mandala of the Wheel of Life and Death, in which the Monster of Impermanence turns the Wheel of Life incessantly.

The Brain is the Screen

The idea that the world is empty is fundamental in Buddhist teachings. In the *Avatamsaka*, it says:

The mind is like an artist
And the world is created by it.
All the spheres of the world
Have been painted by the mind.[57]

The world does not exist but in the mind. 'From the Tantric point of view each being contains the whole universe. There is no separation of the individual and universal mind, the mind not being subject to time and space limitation'.[58] According to *The Avatamsaka Sutra*:

> All the Buddha-lands and all the Buddhas themselves, are manifested in my own being ... [59]

In other words, we should be able to see ourselves in the universe and the universe is contained in us.

It is striking to see how this idea is resonant with Deleuze's claim that 'the brain is the screen'.[60] Gregory Flaxman explains what Deleuze means by saying that '[the brain] is a filter that extracts itself from chaos. This screen is a form of relation, of interchange, of mutual synthesis between the brain and the universe'.[61] We can interpret the claim that the brain is a screen by suggesting that the brain is a projection screen on which we create our world. The world is empty in the sense that it does not have an existence independent of our projection. However, it seems that our existence and the universe's existence are interdependent. Deleuze writes:

> We perceive things where they are, perception puts us at once into matter, is impersonal, and coincides with the perceived object. Continuing on this same line, the whole of Bergson's method consists, first of all, in seeking the terms between which there could not be a difference in kind: There cannot be a difference in kind, but only a difference in degree between the faculty of the brain and the function of the core, between the perception of matter and matter itself.[62]

What Deleuze says in *The Fold* is even more illuminating:

> As an individual unit each monad includes the whole series; hence it conveys the entire world, but does not express it *without expressing more clearly a small region of the world, a 'subdivision', a borough of the city, a finite sequence* ... if the world is in the subject, the subject is no less for the world.'[63] (emphasis in the original)

When Ronald Bogue discusses Deleuze's *Cinema* theory, he cites Deleuze's reference to some recent brain research, that the form of the brain does not follow Euclidean paths, 'but instead tracing dispersed, multiple, and probabilistic passages, such as the inner and outer surfaces of the brain's folds …'[64] He continues: 'If in the modern cinema mind is immanent within the images, and if the images constitute a world, then that world is a topological brain world, in which inside and outside pass into one another …'[65]

I will return to Deleuze's philosophy on cinema in the discussion of time later.

The *Kalachakra Tantra*

The *Kalachakra Tantra* presents three cycles of time – external (outer), internal (inner) and alternative (other).[66] The Dalai Lama explains:

> Outer, or External, Kalachakra constitutes the elements of the universe in which we live; Inner, or Internal, Kalachakra constitutes the psychophysical aggregates, sensory and psychic capacities of the living being; Other, or Alter-Kalachakra is the path of the creation and completion stage yogas that have the power to purify the above two Kalachakra.[67]

The structures of the external and internal cycles are analogous. The most frequently used phrase in the *Kalachakra Tantra* is: 'As it is outside so it is within the body.'[68] The external cycle of time, which is the cosmos, reflects the internal cycle of time, which is the soul and the body of a person.[69] The Dalai Lama further explains the three cycles of time in the Kalachakra:

> Outer Kalachakra is generally explained in the context of this planet Earth. When one meditates on the mandala of Kalachakra, Inner Kalachakra is seen as the body, faces, hands, feet, etc., as well as all the surrounding deities of the mandala, conceived as symbols of the stars, planets, constellations, and so forth.[70]

As it is believed that the Outer and Inner Kalachakra have a macrocosm and microcosm relationship, the Dalai Lama advocates that Kalachakra has a special connection with all the people of this planet. The mandala is not just a creation of art, but an offering for world peace.

When Chögyam Trungpa discusses the mandala, he comments that, 'It is actual space, and we could feel a sense of ' spaceness' all the time .... That total energy – totally creative, totally destructive – is what one might call nowness. Nowness is the sense that we are attuned to what is happening.'[71] When asked to comment on the transformative power of mandala, he says:

> One begins to have an extraordinary panoramic vision with no boundaries. One can afford to associate with particular energies, particular directions then, because one's working situation is not based on a sense of direction anymore. You have a directionless direction. It is an entirely new approach to time and space. You can approach time because it is timeless; you can approach space because it is spaceless.[72]

Chögyam Trungpa's comments on mandala bring forth two important concepts in Buddhist cosmology, that is, time and space.

Time-Image in Mandala

It is very common to divide time into three parts: the past, the present and the future. However, when we try to define the exact meaning of these three times, we are at a loss. One may say that the past is the sum of everything that happened. Is that so? 'This 'past as totality' is a construct: the hypothetical point of reference for the hypothesized entity 'all that there is'.[73] Let's see if it is easier to pinpoint the future. The future is what lies ahead of us and we can make plans for the future. It is also an extension of the 'prerecorded structures of the past'.[74] Not surprisingly, Tulku points out that this 'future' is not the future infinitive. This future will in time become the past, but the future infinitive will never arrive. It is 'in this "never arriving" of the future that the dynamic and power of time make themselves available'.[75] So, this future infinitive is virtual time.

It is perhaps the most difficult to define the present, since '[i]t originates nothing and has no reality of its own. Cut the connection between the present on the one hand and the past and future on the other, and present time – the apparent locus of reality – is left empty: a complete hollow'. Tarthang Tulku suggests another approach to describe the three times: 'gone',[76] 'becoming' and 'not yet'.[77] Nevertheless, he admits that these designations do not tell us more about the nature of time.

Tulku says that '[w]e know *how much* time by reference to other events that also take place in time, such as the movement of the hands of a clock'.[78] This is what we usually think about time – chronological, continuous and objective. However, Tulku thinks otherwise. He raises the notion that '[t]ime in a nonphysical realm might be very different'.[79] He continues:

> Time as it existed before human beings appeared is also a matter for speculation. Our way of measuring assimilates that time to our own, positioning 'our' time on a continuum with 'all' time. But without human beings to provide a basis for measurement, earlier time might well have been quite different from our own.[80]

He asks a fundamental question: how could we touch the body of time directly?[81]

Tulku's notion of 'objective' time is similar to what Deleuze calls 'the movement-image' in his *Cinema* books. However, as Flaxman notes, 'the movement-image is an image of changing space or space covered, that is, an indirect image of time'.[82] When Deleuze analyses time in *Cinema 2*, he puts forward the concept of crystals of time. The first of the four crystals of time is perfect crystal. Deleuze argues that the crystal-image is 'the most fundamental operation of time'.[83] He explains: 'The crystal always lives at the limit, it is itself the "vanishing limit between the immediate past which is already no longer and the immediate future which is not yet … a mobile mirror which endlessly reflects perception in recollection"'.[84] As Bogue describes it succinctly, 'Time in this crystal is circular, rolled in upon itself, perpetually repeating itself'.[85]

Let us turn our attention to the mandala. It is, as Trungpa says, timeless and spaceless because all the times and all the space in this universe are present in it. The 'wheel of time' or 'Kalachakra' as we see in Fig. 6.1, is the ultimate existence of time. When Trungpa talks about the transformative power of the mandala, he notes: 'You can approach time because it is timeless.'[86] In what way could we interpret this 'timeless time' as Deleuze's direct time? The direct presentation of time or time-image in cinema, according to Deleuze, 'does not imply the halting of movement, but rather the promotion of aberrant movement'.[87] We could find examples of direct presentation of time in movies such as *Run Lola Run* (1998), *21 Grams* (2003), *Babel* (2006), *The Discreet Charm of the Bourgeoisie* (1972) and *Prénom Carmen* (1983). We can also see that what these movies present is 'a simultaneity of peaks of the present' – 'a present of the future, a present of the present and a present of the past, all implicated in the event, rolled up in the event, and thus simultaneous and inexplicable'.[88]

Mandalas show a specific image of time – circular in shape – portraying each moment enfolding into another. Considering that Buddhist cosmology believes there are cycles of birth and death of universes, the span of time in which human beings have existed may well take up only a single moment. Tulku writes that '[i]n that case, each "event" that has taken place "within" this span will have to be understood as inseparable from every other "event". We might say that all events are mutually recorded and preserved: equally exhibitions of one another.'[89] This is the perfect crystal of time in which:

> the actual image and the virtual image coexist and crystallize; they enter into a circuit which brings us constantly back from one to the other; they form one and the same 'scene' where the characters belong to the real and yet play a role. In short, it is the whole of real, life in its entirety ...[90]

Notes

1 G. Deleuze and F. Guattari, 1994 *What is Philosophy?* (5th edn), trans. H. Tomlinson and G. Burchill. London and New York: Verso (2003), 89.
2 S. O'Sullivan, 2006, *Art Encounters Deleuze and Guattari: Thought Beyond Representation*. New York: Palgrave Macmillan, 96.
3 B. Bryant, 1992, *The Wheel of Time: Sand Mandala*. Ithaca, NY: Snow Lion Publications, 179.
4 G. Tucci, 1961, *The Theory and Practice of the Mandala: With Reference to the Modern Psychology of the Unconscious*, trans. A.H. Brodrick. Mineola, NY: *Modern Psychology of the Unconscious*, trans. A.H. Brodrick. Mineola, NY: Dover Publications, 25.
5 C. Trungpa, 1991, *Orderly Chaos: The Mandala Principle*, S. Chodzin (ed.). Boston and London: Shambhala, 79.
6 M. Brauen, 2009, *Mandala: Sacred Circle in Tibetan Buddhism*. Stuttgart: Arnoldsche Art Publishers, 183.
7 Ibid. 178.

8 To this extent, 'techno' corresponds with the broadened sense of *techne* (τ έχνη) as Heidegger elaborates it in *The Question Concerning Technology* as denoting not merely the process of making, but as a fundamental mode of revealing. Additionally, this sense of *techne* suggests that the possibilities of an affective topology of the senses that Mark Hansen argues is associated with the greater use of digital technologies (Hansen, 2000, *Embodying Technesis: Technology Beyond Writing*, Ann Arbor: University of Michigan Press) rightly belongs to a much wider variety of practices than digital technologies. To fail to acknowledge this is to restrict the discussion to a range of privileged practices that are simply new – and located in places assumed to be 'advanced'.

9 G. Deleuze and F. Guattari, *What is Philosophy?* 89.

10 Ibid. 93.

11 C. Trungpa, *Orderly Chaos: The Mandala Principle*, 83.

12 D. P. Leidy and R. Thurman, 2000, *Mandala: The Architecture of Enlightenment*. New York: Tibet House, 130.

13 Ibid.

14 J. Hopkins, 1999, 'The Kalachakra Tantra: Introduction' in *Kalachakra Tantra: Rite of Initiation*, His Holiness the Dalai Lama (ed.). Boston: Wisdom Publications, 75.

15 Leidy and Thurman, *Mandala: The Architecture of Enlightenment*, 17.

16 C. Jung, 1972, *Mandala Symbolism,* trans. R. Hull. Princeton, NJ: Princeton University Press, 72.

17 G. Tucci, *The Theory and Practice of the Mandala*, 23.

18 G. Deleuze and F. Guattari, *What is Philosophy?* 89.

19 M. Ricard, 2000, 'Introduction to the purpose of symbolism of the Mandala in Tibetan Buddhism' in D. P. Leidy and R. Thurman (eds), *Mandala: The Architecture of Enlightenment*. New York: Tibet House, 157.

20 Ibid. 158.

21 Ibid.

22 In Buddhism, there are ten directions: North, South, East, West, North-East, North-West, South-East, South-West, zenith and nadir.

23 The construction of Kalachakra Mandala is an elaborate ritual and it is impossible to give a detailed description in this chapter. For details, please see B. Bryant's *The Wheel of Time: Sand Mandala*, 133–45.

24 Ibid. p. 153.

25 Ibid.

26 These seven initiations, again, are very complicated and elaborate and I refrain from describing them in details here. For a step-by step instruction, please see His Holiness the Dalai Lama's *Kalachakra Tantra: Rite of Initiation*. A. Berzin's 1997 *Taking the Kalachakra Initiation*, Ithaca, NY: Snow Lion Publications, also provides a detailed description. He also includes a useful 'Outline of the initiation' in his book 167–90.

27 Sometimes, a small amount of the blessed coloured sand is distributed to the students or the audience as a blessing.

28 For details, please see B. Bryant's *The Wheel of Time: Sand Mandala*, 168–9.

29 V. A. Wallace, 2001, *The Inner Kalacakratantra: A Buddhist Tantric View of the Individual* Oxford and New York: Oxford University Press, 92.

30 *Vimalaprabhā* means *Stainless Light Commentary* or the *Abridged Kalachakra Tantra* written by the Shambhala King Pundarika (176–76 BCE). The Dalai Lamas are said to be incarnations of Pundarika.

31 Ibid.

32 Ibid.

33 Ibid. 93.

34 *Prāṇa* means karmic winds. According to V. A. Wallace's explanation, '[t]here are three types of external karmic winds: the holding (*samdhārmaṇa*), churning (*manthāna*), and shaping (*samsthāna*) wind. The supporting wind holds together the atoms of the earth and the other elements in the same way that a rain-wind holds together the atoms of rain-water. Following that, the churning wind churns the atoms to their very core until the elements become solidified. Just as salt crystallizes due to its exposure to the sun, the elements solidify due to such churning.... Once the agglomeration of the atomic particles of the elements take place, the great shaping wind moves through the entire Buddha-field in the form of the ten winds' (2001, 57–8)

35 His Holiness the Dalai Lama, 2005b, 'The Four Noble Truths' in N. Ribush *Teachings from Tibet: Guidance from Great Lamas*. Boston: Lama Yeshe Wisdom Archive.

36 B. Bryant, *The Wheel of Time: Sand Mandala*, 227.

37 Ibid. The description of the Kalachakra Mandala is far more complicated than my description here, as every symbol, object or animal means something in the mandala. I have included only the most important features and those which are relevant for the discussion in the latter part of the paper here, and left out some important features of the mandala, for example, the chariots drawn by seven animals at each entrance in the Mandala of the Enlightened Body, the offering gardens, the gates of the four entrances of the palace, etc. For a full description of the Kalachakra Mandala, please read B. Bryant's *The Wheel of Time: Sand Mandala*, 202–27.

38 C. Jung, *Mandala Symbolism*, 3.

39 Ibid.

40 R. Thurman, 1997, 'Mandala: The architecture of enlightenment' in *Mandala: The Architecture of Enlightenment*. London: Thames and Hudson, 139.

41 B. Bryant. *The Wheel of Time: Sand Mandala*, 179.

42 C. Jung. *Mandala Symbolism*, 3.

43 G. Tucci. *The Theory and Practice of the Mandala: With Reference to the Modern Psychology of the Unconscious*, 23–4.

44 J. Hopkins, 'The Kalachakra Tantra: Introduction', 69.
45 Wallace, *Inner Kalacakratantra*, 91.
46 J. Hopkins, 'The Kalachakra Tantra: Introduction', 80.
47 E. Laszlo 2006, *Science and the Re-enchantment of the Cosmos: The Rise of the Integral Vision of Reality*, Rochester, VT: Inner Traditions, 16.
48 D. S. Lopez, Jnr, 2008, *Buddhism and Science: A Guide for the Perplexed*, Chicago and London: University of Chicago Press, 207.
49 Ibid. 30.
50 Ibid. 43.
51 Ibid.
52 Ibid. 42–3.
53 Ibid. 44.
54 Ibid.
55 A. Sadakata, 2004, *Buddhist Cosmology: Philosophy and Origins* trans. G. Sekimori Tokyo: Kosei Publishing, 99–102.
56 The division of the *kalpas* is much more complicated than I have described here. For details, see A. Sadakata's *Buddhist Cosmology: Philosophy and Origins*.
57 Quoted in H. V. Guenther, 1977, *Tibetan Buddhism in Western Perspective: Collected Articles of Herbert V. Guenther* Emerville, CA: Dharma Publishing, 168.
58 Quoted in R. Moacanin, 1986, *Jung's Psychology and Tibetan Buddhism: Western and Eastern Paths to the Heart*. Boston: Wisdom Publications, 79.
59 Ibid.
60 G. Deleuze, 2000, 'The brain is the screen: An interview with Gilles Deleuze' in G. Flaxman (ed.), trans. M. T. Guirgis *The Brain is the Screen: Deleuze and the Philosophy of Cinema* Minneapolis and London: University of Minnesota Press, 36.
61 G. Flaxman, 2000, 'Introduction' in G. Flaxman (ed.), trans. M. T. Guirgis *The Brain is the Screen: Deleuze and the Philosophy of Cinema* Minneapolis and London: University of Minnesota Press, 16.
62 G. Deleuze, 1991, *Bergsonism*, New York: Zone Books, 25.
63 G. Deleuze, 1993, *The Fold: Leibniz and The Baroque* trans. T. Conley Minneapolis: University of Minnesota Press, 25.
64 R. Bogue, 2003a, *Deleuze on Cinema*. New York and London: Routledge, 178.
65 Ibid.
66 I am not dealing with the history of the Kalachakra Tantra here as it is too complicated and would take up a book to deal with the topic. To use J. R. Newman's description, the historical account of the Kalachakra represents both actual historical events and myths and allegory. If you are interested in a brief historical account of the Kalachakra, you may read

J. R. Newman's 1985 'A Brief History of the Kalachakra' in *The Wheel of Time: The Kalachakra in Context* Ithaca, NY: Snow Lion Publications.

67 His Holiness the Dalai Lama, 1985, 'Foreword: Concerning the Kalachakra' in R. J. Geshe Lhundub Sopa (ed.), *The Wheel of Time: The Kalachakra in Context* Ithaca, NY: Snow Lion Publications, xvi–xvii.

68 Wallace, *Inner Kalacakratantra* 65.

69 A. Berzin, 1997, *Taking the Kalachakra Initiation*, 27.

70 His Holiness the Dalai Lama, 'Foreword: Concerning the Kalachakra', xvii.

71 C. Trungpa, *Orderly Chaos: The Mandala Principle*, 18.

72 Ibid. 71.

73 T. Tulku, 1994, *Dynamics of Time and Space: Transcending Limits on Knowledge*. Berkeley: Dharma Publishing, 82.

74 Ibid. 92.

75 Ibid. 93.

76 Ibid. 76.

77 Ibid. 9.

78 Ibid. 12.

79 Ibid.

80 Ibid.

81 Ibid. 23.

82 G. Flaxman. 'Introduction', in *The Brain is the Screen: Deleuze and the Philosophy of Cinema,* 19.

83 G. Deleuze, 1989, *Cinema 2: the Time-Image*, trans. H. Tomlinson and R. Galeta, Minneapolis: University of Minnesota Press, 81.

84 Ibid.

85 R. Bogue, *Deleuze on Cinema,* 127.

86 C. Trungpa, *Orderly Chaos: The Mandala Principle*, 71.

87 G. Deleuze, *Cinema 2: the Time-Image,* 36.

88 Ibid. 100.

89 T. Tulku, 1994, *Knowledge of Time and Space.* Berkeley: Dharma Publishing, 17.

90 G. Deleuze. *Cinema 2: the Time-Image,* 83–4.

7

Meditation-Image as Transfiguration of Experience: Bill Viola's Video Art

Nevena Ivanova

Bill Viola's later video-based works conduct an innovative experiment with the workings of the present time-consciousness. Video art shares features with television and cinema and is widely used in new media installations or urban screenings. One approach is to view this technique as a transition medium between analogue and digital technologies. Artists coming from various backgrounds (performance, visual arts, music) such as Bruce Nauman, Vito Acconci, John Baldessari, Peter Campus and Nam June Paik began their experiments with analogue video images and sound recordings in the late-1960s.[1] Their single channel videotapes were usually viewed on small television monitors, even if sometimes arranged into complex architectural settings. Since the 1990s, due to the widespread digital techniques for manipulating audiovisual images, video installations have been transformed into immersive and liquid audiovisual environments, which unfold the present-moment and organize spatial locations in a unique way. The visitor is physically woven into the texture of the piece by entering its audiovisual field. This essay argues that in his later works Bill Viola creates an original type of image, that I will call the 'meditation-image'. The concept of the meditation-image is built on the specific correspondence between the time-image of the video and the time-perception of the viewer. It can be formally defined as a special type of affection-image viewed in extremely slow motion. From the viewer's perspective, it is experienced in a meditative mode of consciousness. In meditation, time is said to stop or slow down extremely, decentring and enriching perceptions. I will elaborate the concept of the meditation-image in several stages. First, I undertake a detailed analysis of the formal and technical construction of Viola's images. Second, their theoretical context will be outlined, drawing upon Deleuze and time/movement-images, and particularly – his affection-image. Third, I will show that the formal/technical specificity and departure of Viola's affection-image from the Deleuzan definition gives it a new perspective. Finally, I explore the modification in the viewer's time-perception, which occurs under the effect of Viola's images.

The Greeting: Formal and Technical Description

The Greeting (1995) is a video interpretation of a Renaissance religious painting by Jacopo Pontormo – *The Visitation* (1528).[2] The canvas depicts the moment when the Virgin Mary visits St Elizabeth and both share the significant news of their pregnancies – Mary with Jesus, Elizabeth with John the Baptist. One of the women seems too old to have a child, but is destined to bear the last prophet of the Old Testament, and the younger of the two is destined to bear the founder of the new Christian era. Their encounter is of higher significance in religious history, symbolizing the change of an epoch, the beginning of a new age. In Viola's video installation, a performance of an ordinary moment, an everyday greeting, is formally and technically transformed into a ceremony. The situation is far from representing a privileged moment in time, it is a generic occasion that can happen to anybody, at any time and any place. The eternal instant of the devotional painting is dissolved into its consequent moments and, in place of the significant and dramatic narrative condensed in the iconic image, nothing of great significance happens in the video. The viewer has no idea of what to expect and, since the image unfolds in an extraordinarily slow manner, every instant of it deepens into itself.

If we compare Pontormo's *The Visitation* with Viola's *The Greeting* in detail, we can follow the ways Viola transforms the painting into a specific type of affection image. In *The Visitation,* the figures merge with the background and, as a whole, all colours are muted. The orange parts outline an additional frame for the prevalent neutral green tone of the painting. The protagonists are well-known personalities from the *New Testament*, and their greeting is an exchange of exceptional information. If read as a frame, the canvas can be classified as a perception-image seen from the point of view of the spectator or the two bystanders.

On the other hand, Viola's *The Greeting* transfigures the colours into bright red, blue and yellow, which stand out against the dark background. The brown buildings and the blue sky are gloomy but clearly outlined from each other. The central figure of the video image is fully dressed in intense red, while parts of the outfits of the other two shows their secondary role – the older woman's skirt is brownish like the buildings, and the blue dress of the young blonde woman is the same as the sky, thus showing her position of the isolated third.

The event itself is an everyday greeting between ordinary women. The emphasis is placed on the affects and their exchange unfolding during the whole scene. The emotions are clearly expressed and their unfolding easily noticeable – the resistance and awkward smile of the woman in blue, the ecstatic affection and maternal tenderness of the older one, and the lively powerful presence of the main protagonist. We can consider the visitor's affect (contemplation, astonishment) as the fourth participant in the larger-than-life unfolding image of *The Greeting*. Thus the accent in viewing is transferred from the image as an independent entity towards the becoming of the assemblage of affects, which includes both the visitor and the video.

The story is not really a narrative (in a strict sense). It is just a short greeting, an ordinary situation, usually enacted without a serious consideration. The protagonists are anonymous, and placed outside of concrete social contexts. The emotions experienced in this scene are rather extracted as pure affects, powers in themselves. When slowed down, the visual image exposes new information, which in normal speed is imperceptible and unreadable. Every single gesture, smile, glance, grimace reveal infinite nuances, their slightest modification is converted into perceptible information; the dynamic fluctuation between affects is easy to follow.

The enacted situation in *The Greeting* takes only 45 seconds recorded time, but it is played back for the duration of more than ten minutes. The piece is made by a static high-speed camera, running at 300 frames per second (instead of the usual 24/30 fps). Thus, although the recorded image is stretched to 12 times its original length, there is no loss of resolution. The highly coloured high-definition video is projected on a larger than human size plasma display mounted on a wall in a darkened room.

The Portraits of *The Passions* Series

The Passions (2000–2003) is a series of 20 video works in different formats, giving an expression to the modification in time of extreme human emotions. They are affection-images by content and form – framing pure affects in close-ups and middle shots. However, they are not typical cinematographic affection-images, being completely extracted out of any context or narrative and unfolded in ultra-slow motion. In the following I will focus on the close-ups of those series.

The first group of *The Passions* series includes several portrait-like projections or diptychs (*Dolorosa, The Locked Garden 2000, Man of Sorrows 2001, Anima 2000, Six Heads 2000*) that mimic the small folding altarpieces of the late Middle Ages. They display a head-and-shoulders view (close-up) of an actor moving through an individual arch of intensity, expressing the four primary affects: happy, sad, angry and afraid. These portraits are shot on 35mm film at very high speed and in continuous 45-second sequence, transferred to digital video. The footage is played on book-size rear displays. The extreme slow-motion alteration of the facial expressions is on the boundary of visual perception – thus placing these high-resolution images between stills and moving pictures. Here as well, Viola employs none of the montage or mobile viewpoint procedures of conventional filmmaking. All video projections of *The Passion* series comprise only visual data without sound.

The close-ups on Viola's video screens are ordinary faces, without specific individuality. They are delocalized in terms of space, time or concrete factual circumstances. The emphasis is on the facial expressions where affects are going through their phases of becoming, only indirectly related to their human carriers. Unlike the stills (or even close-ups in cinema), Viola's videos grasp in an unprecedented way the actual and full transfiguration in time of the expressed affects.

Affection-image: Faciality

According to Deleuze, in cinema 'the affection-image is the close-up, and the close-up is the face'.[3] Against a psychoanalytic or linguistic understanding that the close-up is a magnification, which fragments the body and therefore turns the face into a 'partial object' detached from the whole, Deleuze follows Balázs' and Epstein's ideas that, on the contrary, the close-up abstracts the face from all spatiotemporal coordinates 'and raises it to the state of Entity' (96) which expresses a pure quality. 'Faced with an isolated face, we do not perceive space. Our sensation of space is abolished. A dimension of another order is opened to us'[4]. Unlike Balázs, however, whose understanding of the close-up as absolute entity is limited to the human face, Deleuze expands that conception to all types of close-ups (of other parts of the body, of objects, of spaces, of several faces, etc.) as well as to specific types of middle shots and long shots. Thus, even an image where the space is visible at the background can become an abstracted absolute entity insofar as that space is deterritorialized and turned into what Deleuze, after Pascal Augé's term, calls 'any-space-whatevers' *espace quelconque* (109). In such images, the action-reaction pattern is suspended, and replaced with the expressive power of pure affect.

From Bergson, Deleuze derives a definition of affect as 'a motor tendency on a sensitive nerve' (87), or in other words, 'a series of micromovements on an immobilised plate' (87). The face converts bodily movements expanding in space into locally mapped micro-movements of expression. It can be a 'reflective or reflecting unity' (87) that brings the individual features under the domination of a single quality (minimum vibration, maximum unity, the degree zero of movement) and 'intensive face' (89) whose features escape the contour and 'form an autonomous series that tends towards a limit or crosses a threshold' (89) (the restlessness of desire). The function of the series is to pass from one quality to another, and what is more, to produce a new quality. That passage Deleuze calls 'pure power' *puissance*. Therefore, the intensive face 'expresses a pure Power – that is to say, is defined by a series which carries us from one quality to another', whereas the reflective face 'expresses a pure Quality, that is to say a "something" common to several objects of different kinds' (90).

Affects are not individuated like people and things, but nevertheless they are singularities, which enter in virtual conjunction and each time constitute a complex entity. Deleuze observes that such effects could be achieved not only by the close-up, which is *par excellence* the affection-image, but also via middle or full shot frames. All types of shots – close-ups, middle or full shots – must create 'any-space-whatevers' in order to be affection-images. What Deleuze calls any-space-whatevers is a special haecceity freed from conventional location. In this virtual dimension, all movements are related to other movements. 'What in fact manifests the instability, the heterogeneity, the absence of link in such a space, is a richness in potentials or singularities which are ... prior conditions of all actualisation, all determination' (109). Such space is formed around the conception of movement, which Deleuze, drawing on Bergson's concept of duration [*durée*], distinguishes from space: 'space covered is past, movement is present, the act of covering' (1). Spaces covered by movement are divisible and belong to a single, homogeneous space, while movement 'cannot be divided without changing qualitatively each time it is divided' (1). Deterritorialized, abstracted and deindividuated movements 'unfold with respect to one another rather than occurring within space as a void. They are potential acts of uncovering that are not referred to space conceived as a uniform area of measurable units within which changes occur.'[5] In this respect, any-space-whatevers can be seen as constructed by such deterritorialized movements (expressive qualities and intensive powers) and, therefore, becomes a self-differentiating virtual dimension like Bergson's duration. 'The expression of an isolated face is a whole, which is intelligible by itself. ... For the expression of a face and the signification of this expression have no relation or connection with space.'[6] Middle and full shots construct any-space-whatevers by three techniques: shadows, lyrical abstraction or colours.

Another common feature for affection-images of different kinds is de-individuation of the characters. 'Ordinarily, three roles of the face are recognizable: it is individuating (it distinguishes or characterizes each person); it is socializing (it manifests a social role); it is relational or communicating (it ensures not only communication between two people, but also in a single person, the internal agreement between his character and his role)' (99). The face loses all three in the case of close-up or its equivalents. The close-up suspends individuation for the pure quality-power of the affects to be expressed.

In *The Passion* series (all icon-like portraits, as well as *The Silent Mountain*, *The Quintet of the Astonished*), we observe the emergence, amplification to its threshold point and subsidence of extreme emotional waves (astonishment, anger, fear, grief, joy) expressed in singular close-ups and group middle shots.

In *The Greeting*, Viola creates an affection-image in full shot. The colours in this footage, rather than being representative, become expressive. They are the true carriers of the pure powers, not the individuals. Here, we observe the dynamic exchange between the affects (tenderness, love, resentment, vitality) instead of the becoming of a single emotional wave. 'The affect is impersonal and is distinct from every individuated state of things: it is none the less singular, and can enter into singular combinations or conjunctions with other affects'.[7]

Affection-image is the way in which the subject experiences itself. 'There is a part of external movements that we 'absorb' ... and which does not transform itself into either objects of perception or acts of the subject; rather, they mark the coincidence of the subject and the object in a pure quality.'[8] The movement ceases to be process of transfer or action in order to become an expression. It transforms self-centred subjective perception into acentred and objective, which 'see[s] without boundaries or distances'.[9]

Affection-image Transfigurated into Meditation-image

Although Bill Viola creates a type of affection-image, he does not completely follow the rules of the cinematographic method defined by Deleuze. Instead of a mobile camera or montage, Viola uses fixed camera and single continuous shots, which changes the dynamics of the image. Video installation by definition produces a spatiotemporal environment in present-time, which is continuous, unbroken and congruent with that of the perceiver.[10] Viola's video installations leave the viewer beyond the emotional state. It is not empathy, which is the true effect of his completely de-contextualized affects. As previously mentioned, his approach to the close-up is unlike the classic cinematographic construction of emotions which, following Kuleshov's experiments with montage,[11] is based on contrapositions and a mosaic of associations, usually part of a larger narrative line. We can find, however, stronger similarities between Viola's portraitures and the ones Andy Warhol makes in his *Screen Tests* series.

Warhol's *Screen Tests* are revealing portraits of hundreds of different individuals, shot between 1963 and 1966. They unfold the silent, black-and-white film shots of Factory regulars, Warhol superstars, guests, friends, or anyone he thought had 'star potential'. Factory visitors were seated in front of a tripod-mounted camera, asked to be as still as possible while the camera was running. They were captured in stark relief by a strong key light, and filmed by Warhol with his stationary 16mm Bolex camera on 100-foot rolls of film at 24 frames per second. The resulting two-and-a-half-minute film reels were then screened in (relative) slow motion at 16 frames per second. The subjects include both famous and anonymous visitors to Warhol's studio, along with many other diverse individuals. Each screen test is exactly the same length, lasting only as long as the roll of film. The standard formula of subject and camera remaining almost motionless for the duration of the film, results in a 'living portrait'. What we observe here has a quite different effect from Viola's experimental close-ups. Instead of extremely intensified moment-to-moment experience, Warhol faces us with a test of endurance – both for the subjects in front of the camera and the viewers in front of the monitor. For the extended duration of four minutes, the viewer is confronted not with the pure affects fully depersonalized in Viola's videos, but with the personality of Warhol's subjects. Some of these actors are famous icons of 1960s American culture: Allen Ginsberg, Salvador Dali, Marcel Duchamp, Nico and Bob Dylan. Warhol's portraits are produced more for the sake of the actors' star-oriented self-awareness, rather than for an interaction with a potential viewer. Warhol writes:

> Beauties in photographs are different from beauties in person. It must be hard to be a model, because you'd want to be like the photograph of you, and you can't ever look that way. And so you start to copy the photograph. Photographs usually bring in another half-dimension. (Movies bring in another whole dimension. That screen magnetism is something secret – if you could only figure out what it is and how to make it, you'd have a really good product to sell. But you can't even tell if someone has it until you actually see them up there on the screen. You have to give screen tests to find out.)[12]

Thus, in Warhol *Screen Tests*, the viewer is confronted not with the meditative intensity of his/her own becoming, but with the duration of the Other, closed on itself and unrelated to the process of viewing:

> The resulting films drastically reduced the roles of director and viewer alike.... the viewer, for the first time in the history of the commercial exploitation of persistence-of-vision, was relieved of the obligation – perhaps even a large *part of the desire – to pay attention to the screen.*[13]

In contrast, Bill Viola's video installations embed the viewer in their audiovisual architecture, facing him/her with life-sized and hyper-vivid images unfolding in a continuously unbroken pace. The composed situation produces temporal accordance between the viewer's time-perception and the screen movement. When an ultra-slow motion technique is applied, it transfers the simultaneous unfolding of viewer's and video time into an unusual direction. It transfigures the affection-image into a meditation-image by directly slowing down the time-perception of the viewer.

In text-based construction of meaning, ultra-slow reading[14] would be equal to the total break of any possible synthesis of the temporal object perceived (if you read a word a day from any novel, you lose the meaning even of a sentence or paragraph, not to mention the whole narrative line). According to Viola, however, such a self-understood attitude towards reading a book would rather be abandoned when it comes to the reading of pure affects: in order to decode information condensed in the infinite potentiality of affect's modulations, one must take it very slowly. It is also because the images he creates are not narratives, and their effect is accomplished not through thinking and sense-making, but through visceral experience:

> When you watch time slow down like that, you feel the actions open up, like a flower … I realised that human emotions have infinite resolution – the more you magnify them the more they keep unfolding, infinitely. I began to sense that these feelings, or at least their residue, seem to exist outside of time, in some other eternal dimension.[15]

Slow motion technique's capability to reveal the depth of emotions has fascinated filmmakers since the earliest attempts in cinema. Film pioneers such as Jean Epstein and Dziga Vertov praise it as a means of revealing the invisible dimensions of reality. Vertov initially identifies his 'kino-eye' with a 'slow motion eye':

> Slow motion filming was understood as the opportunity to make the invisible visible, the unclear clear, the hidden manifest, the disguised overt, the acted nonacted, untruth truth … to show people without masks, without makeup; to catch them with the camera's eye in a moment of nonacting. To read their thoughts, laid bare by kino-eye.[16]

In Epstein's 1928 film *La Chute de la Maison d'Usher*, normally acted emotions recorded with speeded-up camera are reported to have unusual expressive power, due to their unrealistic slowness on the screen. Slow motion shots parallel the regular close-ups; they are like temporal close-ups achieving in time what the close-up proper is achieving in space: they magnify the interval so the imperceptible dimensions of change and motion become clearly visible and sensible.

Slow motion is a favourite artistic device for Viola in his earlier videotapes as well. Videotapes such as *Chott el Djerid* (1979), *Hatsu Yume* (1981), *The Passing* (1991) and *Deserts* (1994) create a dream-like temporal flow – fantasies, recollections and perceptions appear in a sporadic, puzzle-like configuration, in non-teleological, reversible, repetitive order. *The Passing* is a silent meditation on the incessant passage of life into death and vice versa. There are three types of images: past recollections, archetypal symbols and what Jacobson termed shifters.[17] An extreme close-up of Viola's sleeping face and breathing sounds appear at almost regular intervals throughout the whole videotape. These close-ups' meta-semiotic and present-time status defines the oneiric origin of all other images. The sleeper awakens in his dream (switching to the present time here and now) and then falls into sleep again (switching to the next sequence of dream-imaginary). These shifters identify the here-and-now departure point, when the dream fantasies take flight, and symbolize the unstable dynamic of dreaming/awakening. Are we ever fully awakened? Aren't we always dreaming, so our dreams are woven into another dream? It seems that the repetitive awakenings and fallings into sleep again could be interpreted in a more existential way as an attempt to awaken from the world of illusions, from death-life cycles or *samsara*. Or just to awaken, to see, to be aware of the transition. All types of images mix into small sequences, fragmentary and repetitive, which recur in circles over and over again. The breathing sound overwhelms most of the video piece as well as the sounds of nature, the sound of water. Unlike cinema, any kind of scenario, script or linguistic semiotic level is absent.

Most of the visuals are without detail, dissolved in darkness, slightly visible. In contrast to cinema, where the emotions are dramatized in one respect or another, here they are subdued, the overall feeling is meditative, more like a quiet struggle of one to face the whole complexity of life and death and their constant transition into each other. The image invites contemplation: with its vast empty landscapes, depersonalized bodies floating underwater, de-contextualized faces, minimalist clear-cut montages, diffused light, slow motion.

Hatsu Yume, The Passing, Chott el Djerid and *Deserts* might be regarded as transitional images on the boundary between dream-like representations, characteristic of cinematographic use of slow motion, and meditation-directed praxis, characteristic of ultra-slow motion in some video installations. The visuality in these videotapes lacks detail, the colours are subdued, somehow out of focus. In *Hatsu Yume* the camera is floating, thus producing fluid, unstable images. *Chott el Djerid* is shot in the Sahara Desert in Tunisia and captures mirages formed in the midday sun. Viola describes the production process in this way:

> the intense desert heat manipulates, bends, and distorts the light rays to such an extent that you actually see things that are not there. Trees and sand dunes float off the ground, the edges of mountains and buildings ripple and vibrate, colour and forms blend into one shimmering dance. The desert mirages are set against images of the bleak winter prairies of Illinois and Saskatchewan, Canada, some of them recorded in a snowstorm. The opposite climactic conditions induce a similar aura of uncertainty, disorientation and unfamiliarity. Through special telephoto lenses adapted for video, the camera confronts the final barrier of the limits of the image, the point when the breakdown of normal conditions, or the lack of visual information, causes us to re-evaluate our perceptions of reality and realize that we are looking at something out of the ordinary—a transformation of the physical into the psychological. If one believes that hallucinations are the manifestation of some chemical or biological imbalance in the brain, then mirages and desert heat distortions can be considered hallucinations of the landscape. It was like physically being inside someone else's dream.[18]

Although slow motion is predominant in these pictures, its role is to imply a dream-like state of consciousness on the boundary between fantasy and perception. The details of the image are unclear, the colours are diluted. The function of slow motion employed in *Chott el Djerid, Hatsu Yume, The Passing* and *Deserts* differs greatly from the function of ultra-slow motion employed in *The Passion* series, *The Greeting*. The former conveys an image beyond the physical reality – it is situated in dream, in memory, in fantasy. Accordingly the viewer's imagination wanders in the same direction, while the latter places the visitor into his/her direct physical environment, confronting him/her with the image in a meditative mode of the here-and-now alert awareness. The difference comes through in several ways: the video installations create a life-size audiovisual environment, where the body of the visitor becomes part of the image; they expose high-definition details, intensify colours to an explosive degree, unfold affection-images in ultra-slow motion, employ a fixed camera view and a continuous shot, as well as completely lacking context, narrative and personified characters. Nowadays, ultra-slow motion is achieved via digital or other emergent devices and captures phenomenal events at speeds faster than 3,000 fps. However, Viola's experiments with ultra-slow motion were conducted first in 1995 (*The Greeting*) and were among the first to slow down emotion to such an extended degree. He shot 45 seconds of 35mm film at the speed of 300 fps and processed it farther in digital format.[19]

Viola's Meditation-image and Noh Drama

In mystic and religious ceremonies, as well as in some ritualistic performances (like the Japanese Noh drama or tea ceremony), similar characteristics are essential for the event to maintain its meditative effect. Let us draw a brief comparison between Noh drama and Viola's later video installations in terms of their composition and effect. Although vastly different as media, those artistic practices share important formal characteristics: ultra-slow rhythm, ceremonial atmosphere and a meditative effect on the viewer.

Noh drama grows out of Shintoist ritual dances, festival entertainment arts (*sarugaku*) and Zen thought. The Noh play comprises elements of dance, chant, drama and poetry, performed at a specific tempo. The costumes are highly elaborate and vividly colourful. The stage is bare and subtly lit with minimal dramatic sets. The formal structure and experience of Noh invites comparison with *The Passions* series in several respects, and I will outline the similarities in the following discussion.

The Process of Creation

There is a common repertoire of plays and an established system of rules in Noh, which regulates all acting, chanting and dancing. All actors have been trained since childhood to master these patterns. Thus, they do not need a director to organize their acting and 'do not conduct stage rehearsals but meet and discuss briefly or talk through, in the dressing room, any changes or variations'.[20] In this way, each performance is a unique spontaneous encounter between the expressive powers of the performers, regulated by their 'group consciousness'. 'A Noh play is given life only through a sharing of the wills of all performers, each anonymous [...] the only real stars are the characters born on the stage'.[21] It is not the quite simple plot around which the characters are built, but the affects and the energy field generated on the stage.

Similar improvisation in acting-together can be observed in Viola's group video installations: *The Raft*, *The Quintet* series and *Observance*. All these works represent groups of people, depicted by fixed camera on a neutral background. The performers seem ruptured from head to toe by waves of emotion – astonishment, pressure, tension, shock, bewilderment, etc. – as they emerge, manifest themselves, and leave the body. One-minute real time is stretched in the video over a 15 minute continuous loop. The individuals are depicted in close physical proximity, but they seem completely detached and unrelated to one another in emotional or narrative dimensions. What happens in all these groups, however, is that what begins as singular becoming of disconnected affects produces its own complex dynamics of energies and assemblages. Such interaction occurs spontaneously, following the curves of becoming of the emotions, without much preliminary direction on the part of the artist.

The approach of Viola as an author and director is to distribute the affects or roles among the actors, but without any detailed script or orchestration during the piece. As was shown in the analysis of *The Passions,* all the actors are not individual characters, but singularities of affects. The becoming of affects and their interaction on an almost visceral level produces unpredictable assemblages of intensities and harmony-in-discord. 'Each of us, even though we were feeling different emotions – joy, sorrow, anger, fear – were following the same arc of intensity, so the piece had an emotional and physical shape.' 'For an actor, this was a totally anti-theatre experience! There were five of us shoulder to shoulder but having no eye contact at all ... We had no choice but to interact physically. There was an amazing energy generated by the five of us – amazing force and intensity – though we weren't acting together.'[22]

The space

The manipulation of space in Noh plays and Viola's video art installations creates a condition in which the visitor occupies the fluid space of the characters and enters into symbolic interaction with them, or even takes a role in the scene. Both create the type of Deleuzan 'any-space-whatevers'. As Deleuze explains it:

> Any-space-whatevers is not an abstract universal, in all times, in all places. It is perfectly singular space, which has merely lost its homogeneity, that is, the principle of its metric relations or the connection of its own parts, so that the linkages can be made in an infinite number of ways. It is a space of virtual conjunction, grasped as pure locus of the possible.[23]

The face

Face expressions play an essentially different role in Viola's later video art installations (*The Greeting, The Passions, Ocean Without a Shore*) and in the Noh drama. The leading character in Noh usually wears a highly refined mask (*omote*), capable of subtle expressions, varying with the change of light and angle. There are some plays in which masks are not used, but the actor's face is required to stay completely impassive and to function as a mask instead. By covering the biological facial articulations of the actor, the Noh mask erases his original self and frees him to communicate only the state of mind of the character through the movements of a highly trained body. 'The actor uses moments of stillness and variations of the speed of the walk to give character to the role and express modulations in feeling.' [24]

In contrast to Noh, it is exactly the mobility and gaze of the face which articulates all the imperceptible gradations of affect in *The Passions* series. In cinema, as Deleuze suggests,[25] the expressive power of the face replaces the body's power of extension (action-reaction) in movement. In everyday discourse, the face is regarded as a manifestation of the individual self or its social role, and serves as mediator in communication. That is why, in Noh, it is effaced by the mask. However, in the close-ups and middle shots of Viola's installations, the face is fully extracted out of its context (spatiotemporal and social) and thus de-individualized. Only its ability of expressiveness – being a composition of intensive singular micro-movements on an immobile surface – is left. In Western culture the face is considered as the only part of the body capable of these invisibly fast vibrations of affect. In distinction, the body in the Noh play takes all the functions of the face and executes the same high intensities of non-movement. The rationale behind this difference can be found in the opposite ways in which the modern Western civilization utilizes body discipline as a form of social control and submission,[26] in contrast to the Zen-based practices where rigorous self-discipline served to liberate the individual body's potential.

Foucault observes that highly refined forms of body technologies were developed in Europe during the eighteenth and nineteenth centuries, replacing the explicit violence of punishment in the Middle Ages and the Renaissance. Through the knowledge of medicine, psychiatry and education, the new meticulous disciplines manipulate the body on a molecular level (in the ubiquitous distribution of micro-powers), turning it into an effective labour machine. These social politics work on the principle of the Alter Ego: the subject, who is produced in this process, accepts them as internal regulations, normal and natural patterns of self-restraint. Such 'negative' economics of control lead to a process of automatization of motor, perceptual and conceptual behaviour.

'[A]utomatization is assumed to be a basic process in which the repeated exercise of an action or of a perception results in the disappearance from consciousness of its intermediate steps'.[27] Automatization normally accomplishes the transfer of attention from a percept or action to abstract thought activity, which explains the observation of Foucault that the bodies disciplined in this manner are individualized (for a specific role) and generalized (as in the army) at the same time, like machines.

The case with all Zen arts (the ways) displays the reverse practice of body/mind discipline. Martial arts, calligraphy, flower arrangement, tea ceremony and Noh drama, all require a life-long rigorous and repetitive training in meditation, breathing and concrete artistic skills. The result is an open and flexible egoless self, who identifies with all phenomena, seeing them not from a self-centred perspective (as a centre of indeterminacy – Bergson, Deleuze) but from their respective centres (gaseous/molecular perception – Deleuze). The result of such 'creative' technologies of the body is rather de-automatization: de-automatization is the undoing of automatization, presumably by reinvestment of actions and percepts with attention.[28] Contemporary digitization and electronic technologies open a field for a more fluid economy of the body as conjuncture of potential intensities. The works of Bill Viola can be taken as an artistic illustration of this process.

The temporal flow

The composition of temporal passage in Noh is complex: in accordance with the narrative, time is condensed, slipped, vanishing, reversed or split.[29] It unfolds around a drama of reminiscence and dreams, where imaginary scenes from the past mix with present-time situations. In this respect, Noh time differs greatly from the temporal flow in Viola's late video installations (*The Passions* series, *The Greeting* and *Ocean Without a Shore*) which is continuous and uninterrupted. However, since the settings on the Noh stage are kept to a minimum, all changes in space and time during the play are indicated by voice narration instead of visual evidence. Chanted description directs the imagination of the viewers and transfers it into the appropriate for the momentary time-space continuum. Therefore, '[a]s we watch, the time is always right now'.[30] In order to evoke deep pensive responsiveness in the audience, Noh plays rely mostly on the rhythmic movements, ceremonial dancing and repetitive chanting, rather than on the progression of the plot. Therefore, for the purpose of this study we can bracket the narrative time and take for speculation only the temporal flow of the movements.

Movement

The conduct of movements is the most striking correspondence between Viola's more recent video installations and Noh drama. Viola's ultra-slow motion technique and Noh actor's movements without movement produce a unique type of present-time temporal flow. Both utilize simple gestures, body postures and body-motion, and transform them into ceremonial ones. A ceremony of life and movement full of possibilities, yet essentially devoid of content and meaning. This transformation is due to the high level of attentive concentration these gestures receive. To participate in a Noh play as a spectator, especially one who does not understand the meaning of the narration and lacks a preliminary acquaintance with the story (no ready-made deposits in memory – what Zen calls 'the beginner's mind') means that you concentrate on the rhythm and atmosphere of the performance. All gestures, dances, tonality of the chanting and music are performed in a highly stylized, elegant and slow manner. The movement seems to stop at the very moment when the muscles are tensed the most. In this way, the Noh actor performs just sufficiently to generate a blank interval full of potential, when 'nothing happens'. Thus, the movement patterns concentrate dramatic power in moments of stillness. The impression is very close to the extremely stretched unfolding of *The Greeting*, *Observance*, *Ocean Without a Shore*, *The Raft*. All these pieces build their image not only through face expression but also through body postures and gestures. The colours are vivid and living for themselves, the hand or legs move at incredibly decelerated speeds.

The meditative effect

Being a pensive participant in the praxis of Noh drama or Viola's video installations, one learns to deconstruct their present conceptual system and habitual way of seeing, and unlearn all previously learned and conditioned responses. Viola's technique intensifies not only the affect (of the image), as argued here, but also the percept (of the viewer's consciousness). The visual perception of movement stretches to unusual dimension and comes in direct resonance with the viewer's time-perception. The habitual mode of visual and time-perception is deterritorialized, deconstructed and modified into a meditative experience:

> I think the thread that goes through all of the works isn't even necessarily about time. It's really about waking up, about being aware. [...] There's a new perception at that point. Anybody who's ever been in an accident knows that right away. Your reality, your sense of time, everything changes; your life changes. In a way, a lot of spiritual disciplines – particularly in Eastern cultures – deal with the body: fasting, walking on fire. In some ways, you can look at them as sort of very controlled accidents.[31]

Transfiguration of Viewer's Time-perception

I now turn to the ways Bill Viola's slow motion images enter into direct resonance with brain vibrations, slowing them down. As argued earlier, Viola constructs a kind of affection-image in present time. The life-size projections and the viewer seem to share the same spatiotemporal dimension. When the time of the image is slowed down to an extreme level, time-consciousness alters its mode in order to keep the illusion of congruent time, thus slowing down its own pace.[32] Slowed down time-perception is said to be characteristic of the mind in meditation. The experience is supposed to bring intensification of the present moment, enriched and sharpened visual sensitivity, acentred awareness of the self and the object at once. The same characteristics hold for the affection-image as described by Deleuze, but in Viola they are achieved on the level of consciousness, not just on the level of the slowly moving image. The experience is holistic, receptive and beyond language or logic.

Meditation is a form of mental exercise to calm the mind and open it beyond the conditioned habitual patterns of thought, thus regaining the primary nature of perceptions and events. The results are higher spiritual awareness (in religion), higher attention to the present moment (mindfulness), relaxation, self-awareness, better concentration, creativity, peace of mind. Various audiovisual stimuli can facilitate meditative awareness. Visualizations, music, rhythm, dance and chanting have been important components of almost all mystical and religious cults. Via contemplation and prayer to the direct image of the divine, chanting spiritual poems in a repetitive manner or performing ritualized rhythmic movements, the practitioner enters meditative modes of consciousness. The predominant meditation practice in Buddhism is 'just sitting' for long periods of time, and concentrating either on the surrounding sounds, or on the free flow of consciousness, or attempting to completely stop the workings of the mind.[33]

Basic research using powerful neuro-imaging techniques, such as electroencephalograph (EEG), magneto-encephalograph (MEG) and functional magnetic resonance imaging (fMRI) are being used to analyse changes in brain dynamics during meditation.[34] Scientists have observed that there are basically four states of mind depending upon the frequency of mind waves. These states are named alpha, beta, theta and delta. With most meditative practices, the EEG patterns exhibit a slowing and synchronization of brain waves, with alpha waves predominating. More advanced practitioners of meditation demonstrate an even greater slowing of their brain waves, with the possible emergence of theta wave patterns.

Alpha mental state is slower (8–13 cycles per second) than the normal in everyday activity beta state (13–30 cycles per second), and is often known as the state of mind in meditation. The EEG tracings revealed that, about ninety seconds after an accomplished Zen practitioner begins meditation, a rhythmic slowing in the brain wave pattern occurs. This slowing progresses with meditation, and after 30 minutes, one finds rhythmic alpha waves of seven or eight per second. In meditation mode, not only horizontal time-phase frequency slows down but also the present moment (vertical axis) deepens and intensifies. That means that information perceived per now-phase increases. The present moment becomes a departure point, line of flight towards eternity. Eternity in the case of meditation means that time perception stops or extremely slows down, but not the present awareness. This could be proved psychologically by the phenomenon called 'alpha blocking'. A normal subject with closed eyes produces alpha waves on an EEG tracing. An auditory stimulation, such as a loud noise, normally obliterates alpha waves for seven seconds or more; this is termed alpha blocking. In a Zen master, the alpha blocking produced by the first noise lasts only two seconds. If the noise is repeated at 15 second intervals, we find that in the normal subject there is virtually no alpha blocking remaining by the fifth successive sounding. This diminution of alpha blocking is termed habituation and persists in normal subjects for as long as the noise continues at regular and frequent intervals. In the Zen master, however, no habituation is observed. His alpha blocking lasts two seconds with the first sound, two seconds with the fifth sound, and two seconds with the twentieth sound. This implies that the Zen master has a greater awareness of his environment as the paradoxical result of meditative concentration. One master described such a state of mind as that of noticing every person he sees on the street but of not looking back with emotional lingering.[35] Meditation produces a heightened awareness that resists habituation and maintains spontaneous freshness of perceptions. Consciousness in a slow time-mode experiences high-speed perception and full awareness of the details in the surroundings, and could be compared to a video taken at 300 frames per second and then projected in very slow motion-mode.

The technique of meditation seems to constitute such a manipulation of attention, as it is required to produce de-automatization. The percept receives intense attention while the use of attention for abstract categorization and thought is explicitly prohibited. Since automatization normally accomplishes the transfer of attention from a perception or action to abstract thought activity, the meditation procedure exerts a force in the reverse direction. Cognition is inhibited in favour of perception; the active intellectual style is replaced by a receptive perceptual mode.[36] In an attempt to explain the automatization of thought and visual abstraction observed in contemporary adult individuals, the psychologist Heinz Werner studied eidetic imagery in primitive, pre-analytic cultures and the perceptual development of children. The perceptual and cognitive functioning of children and of people of primitive cultures have been described as vivid and sensuous, syncretic, animated and holistic. Werner discovered that in modern-day imagery, the image is in the service of abstract thought and, as such, it loses its richness:

> The image gradually changed in functional character, it becomes essentially subject to the exigencies of abstract thought. Once the image changes its function and becomes an instrument in reflective thought, its structure will also change. It is only through such structural change that the image can serve as an instrument of expression in abstract mental activity. This is why, of necessity, the sensuousness, fullness of detail, the colour and vivacity of the image must fade.[37]

Other experimental evidence shows that, while growing older, children pay less and less attention to the sensual aspects of images, such as texture and colour, and progressively more attention to their meaning, and to their formal qualities, such as shape and size.[38] Meditation, on the other hand, performs the opposite effect – de-automatization of perceptual apparatuses, their release from abstraction, and goal oriented action-modes. As William Blake's renowned expression goes, meditation 'cleanses the doors of perception' and the effect is a vivid, bright, ever renewed vision of the world. Such awareness corresponds to the impression of Bill Viola's ultra-slow motion video images.

Bill Viola's art is about the flux of emotional and spiritual time. By his technique of extremely slow motion applied to the affection-image in the medium of video, Viola creates a new type of image, which I refer to as the *meditation-image*. The meditation-image is defined as such not only formally (by the intrinsic dynamics of its elements) but also by its ability to modify directly the viewer's time-consciousness. Viola's video art installations 'pursue an absolute limit of visual perception until that perception becomes something else'.[39]

My approach in defining meditation-image is based on practical and theoretical methods. The practical method is phenomenological observation of time-perception during participation in Viola's video art installations combined with technical and formal analysis of his art. Theoretically the observations are supported by the interviews and talks given by the author, as well as the Bergson-Deleuzan theory of images, Husserlian theory of time-consciousness and neuro-scientific investigations of brain waves during the state of Zen-meditation.

Notes

1 For more information on video art refer to D. Hall, S. J. Fifer and D. Bolt (eds), 2005, *Illuminating Video: An Essential Guide to Video Art*. New York: Aperture Foundation; J. Jäger, G. Knapstein and A. Hüsch (eds), 2006, *Beyond Cinema: The Art of Projection. Films, Videos and Installations from 1963 to 2005* Ostfidern: Hatje Cantz; Y. Spielmann, 2008, *Video. The Reflexive Medium*, trans. A. Welle and S. Jones Cambridge MA: MIT Press.

2 The oil-on-wood painting is located in the Church of Santi Michele e Francesco in Carmignano, Tuscany.

3 G. Deleuze, 1986, *Cinema 1. The Movement-Image*, trans. H. Tomlinson and B. Habberjam Minneapolis: University of Minnesota Press, 87.

4 Balázs, quoted in Deleuze 1986, 96

5 I. Buchanan and L. Gregg (eds), 2005, *Deleuze and Space* Edinburgh: University of Edinburgh Press, 165.

6 Balázs, quoted in Deleuze 1986, 96

7 Deleuze, 1986, 98

8 Ibid.

9 Ibid, 81

10 On presentness of the video medium, see D. Graham, 1979, *Video-Architecture-Television: Writings on Video and Video Works 1970–1978*. Halifax: Press of Nova Scotia College of Art and Design; New York: New York University Press; B. Kurtz, 1976, 'The present tense' in I. Schneider and B. Korot (eds), *Video Art: An Anthology*. New York: Harcourt Brace Jovanovich, 234–5; Y. Spielmann, 2008, *Video: The Reflexive Medium*.

11 J. Nelmes, 2003, *An Introduction to Film Studies*. London: Routledge, 394–5.

12 A. Warhol, 1975 *The Philosophy of Andy Warhol (From A to B and Back Again)*. New York: Harcourt Brace Jovanovich, 63.

13 T. Rayns, 1990, cited in The Andy Warhol Museum, The Warhol: resources and lessons www.warhol.org/education/resourceslessons/Screen-Test-Activity accessed November 2014.

14 Take as an example a comic strip from *Peanuts*, where Snoopy decides to read Tolstoy's novel *War and Peace* at an extremely slow pace – just a word a day.

15 J. Walsh (ed.), 2003, *Bill Viola: The Passions*. Exhibition Catalogue. Los Angeles.

16 A. Michelson (ed.), 1984, *Kino-Eye: The Writings of Dziga Vertov*, Oakland, CA: University of California Press, 173.

17 R. Jakobson, 1957, 'Shifters and verbal categories' in L. R. Waugh and M. Monville-Burston (eds), *On Language*, Cambridge, MA: Harvard University Press (1990), 386–92.

18 Bill Viola cited on MOMA's website www.sfmoma.org/media/features/viola/fr_videotapes1.html accessed January 2014.

19 www.arts-in-company.com/ArtHistorySurvey/29-10-mod12-video/03B-05-viola-mod-3.htm

20 K. Komparu, 1983, *The Noh Theatre: Principles and Perspectives*, trans. J. Corddry and S. Comee, New York and Tokyo: Weatherhill, 165.

21 Ibid. xx–xxi.

22 Walsh, *Bill Viola*.

23 Deleuze, *Cinema 1*, 109.

24 Komparu, *Noh Theatre* , 220.

25 Deleuze *Cinema 1*, 87.

26 M. Foucault, 1977, *Discipline and Punish: The Birth of the Prison*, trans. A. Sheridan, London: Allen Lane.

27 H. Hartmann, 1958, *Ego Psychology and the Problem of Adaptation*, New York: International Universities Press, 178.

28 A. J. Deikman, 1966, 'De-automatization and the mystic experience'. *Psychiatry* 29, 324–38.

29 Komparu, *Noh Theatre* , 81.

30 Ibid. 83.

31 Viola, quoted in Walsh, 2003.

32 On phenomenology of time-consciousness, see E. Husserl, 1991, *On the Phenomenology of the Consciousness of Internal Time (1983–1917)*, trans. J. Brough Dordrecht: Kluwer Academic Publishers.

33 For more information on Viola's connection to Zen Buddhism, see his 2004 interview in 'Bill Viola. The Light Enters You,' *Shambhala Sun*, November www.shambhalasun.com/index.php?option=com_content&task=view&id=1357 accessed January 2014.

34 See series of research articles: T. Hirai, 1960, 'Electroencephalographic study of Zen Meditation (Zazen): EEG changes during the concentrated relaxation', *Psychiatrica et Neurologia Japanica* 62, 76–105; J. P. Banquet, 1972, 'EEG and meditation', *Electroencephalography and Clinical Neurophysiology* 33, 449–58; D. M. Eagleman, 2010, 'How does the timing of neural signals map onto the timing of perception?' in R. Nijhawan and B. Khurana (eds), *Space and Time in Perception and Action*, Cambridge: Cambridge University Press.

35 Hirai, 1960, 'Electroencephalographic study of Zen Meditation', 76–105.

36 Deikman, 'De-automatization and the mystic experience'.

37 H. Werner, 1957, *Comparative Psychology of Mental Development* New York: International University Press, 152.

38 D. Shapiro, 1960, 'A perceptual understanding of color response' in M. A. Rickers-Ovsiankina (ed.), *Rorschach Psychology*, New York: Wiley, 154–201.

39 M. Nash, 1990, interview with Bill Viola, *Journal of Contemporary Art* 3:2, 63–73; www.jca-online.com/viola.html accessed 3 February 2014.

Section 3

Experiencing

8

Tracking the Screen in Public Spaces: Everyday Dis/Enchantment

Chris Berry and Janet Harbord

'Ubiquitous media' is one of the most infectious, and indeed ubiquitous, catchphrases of the current era.[1] Whether imagined as utopia or dystopia, this 'mediatized' environment is manifested in ideas like the Smart Home, where refrigerators know their owners' habits and you can start the oven from your office.[2] Ubiquitous media are not confined to domestic space. Technologies that were once mostly found within buildings and fixed, such as the telephone, have migrated and/ or become mobile. Moving image screens have also come out of the movie theatre and the living room, and proliferated in publicly accessible spaces. Their forms and functions range from the ATM machine's touchscreen to huge advertising screens on the sides of buildings and television screens inside public transport. These fixed moving image screens co-exist in the mediatized urban environment with mobile screen technologies, such as the mobile phone, and also other screen-based technologies, like CCTV, with its surveillance cameras leading to moving image screens based elsewhere.

This essay is an initial foray into developing a framework for thinking about screens and screen technologies in publicly accessible spaces, whether those spaces are publicly owned like streets or open to the public like shopping malls and museums. It grows out of the pilot project for an ongoing and larger piece of research on moving image screens in the public spaces of Cairo, London and Shanghai.[3] Looking at the transformation of the urban environment under conditions of globalization, digitalization and rapid development, eminent architect and Harvard professor Rem Koolhaas has claimed that 'The Generic City is what is left after large sections of urban life crossed over to cyberspace'.[4] No doubt Koolhaas is onto something, but does this really mean that new media usage is making all cities the same? Are the new public screen technologies being taken up in the same way in Cairo, London and Shanghai? Are they really 'ubiquitous'? And if not, where are they and where are they not, in each city? Does the moving image screen no longer play any role in public life, and what is public life in these different places? What kinds of roles does the moving image play, now that its locations, sizes and modes of engagement are so diverse? These are some of the questions that animate our larger project.

How can we begin to answer these questions? Screen Studies has developed key concepts such as 'texts' and 'reception' on the assumption that audiences are (or at least should be) sitting still and watching films or television programmes from beginning to end. Practices such as channel switching have made that assumption dubious for a long time. But when the field is stretched to include screens in public spaces, with multiple frames, touchscreens and more, which function as portals to a variety of materials, it may be necessary to re-think these assumptions. Before talking about the text, perhaps we need to think about the archive as the multiplicity of materials that we may call upon or that may be called up for us. Even more radically transformed is the mode of engagement with the screen, as it is very rare for anyone to sit still and watch a public screen outside the movie theatre. In these circumstances, we may be better off following Jonathan Crary and speaking of regimes of attention (including lack of attention).[5]

We also need new methods to explore these public screens. Neither textual analysis (which assumes the attentive and passive viewer) nor focus groups or interviews are likely to yield much understanding of situations where people pass by or engage with screens almost without conscious awareness of their existence. One of the first things we realized when we started this project was how many more screens and screen-based technologies permeated public space than we had noticed before. Once we were looking for them, they seemed to be, if not quite ubiquitous, certainly much more common than we had imagined.

In what follows, we outline our decision, on the basis of this initial observation, to engage with the everydayness of public screens. That initial observation also made us realize the importance of abandoning as many preconceptions as possible and engaging with our object of study. Then, we describe in detail our 'walking method' as we have come to call it, and the results of our four London walks. (Focusing on London alone here means deferring the issue of difference between cities for later accounts.) By taking the reader with us as we retrace our steps, we aim to communicate how and why we have come to think about the everydayness of public screens through enchantment, disenchantment and re-enchantment. This may seem surprising. After all, it might seem odd to invoke ideas of wonder and magical belief at the same time as the everyday, the ordinary and the taken for granted. Yet, we think it is precisely this comingling and the tension between these qualities that is one of the characteristics of public screen environments.

Everyday Screens

In the small but rapidly developing literature on the use of screen technologies in public spaces, their everydayness has received comparatively little attention. For example, the website for the Urban Screens 2008 conference shows an image of a huge public screen with a fireball exploding on it. This sort of exceptional instance is eye-catching and important, but quite different from what we are investigating here.[6] In Hong Kong, Helen Grace has written about the use of YouTube and mobile phone cameras during the protests and other activities around the demolition of the Star Ferry Pier, arguing that the images and videos collected and posted in cyberspace create a virtual monument that enables the pier to live on in an electronic elsewhere.[7] But this again is a special event rather than a quotidian use of screen technology in public.

We are also interested in these and other unusual and eye-catching deployments of screens and screen technologies in public. But we want to focus here on the taken-for-granted-ness of screens, a quality that has perhaps made them unseen and uninterrogated except in unusual circumstances. Screens are now mixed in with everyday life; they are part of our experience of the bus stop, of buying a certain object, and of traversing the world in numerous ordinary ways. They complicate our sense of presence by mixing the here and now with images of elsewhere, the 'there and then'. And where the cinema was once the delimited sphere of public dreams, this imaginary landscape is now part of the everyday milieu of city life. These technologies are variously placed in urban environments and establish differentiated modes of presence. Screen technologies may be discretely embedded in the architecture of place (the ATM machine), or loudly advertising a connection to other sites (screens advertising a holiday destination), or transient devices moving through place (the Blackberry). More than the simple fact of their presence in an urban environment, their significance lies in the various ways in which they engage us, facilitate our demands and connect with various states of attention and consciousness. The experience of urban location today cannot be extracted from the multiple texts and images circulating on screen technologies. It is precisely the everydayness of screen technologies, their appearance not only as objects within the quotidian but *as a naturalized and designated part of* the quotidian, that requires us to rethink our approach to the study of screens as simultaneously the study of particular environments. In other words, we cannot take screens out of place any more than we can extract place from its mediations and elaborations in our analyses.

In what Francesco Casetti calls the 're-location' of screens from the bounded site of the cinema to their dispersal across urban terrain, screens themselves undergo transformation.[8] The scale of the image is variable, sound is often (although not always) absent, and the screen increasingly acts as an interface for a range of rapidly changing subjects (news, weather, advertisements, film, to name a few). The process that Bolter and Grusin have called remediation goes some way in providing an understanding of the mixing of media formats and their content. In the first instance, remediation refers to the possibility with digital media of importing and re-presenting other, older forms of media. Digital media refers not just to the codification of information as a new materiality, but also to the process signalling the defining properties of each medium. Thus remediation is a re-perception of media itself.

However, there is a second part to the description of remediation that draws closer to our question of how urban screens enchant. Bolter and Grusin argue that there is no thing outside of mediation (we have no pure access to things), and that mediated states are therefore real. In this line of argument, remediation is not only a retooling of media forms, but a retooling of how we apprehend and understand reality itself. They write, 'Mediation is the remediation of reality because media themselves are real and because the experience of media is the subject of remediation'.[9] The reality referred to is not the representation of the real (another claim to present a truth). Far more radically, remediation is the making 'real' of relationships between artefacts, practices and humans. 'Media hybrids', by which they mean 'the affiliations of technical artefacts, rhetorical justifications, and social relationships', are 'as real as the objects of science'.[10]

The Walking Method

It is one thing to note how everyday screens in public spaces are. But how should we research them and their roles as elements in these 'media hybrids'? As already indicated, many of the existing approaches in the fields we were familiar with seemed completely inappropriate. Our initial decision was to select starting points and then undertake unplanned walks in the city. This method draws from multiple heritages. Digitization and other contemporary technological and ontological changes in the nature of cinema have taken other scholars back to the pre-history of cinema to understand the conceptual and theoretical impact of these reconfigurations.[11] Similarly, we are inspired by those earlier observers of everyday life in the burgeoning cities during the tumultuous social (and technological) changes of the 1920s and early 1930s, such as Walter Benjamin and Siegfried Kracauer. In the face of the new, they did not turn to the collection of large bodies of statistical data from which objective generalizations could be proposed. Inka Mülder-Bach notes that Kracauer wrote explicitly against such methods in his early 1922 work *Soziologie als Wissenschaft* (*Sociology as Knowledge*). He felt such an approach missed social reality, which consists of singularities that cannot be divorced from experience and subjectivity.[12] For Kracauer, the need to apprehend that social reality through direct experience of its 'surface-level expressions'[13] and then analyse that experience, led him out onto the streets, into the restaurants, hotel lobbies and bars of Berlin, before writing his essays for the *Frankfurter Zeitung*, many of which are collected in *The Mass Ornament*, and his book, *The White Collar Masses*.[14] We also felt we needed to find out about the new screen environment by going out into it rather than trying to observe it from an objective distance.

The idea of using walking to experience the new screen environment also draws on the Situationist International's *dérive* and psycho-geography, although without the particular political or occult manifestations of these traditions.[15] We share the Situationist hope of observing

Lefebvre's *vie quotidienne*, or everyday life in its experienced singularity. But we also drew on the Situationists' effort to incorporate an unplanned element in their walking method. We wanted to maintain the distinction Thomas McDonagh draws between the Situationist *dérive* and the ethnographer's participant-observation paradigm. He points out that whereas the latter pursue 'the building of a shared experiential world', the former seek 'behavioural disorientation.'[16]

Thinking about where to begin, we identified contexts in which screens are likely to provide different functions. In London, we selected a transport hub and its surrounding neighbourhood (St Pancras International Station); a shopping centre (Brent Cross); an exhibition space (the Science Museum); and a tube (subway) station none of us had used before (Bromley-by-Bow) as our departure points. We undertook a form of loose visual ethnography. We set out taking written notes of where we went, and also intending to take notes of what we saw, along with video footage and some photographs as *aides-mémoire*. However, it became clear on the first walk that to walk, observe and take notes all at once would not only slow things down but also interrupt the process and make it less effective. The video footage was both too much material and also did not adequately capture the simultaneous process of looking and selecting that we were engaged in. Ironically, we had not anticipated the value of the still photograph, possibly because we thought it is an 'old' technology inappropriate to our interest in 'new' media, and possibly because we assumed that video would be most appropriate to our interest in the moving image. As a result, we only had a very basic still camera without a zoom on these walks, we used it rather sporadically, and we only started using it well into our first walk, when we were at King's Cross Station. However, these still photos were perhaps the best at capturing and even facilitating the moment of noticing something.

Our effort was not to record 'scientifically'. Rather, we recorded wherever and whenever screens and screen technologies encroached on our consciousness or eye-line. As Jane Rendell writes, 'Walking provides a way of understanding sites in flux in a manner that questions the logic of measuring, surveying and drawing a location from a series of fixed and static points.'[17] She continues, 'When we walk we encounter sites in motion and in relationships to one another, suggesting that things seem different depending on whether we are "coming to" or "going from" ', and it is precisely this sense of the relational quality of screens and place that we intended to trace: how does perception rove across the textures of screen images and brick walls, and how do screens affect dynamics of the city as they appear in thoroughfares or punctuate space as meeting points? And how do we, as bodies moving through an urban landscape, take cognisance of their presence? Next, by retracing our steps, we hope to provide an account which enables the reader to understand how we went from observation of the everyday to turn to ideas of enchantment, not as an escape from the quotidian but as part of it.

Walk 1: St Pancras International

We began our first walk at the new St Pancras International Station, which is the London terminus for the Eurostar train to Paris, Lille and Brussels. St Pancras is owned by Network Rail and is part of a 'location library' of venues owned by the company and actively promoted for film and television shoots.[18]

Route of Walk 1 (17 July 2008):

Begin 11.15. Café des Vins, St Pancras Ground Floor → Eurostar check-in and entrance area → upstairs to Level 1 in St Pancras, where we play with an interactive screen → platforms for trains to the Midlands → downstairs and out the back, across the street to the back entrance of King's Cross → King's Cross lobby → along Pentonville Road to Houseman's bookstore, 5 Caledonian Road → Gray's Inn Road → St Chad's Street → Argyle Square → south via side streets to Cromer Street and into St George's Gardens → Regent Square → pathway to Heathcote Street → Mecklenburgh Street and Mecklenburgh Square to back of Coram Fields, double-back and walk down to Guilford Street → Lamb's Conduit St.

Lunch break.

Lamb's Conduit St → Red Lion Street → High Holborn → Holborn Circus → Charterhouse Street → Smithfield → St John Street. Coffee at café, summing up discussion, and disperse, 15.30 approx.

St Pancras International architecturally has the structure of a Victorian railway station inflected by the modern design of an airport; the new glass ceilings and multi-level platforms open the space to different levels of travel. Originally designed by William Barlow in 1868, it was redeveloped and a glass extension added to house the lengthier Eurostar trains in 2007 (the extension designed by Norman Foster).[19] On the ground floor, a range of cafés and shops feature the signs of global brands, with a few information point screens that seemed little used. Halfway along the concourse, the signs direct passengers towards the Eurostar terminal, where a significant presence of security guards oversee entry to the security check system and passport control. Over the entrance are several monitors featuring instructions on the process ahead. This is the site of a border, and the screen devices both mark it and prepare passengers for their necessary submission to luggage and body screening.

Above the concourse, the higher level affords a view of the Eurostar trains through glass barriers. There are a few interactive screens that allow people to explore archives of information about the neighbourhood, but we seemed to be the only people using these. Furthermore, they were not internet-enabled, and so the 'choice' enabled by interactivity was comparatively limited and guided. Both passengers about to depart and those who have just arrived know where they are going, and are unlikely to want to wander around the neighbourhood with their luggage even if they do have time between trains. It may only be 'abnormal' visitors like us who might find this information useful. And, indeed, we made our decisions about where to walk on to next after consulting these screens.

On the lower floor of St Pancras, walking to the rear of the station, the point of departure for a small number of local trains was fronted with departure boards and a large screen displaying a loop of Sky news, sport, weather and advertising. This screen acts as an antithesis to the Eurostar information screens. The space is dimly lit so that the screen's ambient glow is notable, and the position of the screen ensures that travellers look up to a place 'above' (see Fig. 8.1). This physical space becomes a temporal space, a holding ground between anticipation (of travel) and boredom (waiting). Its purpose is to mark the place of non-time, to fill the pause between work and the commute home with images of current happenings. At King's Cross station next door, we found a similar situation with a large cinema-scale screen. However, where the screen at St Pancras is next to the departures board, the screen in the King's Cross foyer is situated at right angles to it, providing the same loop of Sky news,

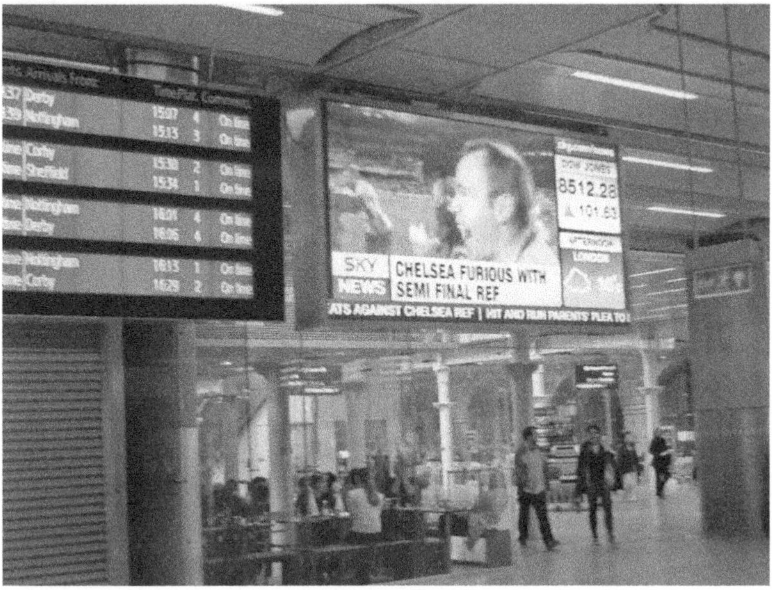

Figure 8.1. St Pancras international departures board and screen.

sport, weather and advertising as at St Pancras. Where passengers at St Pancras catch this screen in the corner of their eye as they watch the departure board, at King's Cross its light may bathe the passengers, but mostly they look away from it and towards the departure board (see Figure 8.2).

The environment outside King's Cross is a busy road, and here we found ourselves under heavy surveillance from a number of cameras. The path we took led away from the noise of the traffic and into smaller streets lined by down-market hotels and a few corner shops and the odd traditional pub. The heavy surveillance camera presence continued (see Figure 8.3). Inside, the shops had their own type of intimate ambience of conversation, and low-grade surveillance screens that seemed largely ignored. One pub had a large screen showing a live sporting event. As we walked on into Bloomsbury and Clerkenwell, we noticed far fewer security cameras than in the immediate vicinity of the station, and a number of smaller screens in shop windows, a window within a window displaying looped films of holiday destinations or beauty products, an invitation towards the future in both respects.

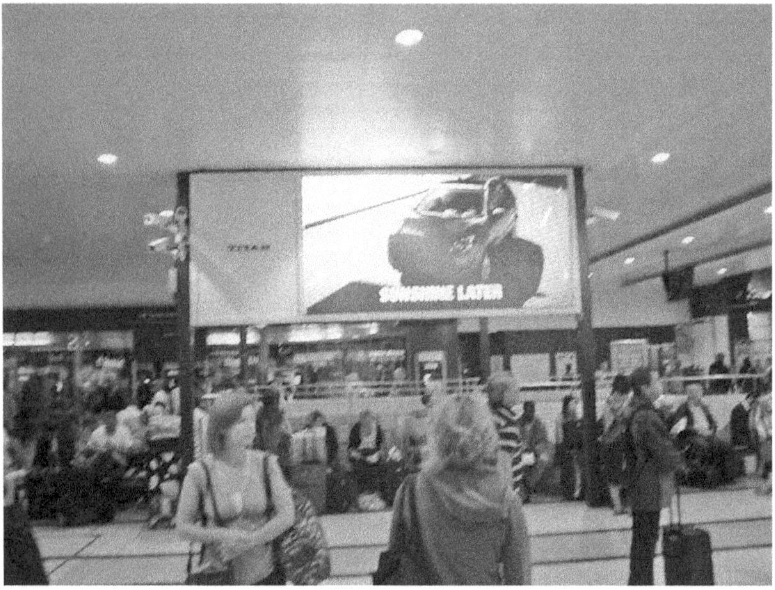

Figure 8.2. King's Cross Station. The departures board is off-screen to the right. The only person looking at this screen is one of us.

At the end of our first walk, our impression was of a very instrumental and functional deployment of everyday screens. At the Eurostar and through much of the station, they remediated noticeboards, giving information to guide passengers, or remediated billboards and network television receivers, directing advertising at passengers. Even the little-used interactive screens had instrumental aims. Perhaps the surveillance cameras invoked a sense of mystery about who was watching and where from for those who noticed them, but we neither experienced nor noticed any expressions of wonder in response to the screen-dense environment of St Pancras.

Walk 2: Brent Cross

The second walk began at Brent Cross tube station, North London, from which we negotiated our way across the North Circular Road into Brent Cross shopping centre. In contrast to the newly refurbished St Pancras International, Brent Cross is a shopping centre dating from 1976, the first of its kind nationally.[20]

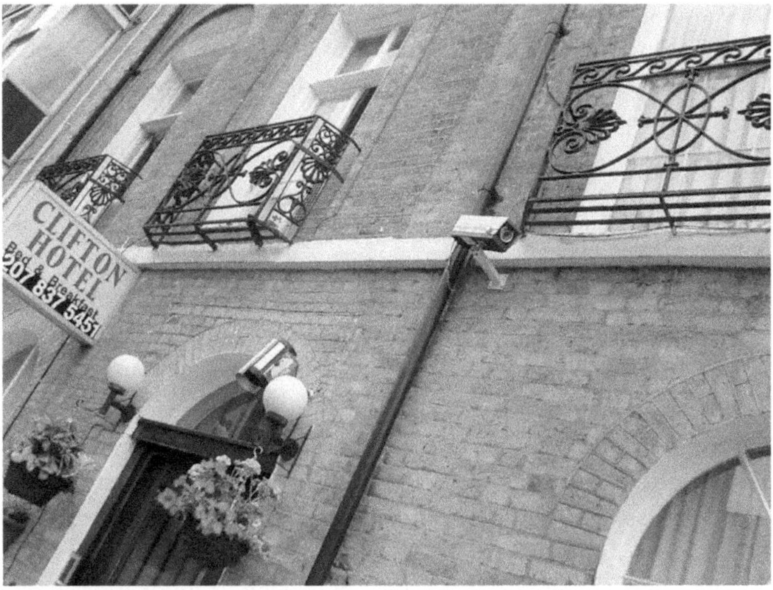

Figure 8.3. Two examples of heavy surveillance presence on St Chad's Street near King's Cross. The cameras were on the sides of buildings, on posts in the street, and over doorways.

Route of Walk 2 (24 July 2008):

Begin midday, Brent Cross Tube Station → Heathfield Gardens → North Circular & Hendon Way intersection → Prince Charles Drive → south-east entrance to Brent Cross Lower Level → escalators next to Fenwick (up to Upper Level) → Information Desk, centre of mall → restaurants near multi-storey car park (lunch in Café Alba) → car park → Fairfield Avenue → Park Road → Hendon Way → Spalding Road → North Circular & Hendon Way intersection → Highfield Avenue → Brent Cross Tube.

Tube to Colindale

Colindale Avenue → Edgware Road → Capitol Way → ASDA café, for summing up discussion, 15:30.

Unlike later out-of-town shopping centres, Brent Cross shopping centre is built in a conurbation. Yet travelling to the site on foot is clearly not expected. Brent Cross tube station delivers travellers to suburban streets close to main traffic arteries. We followed signs from the station, towards the North Circular Road, over and under concrete bridges above and below roaring traffic. This took us to the outer edges of the shopping centre. Notable in this experience was the lack of surveillance cameras, with the exception of traffic surveillance cameras fixed above roads, and an absence of information screens of any kind.

However, crossing the roads that circle the centre and lead into its car parks, we found ourselves in an environment that is saturated with surveillance cameras and signs warning us that they are in use. It is often said surveillance cameras will increase our personal safety. However, the lack of cameras in public spaces where individuals would be very vulnerable to attacks undermines the credibility of the dominant rhetoric. Furthermore, the clear increase in surveillance on the property of the mall suggests the priority may be protection of private property against theft and perhaps even giving the owners of the site evidence in case of law suits by visitors.

The location design, traffic system and architecture of Brent Cross shopping centre speaks to the ideals of another age, the decades of the 1960s and 1970s when mobility meant cars, when shopping became positioned as a specialized leisure activity, and its purpose was separated from the social relations of urban life and relocated to new 'centres'. The 'centres' are now notable peripheries to metropolitan city hubs where the complex dynamics of mixed and overlapping activity is conceived as a desirable feature of urban design. Brent Cross is jointly owned by Hammerson UK Properties and Standard Life Investments. Hammerson is one of the largest property developers nationally and the owner of a portfolio of shopping malls. The site has 8,000 free car parking spaces, and is visited by 15 million people annually.[21]

Brent Cross's peripheral and dated status was signalled, in part, through its lack of screen interfaces. More than a statement of 'low tech' capacity, the absence of screens delimited the horizons of the Brent Cross consumer. Compared to King's Cross, for example, where the visitor was able to access information about transport, and about the environment, using a screen to access local history and navigate pathways through, in, and out of the location, Brent Cross appeared to seal the visitor into its bubble. In a sense, the relative absence of screens enacted a spatial and temporal immobilization. The screens that visitors did have access to were of course their own mobile phone devices, yet these looped visitors back into familiar systems of circulation, rather

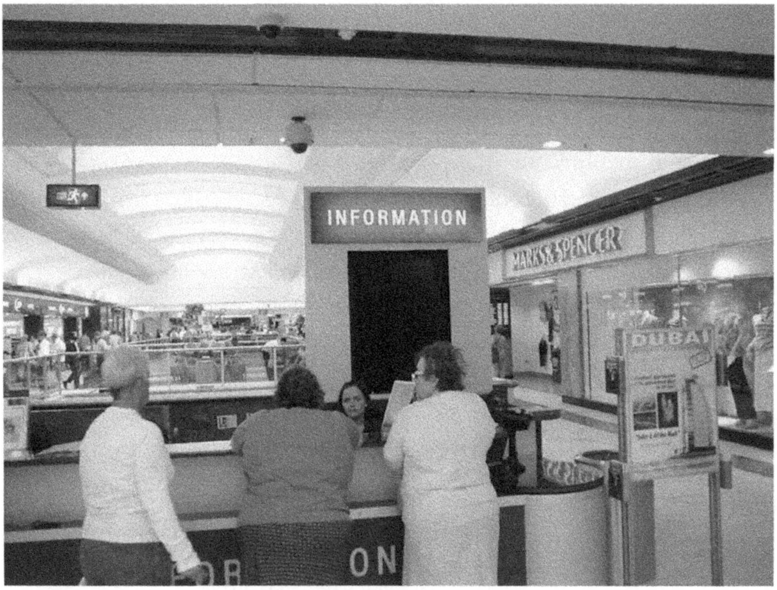

Figure 8.4. Brent Cross shopping centre. Information display screen plus two surveillance camera emplacements above.

like the traffic system, rather than allowing roaming, and access to the unfamiliar. The only prominently displayed screens were at an information booth, working as part of the design encouraging us to think and behave as consumers (see Figure 8.4).

On entering the shopping mall, we embarked on our visual ethnography of recording and photographing the environment, using domestic appliances like those sold in the mall. Within ten minutes we were approached by a security guard and told to stop filming. We were not offered an explanation why. While the increased vigilance of terror-risk assessment might play a part, it is notable that at St Pancras International and King's Cross, far more likely to be considered terrorist targets, we were left undisturbed. In photographing and filming the interior of the Brent Cross shopping centre, we were out of place. And in this location, in which the only screen technologies other than personal phones are objects to buy in shop windows or surveillance cameras, we were redirecting the uni-direction of information. To expand the metaphor of the information super-highway, at Brent Cross we were navigating a one-way street against the current.

From here we walked back to the underground station and took the train to Colindale in search of another shopping centre, Oriental City. The site of the shopping centre was, however, boarded-up, having closed since one of us had last visited it. We retired to the only venue nearby to conclude our walk, an Asda store with a café. Again, we reflected on the instrumental use of public screens, although we noted different purposes at work. Where they directed movement through St Pancras, they encouraged absorption into the shopping centre. Once inside Brent Cross, there is nothing to indicate an outside world even exists. And we also noted how, at both St Pancras and Brent Cross, once away from the core venue, screens and screen technologies became rare, challenging the assumptions of media ubiquity.

Walk 3: Exhibition Road and the Science Museum

From the very beginning of our project, we had highlighted the Science Museum as somewhere to visit, because we knew interactive screens were present in profusion. We acknowledge that this makes it exceptional rather than ordinary and everyday. Leaving the underground, we walked up to Exhibition Road, a street in an affluent area of Kensington and Chelsea where a number of museums perform the name of the road (the Victoria and Albert Museum, the Natural History Museum and the Science Museum). Although built in the twentieth century, the exterior of the Science Museum has a classical-style façade. At the time of our visit, it was hung with posters attached featuring key attractions such as the Imax cinema.

Route of Walk 3 (31 July 2008)

14:00 approx. Entrance to Science Museum → Ground Floor ticket booth for Imax → Mezzanine exhibition on Films of Fact → Stairs up to Level 2 Computing → Computing section (in search of computer with a heart) → Level 2 energy exhibition related to big loop screen → stairs (kind employee tells us where computer with a heart is) → Ground Floor → Wellcome Wing antenna section, computer with heart → Ground Floor → Store → Exhibition Road north → Serpentine Pavilion → Serpentine entrance (Cao Fei's RMB City exhibition) → Serpentine Bookshop, where the walk finished at 16.30.

The museum evolved from the Great Exhibition of 1851, housing many of the artefacts from this event, and became an independent museum in 1909.[22] It has continued to update its collection with technologies that conform to the museum's remit to teach science in an entertaining fashion. The presence of screens in the museum created a remediation of both science (ideas and concepts), and the nineteenth-century idea of the museum as a pedagogic institution.[23] From the architectural frontispiece of the exterior that signalled a type of elaborate architecture similar to religious buildings, the interior leads via a space for security checks and a few screens advertising specific attractions, to a display of the museum's fabric. The iron and glass structure built around a central well allows the visitor a view of the platforms of the museum as a vista, a panorama. A large LCD wheel filled the centre of the well, rotating messages that circled above the entrance desk. The theatricality and ambience of the entrance hall was generated across the different historical fabrics of architecture, lighting and display (see Figure 8.5).

Inside the museum, we broke into two groups, one pair of researchers moving through the museum, with the other pair concentrating on the Science Museum's Imax screenings and simulator ride. In walking through the museum towards our designated exhibits, we were drawn past a number of themed rooms on different floors of the building. Notable to all exhibits was the presence of a screen or multiple screens. For example, the main hall housed a number of brightly painted and large steam engines, each with a screen interface attached, allowing the visitor to navigate through what were effectively a series of information cards. The space travel room contained the original shuttle to have returned from the Apollo 10 mission, an object roped off by a barrier containing a looped film of the Apollo aircraft launch, journey and return. The entire historic journey was edited down to under a minute. The screen interface offered a choice of pathways for the visitor to navigate through, but fell short of an interactive exchange where the display would be transformed by the actions of the visitor, via the screen.[24] Therefore, the majority of the museum utilized a sense of restricted interactivity, confined to the relation between the visitor and screen (the visitor may affect the screen contents but not the exhibit).

There was, however, a sense of an emerging culture of screens allowing interaction with the environment in a few places within the

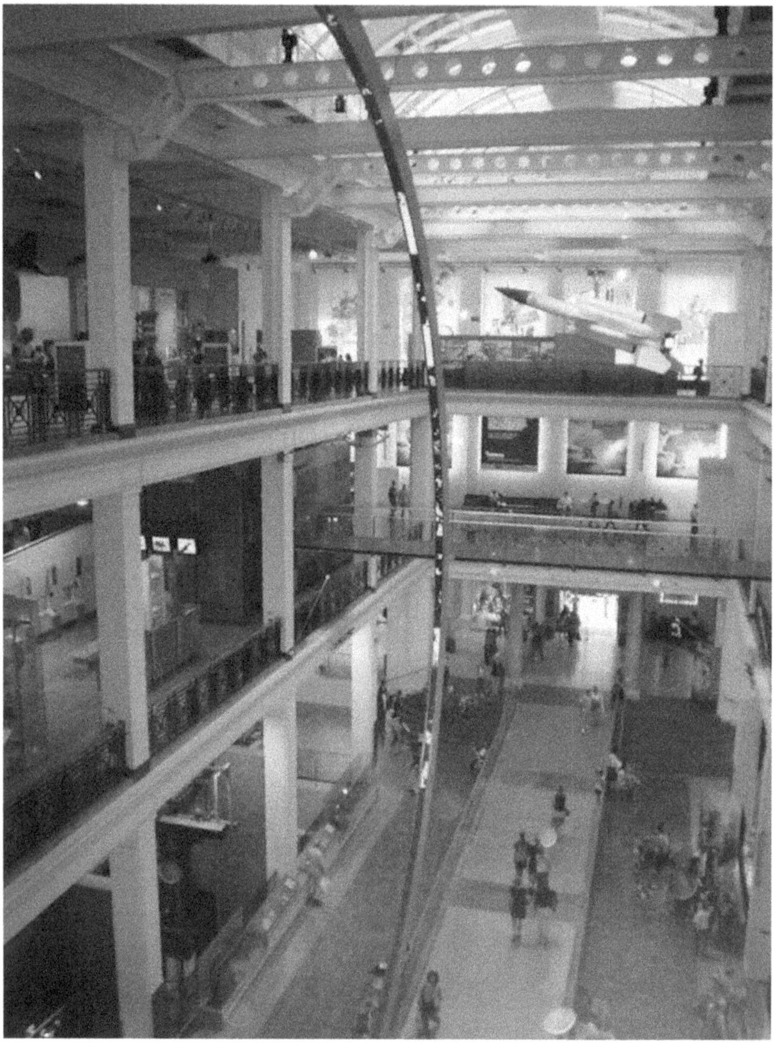

Figure 8.5. Entrance hall of Science Museum, viewed from second floor. The LCD wheel arcs across middle of picture. The box office for the IMAX theatre is below. Screens and light from screens can be seen at various levels through the building.

museum. For example, one of the most densely packed areas on the day we visited was an exhibition called 'Energy Fuelling the Future', located on the second floor of the building on a balcony overlooking the main foyer. Not only was it popular, but the visitors were mainly young children actively engaged with a larger number of interactive screens in the area. Particularly popular was an exhibit where the visitor could enter a message onto a screen that would appear moments later on the huge circular LCD display in the main foyer (see Fig. 8.6). We might speculate that this is a second generation of interactive screens emerging in museum culture, with appeal for a new generation that cannot remember a time before interactivity. How meaningful or pedagogical this interactivity is cannot be considered here. But this LCD wheel public screen – exceptional in size, design, placement and use – was the first time we noted a sense of wonder among those observing it. In this case, the screen itself was also the exhibit. But even in cases where most attention was directed to the object displayed, touchscreens in the Science Museum seemed to draw the public to play with them without inhibition and with enthusiasm, often fascination, and sometimes delight.

If the museum itself is an archive of science and science-related curiosities, screens both constrain and enable access to that archive. They constrain in that they often explicitly screen off direct physical access to objects, even those like steam engines that are robust objects, and by directing perception, they narrow the choice of responses that we may make to things in this environment. Conversely, they enable relations to things by providing contextual and historical information, in effect drawing on a larger range of behind-the-scenes archival knowledge and material that the object 'stands in' for metonymically. Both the screen and the object therefore act as portals into a spatial and temporal elsewhere: the archive of scientific collections located out of sight (in specialized access-restricted zones), and the past as it resides in our relations with objects and texts. In the context of the Science Museum, screens facilitate forms of temporal and spatial mobility, whether we characterize that mobility as a form of tourism, education or entertainment.

In the particular exhibits that we visited (as paired researchers), the museum provided another mode of archiving: the explicit archiving of the artefacts of film and the institution of cinema. Film was made an exhibit, thematized scientifically as 'Films of Fact', an exhibit of approximately 30 documentaries from 1903 to recent times. Cinema itself was archived in the form of the Imax cinema, a steeply raked venue with a capacity to seat two hundred viewers. This cinema-within-a-museum screened a 30 minute film made in 2006, with a subject matter of ocean-life. Its purported pleasure was, however, nostalgia.

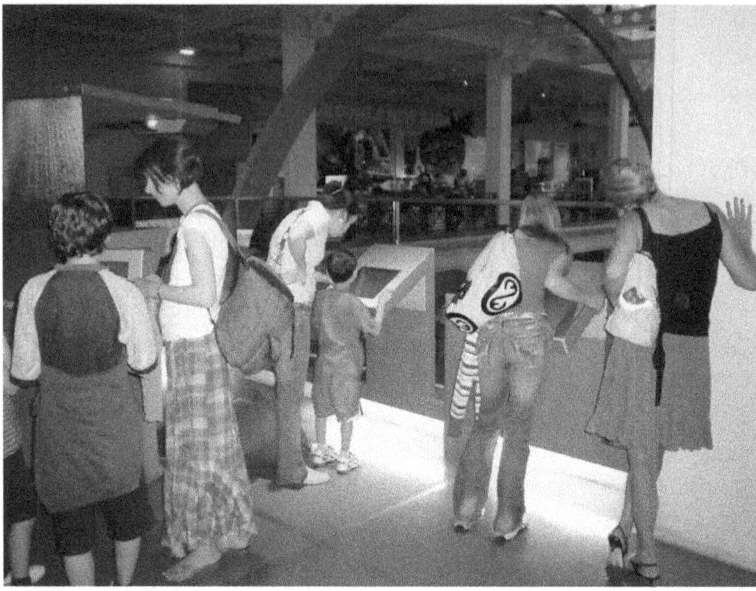

Figure 8.6. Science Museum visitors to 'Energy: Fuelling the Future' display, with screens for inputting messages to LCD wheel in centre and on right.

Where we might have presumed that the museum would dazzle with a new immersive form of cinema, the Imax delivered 1950s 3D cinema, handing out glasses to all spectators at the entrance. Like the LCD wheel, here again the screen itself was part of the exhibit and not just an interface with it. The experience of the ocean-bed and the film was overlaid with a sense of the curiosity-value of this cinematic experience: cinema as spectacle, attraction, theatre of the senses. Similarly, the simulator ride situated the visitor in a bodily relation to the screen, but through a computer-based technology that felt dated, retrospective and nostalgic. These exhibits evoked and revisited historic moments in cinema's magical past, and in tandem with the factual exhibition, kept in play the dual trajectories of Méliès and the Lumières, but almost as miniature, scaled-down versions.

The walk concluded at the Serpentine Gallery, travelling up Exhibition Road and its concentration of museum buildings, across the road to Kensington Gardens and Hyde Park, the nineteenth-century tailoring of leisure, health and education through the physical activities of walking and visiting public sites. Again, there were no public screens and only a scattering of surveillance cameras en route. On entering the gallery, we noticed one flat-screen monitor in the lobby displaying an artwork, the only screen evident inside the gallery. In the space outside, a temporary pavilion designed by Frank Gehry, a projection screen was set up for evening performances and screenings.

Walk 4: Bromley-by-Bow

If our visit to the Science Museum had been more planned and purposeful than the Situationists might have liked, our final walk came closer to the spirit of the *dérive* than any other. None of us had ever got off the tube at Bromley-by-Bow before, therefore our meanderings, first to the North and then to the East, before returning to the tube station, were largely random.

Route of Walk 4 (7 August 2008)

14.00. Bromley-by-Bow tube → north along Blackwall Tunnel North Approach → north up St Leonard's Street → right/east on Bromley High Street → stop at shops on Stroudley Walk → meeting Bow Road via Bromley High Street → continuing east/right along Bow Road → stop at Dawn's Café in workshops off Bow Road → return to Blackwall Tunnel North Approach underneath flyover → turn onto River Lea via Global Approach → continue along towpath until Three Mill Lane → entering Three Mills and then turning left/north into Three Mills Green to climb landfill-type hillocks → returning to Bromley-by-Bow tube via Three Mills studios and Tescos → continuing south and turning left on Devas (then Devons) Road past demolished hospital → turning right/north on Campbell Street → turning left/west on Bow Road and stopping at Bow Road tube station around 16.30.

This walk was perhaps the most remarkable because of the striking absence of public screen technologies. There were even fewer of London's supposedly ubiquitous surveillance cameras than we saw anywhere else, although there were of course quite a few. Shopping malls, museums and transport hubs are all sites in which the deployment of public screen technologies can reasonably be anticipated. Because none of us had ever been to Bromley-by-Bow before, we had no idea what to expect.

On exiting the Bromley-by-Bow Tube station, we turned round and noticed a television screen above the entrance. It carried notices to

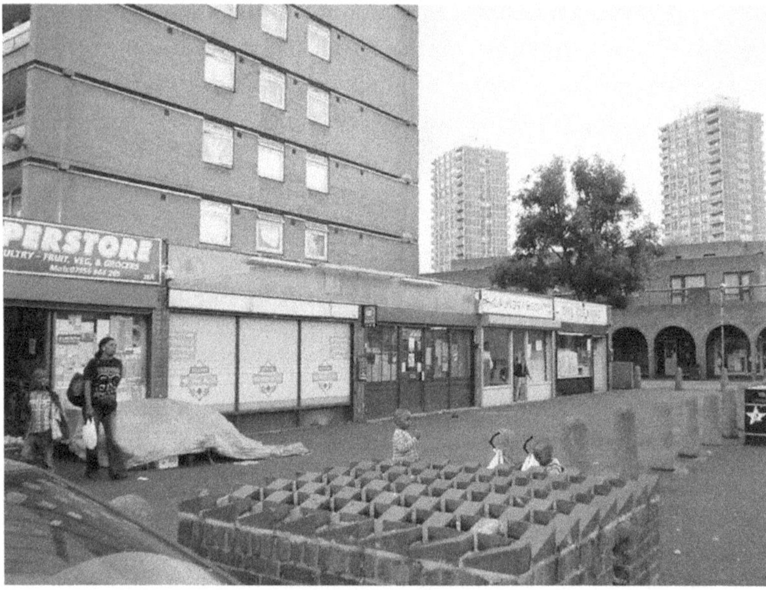

Figure 8.7. Shops in Bromley-by-Bow. If you look very carefully, you may be able to make out surveillance cameras over some of the entrances.

the public and details of train times. As it turned out, this was the only public screen we encountered during the entire afternoon. Bromley-by-Bow appears to be a poor inner city neighbourhood. Although we located one small cluster of shops (see Figure 8.7), there does not appear to even be a high street in the neighbourhood. Even the convenience stores did not all use surveillance cameras, although we did encounter these at strategic traffic intersections and guarding the entrance to some stores and other private sites where theft might be an issue, such as the Three Mills Studio (London's largest film and television studio). Just as there were no visible surveillance cameras on the walk under the North Circular to get to Brent Cross shopping centre, we observed none along the section of the canal path that we walked. The only other public sign of screen activity was the presence of satellite dishes on the walls of many houses and flats. Not only was there little sign of public screen culture in Bromley-by-Bow, there was little sign of much public culture at all. There were few people on the streets, even in the more residential sections of the area.

It was here, in the absence of any public screens, that we began to think back to the screened environments we had encountered on our other walks. Although we had readily noted the instrumental and functional qualities of public screens in these places, it was only when confronted with a neighbourhood devoid of these everyday screens that we really began to think more about what else they did.

Everyday Dis/Enchantment

At first sight, the everyday seems far removed from the discourse of enchantment. However, the alignment of the everyday with the secular invokes a relationship with the idea of enchantment. For both Kracauer and Lefebvre, their interest in the everyday is part of a larger conceptual and theoretical engagement that encompasses modernity and the related dilemmas of enchantment and disenchantment. To understand our own engagement with the everyday and enchantment, we need to locate our work within this discursive lineage.

The argument that one of the characteristics and even requirements of modernity is 'the disenchantment of the world' is associated with Max Weber, who held that the acceptance of science and rationality meant the disappearance of mystery in all its forms ranging from religion to magic.[25] There are many differences and disagreements among those writing on disenchantment and modernity. For many, disenchantment meant the liberation of humanity. For others, including Weber, disenchantment robbed the world of meaning and was a profoundly alienating experience. Marxists shared Weber's negativity about existing modernity, but they believed that disenchantment had not gone far enough. As Marx's use of terminology like 'the commodity fetish' indicates, Marxism holds that capitalism has installed its own forms of enchantment as part of the process of maintaining willing exploitation. And where Weber is pessimistic about modernity in general, Marxists are hopeful that revolution will dispel these forms of enchantment. Depending on one's perspective, this is either a path to restore fullness of being without enchantment, or an enchantment itself.

For both Kracauer and Lefebvre, the turn to the everyday occurs in the face of an at least temporary absence of revolution. For Kracauer, everyday life in the Berlin of the 1920s is where the processes of modernity manifest themselves at their most intense, promising the possibility of avenues towards the more intense disenchantment that he wanted to promote. Henri Lefebvre, writing in the 1960s, turns to the everyday in response to a sense of disappointment, communicated when he writes, 'We are only too conscious of the fact that the world as currently established is not the product of revolution'.[26] Lefebvre's compatriot of the times, Guy Debord, famously denounces the totalizing effects of the image as commodity in *The Society of the Spectacle*.[27] Lefebvre's distance from this position can be sensed towards the end of his trilogy on everyday life, albeit obliquely, when he writes, 'Refutation of the commodity as a world, and of the global as a product of the market, still has sense. Unfortunately, however, this sense also implies the non-sense of refutation.'[28] For Lefebvre, there is something pointless and shortsighted about outright condemnation, that fails to see that 'something' gets away from the totalizing effects of the political system and a corresponding alienation, that seems to leak out of the 'politico-bureaucratic-state-edifice' in the 'cracks, chinks, spaces':[29]

> What escapes the state? The derisory, miniscule decisions in which freedom is rediscovered and experienced: taking the bus to this or that stop; speaking or not speaking to a particular person; buying such and such an object; and so on. Starting from these micro-decisions, freedom starts to gather momentum.[30]

Both Kracauer and Lefebvre turn to the everyday in the search for liberation, but for different reasons. Kracauer hopes to use it to further revolution, whereas Lefebvre turns to it as his faith in revolution declines. But what they share is the assumption of a fundamental opposition between modernity and enchantment. As Michael Saler points out, it is this position that has changed in the last decade and more. With it has changed the status of the enchanting in everyday life. It is no longer necessarily opposed to modernity, either as a remnant from the pre-modern or as a perversion of modernity. For some, this can mean trying to work out a space for religion and the supernatural within modernity, or accounting for 'modern religion'. For others, it means engaging with what Saler calls 'disenchanted enchantment'.[31] In public screen environments, we believe this disenchanted enchantment meets and mingles with the everyday and taken for granted.

In Saler's account, a primary area of work where 'disenchanted enchantment' is found is the discourse of wonder around science itself. Seemingly magical effects are used to excite audience interest and then explained in a dialectic of the mysterious and the rational employed to pedagogical ends. Michelle Pierson has also investigated this interest in scientific 'phantasmagoria' as part of the heritage of today's excitement and interest in cinema's special effects. These themselves inspire disenchanted enchantment manifested in magazines and websites devoted, and in almost fetishistic manner, to effects and their explanation.[32] The enchantment of science as both mysterious and rational certainly helps to explain the intensity of engagement we saw in the Science Museum. To what extent this is attributable to the touchscreens is hard to tell. But rather than trying to draw lines, it may be wiser to understand the sense of wonder or enchantment of screens in the Science Museum as being enhanced by their location. We take it for granted that somehow when we touch the screens, something is activated, or that an LCD screen can show moving images. But how many of us really know how they work? In the atmosphere of the Science Museum, we trust that this mystery can be explained rationally.

Outside the Science Museum, the moving image screen relocates some of the wondrous qualities of the cinema, itself a model of 'disenchanted enchantment' in the everyday. Writing in the post-digital era when the ontological distinctiveness of celluloid has disappeared and the definition of cinema is once again up for grabs, Sean Cubitt returns to the Lumière Brothers' famous *Sortie d'Usine* (*Leaving the Factory*, 1895) to argue for the idea of a quality that he calls '*le vif*' as the quintessentially cinematic. This is the 'magical transformation' that puts things into movement.[33] When cinema first appeared, it inspired amazement. Although it rapidly became quotidian, its special quality as the site of *le vif* did not disappear. By extension, when moving image advertisements and notices are brought into public spaces, however banal their content and taken for granted the technology is, this magic of *le vif* is also present.

Some 50 years ago, the French critic and social theorist Edgar Morin also argued for an understanding of cinema as magical. He claimed this lay in a double consciousness, where the 'reality' of the image presented, its re-presentation of something that has occurred, co-exists with recognition of its status as an illusion.[34] This willing suspension of belief presages the idea of 'disenchanted enchantment'. And in this double knowledge, Morin locates the enchantment of the cinematic image. For him 'the technical and the dream are linked at birth'.[35] The cinema holds a particular significance in his examination of the social, for it facilitates what he calls 'projective identifications', a taking into the self of the external world, and a projecting of the self onto the external environment. In reading Morin, his ideas seem to map out a relationship to images that prefigures the dispersal of the screen into the landscape of the everyday. His work describes a kind of ambivalent relation to the image that is closer to the states of encounter with screens across the city than to the concentrated environment of the cinema. He writes: 'The zone of affective participation is that of mixed, uncertain, ambivalent projective-identifications. It is equally that of magico-subjective syncretism'.[36]

Encountering screens on a daily basis in places where we least expect to find them is both startling and banal, and it is precisely the syncrisis of these opposing states of experience that for Morin, produces the magical. Magic in this context is not matter to be added to a context, but a product of relationality, for 'Magic has no essence'.[37]

In the public spaces we walked through for our pilot project, the possibilities for fleeting, rapid, projections of here to there were multiple. And this multiplicity was not only the product of multiple screens enabling the watcher to be both here and there in multiple places and conceptualizations at once and in quick succession, but also the knowledge that we were being looked at from unknown elsewheres through surveillance cameras. The result is that no matter how everyday they are, public screen spaces also carry a charge of enchantment, even if it was only when we were in spaces without public screens that we began to notice this.

However, to return to the beginning of this essay, we must also ask how this production of enchantment is caught up with issues of power. For it is clear from our walks that public screens are not ubiquitous but unevenly distributed, and used in different ways in different places.

Areas rich in screens were literally more affluent and were also the sites for international visitors as well as local citizens. In these locations, screens are both a marker of an effective global economy, and part of the mechanism for processing human traffic, as the management of a commuting labour force and tourists. These sites were also areas where people gathered, where a sense of publicness was evident, in comparison to the deserted streets and walkways of Bromley-by-Bow, Colindale and Brent Cross. From this we may deduce that an experience of 'publicness' is now assured by the presence of screens, providing information and entertainment, and a situation accompanied by a sense of being watched over by cameras leading to absent screens. Both watched and watching, the relay of looks defines the dense urban space where the public gathers. And yet this publicness is also far from either the original coffee house face-to-face gatherings imagined in Habermas's 'public sphere' or modern mediated variations thereof, especially if the screen is likely to distract members of these publics from each other rather than encourage interaction between them. And in today's context, the presence of surveillance cameras resonates in two ways. Cameras monitor public behaviour in sites where collective unrest could threaten the effective functioning of the city. Conversely, swathes of the city and its populace are abandoned to their own security measures in areas that 'don't seem to matter'.

If locations rich in screens offer an experience of enchantment, we need to ask what kind of magic operates here in images and text that move, appear and disappear, that at times can be touched via an interface and manipulated? For Morin, enchantment was connected to alienation in its modernist sense, an experience of the abstraction of value and relationships into signs and commodities. Yet the force of alienation in his thought has the potential for something more creative, akin to the capacity for projection, that is, the potential to create a relationship to the environment and the world outside of the self. The screen image is a doubling of the world and the individual psyche, and it is the alienated image that becomes magical in its affective capacity, providing a fluid relation of projection-identification, which, for Morin, is also affective-participation. He argues of the image, 'We cannot dissociate it from the presence of the world in man, from the presence of man in the world. The image is their reciprocal medium'.[38]

Critical to Morin's thought is the quality of movement, which in film carries the spectator through a flux of states rather than a sequence of realist representations, for the image in its moving form doubles or even mimics the selective process of perception and its attunement to affective images. Morin, like Epstein, draws on the multiple perspectives that cinema provides in mixing scale (micro and macro images), speed (slow motion and time-lapse photography), and the cutting together of vision through montage. In the parallel workings of the cinema and the psyche, where the cinema mimics perception and consciousness, Morin locates a movement back to the individual who reworks the selective perception of cinema into a subjectivized version. In taking the world back, via the cinematic image (a relation of reciprocity as an endless feedback loop), an affective relation between the individual and the image is at play.

Taking Morin's notion of affective-participation and applying it to the dispersed sites of our walks, we can locate another doubling, one conditional on the relocation of screens to public space. The movement of the image is doubled by the movement of the individual, increasing the randomness of perception, multiplying the range of 'cuts' as we move towards and away from screens. The fragile continuity of energies that cinema appeared to offer writers such as Epstein, is looped back into the scene of transmission. The content of the screen may be secondary to the process of engagement, evident in the Science Museum where visitors approach screens prior to objects, whose point of gravitation is now the interface of the screen itself. If the museum provides a distilled example of affective-participation, the station at St Pancras provides an environment of potentiality, where we stumble upon screens in a less conscious way. The fact that screens barely register on our consciousness in this environment, that it takes a particular effort of research to note their presence, is testament to their established participation in public life. That screen-dense sites are sites of enchantment, rich in the potential of affective-participation, has implications of course for screen-poor environments in the inverse.

However, although this suggests clearly that public screens are marked as to-be-desired for what they signify, for the affects they induce, and for the possibilities they open up, whether or not they merit that desire and what exactly screen-poor areas are missing out on requires further consideration. Indeed, whether or not sites rich in everyday screens deploy enchantment as a means of mystifying, pacifying or directing the public, or allow its allure to open up to the kinds of 'derisory, miniscule decisions in which freedom is rediscovered and experienced', as Lefebvre puts it, varies from site to site. In these circumstances, although we affirm that 'disenchanted enchantment' is part and parcel of the modernity embodied in every public screen, we also believe that whether it is emancipatory, mystifying or of more fleeting significance varies. What matters then is when and under what circumstances it participates in the production of these different results, and that is one of the topics of our further project.

Notes

1 W. A. S. Buxton, 1997, 'Living in augmented reality: Ubiquitous media and reactive environments' in K. E. Finn, A. J. Sellen and S. Wilber (eds), *Video Mediated Communication*, Hillsdale, NJ: Erlbaum, 363–84.

2 L. Spigel, 2005, 'Designing the smart house: Posthuman domesticity and conspicuous consumption', *European Journal of Cultural Studies* 8:4, 403–26.

3 This is a Leverhulme funded project that forms part of the Goldsmiths Leverhulme Media Research Centre: Spaces, Connections, Control. The four researchers are Chris Berry, Kay Dickinson, Janet Harbord and Rachel Moore.

4 R. Koolhaas, 1995, 'The generic city', in R. Koolhaas, B. Mau, J. Sigler and H. Werlemann (eds), *S, M, L, XL*, New York: Monacelli (1250).

5 J. Crary, 2001, 'Modernity and the problem of attention' in *Suspensions of Perception: Attention, Spectacle, and Modern Culture*, Cambridge, MA: MIT Press, 11–80. The term 'regime of attention' occurs in footnote 15 on p.17.

6 www.urbanscreens.org/us08.html accessed 15 November 2013. The Media Facades conference in Berlin also attests to this eye-catching quality of the big public screen: www.mediaarchitecture.org/mediafacades2008/.

7 H. Grace, 2007, 'Monuments and the face of time: Distortions of scale and asynchrony in postcolonial Hong Kong', *Postcolonial Studies* 10:4, 467–83.

8 F. Casetti, 2007, 'Theory, post-theory neo-theories: Changes in discourses, changes in objects', *Cinémas: revue d'études cinématographiques / Cinémas: Journal of Film Studies* 17:2–3, Spring, 33–45.

9 J. D. Bolter and R. Grusin, 2000, *Remediation: Understanding New Media*, Cambridge, MA: MIT Press, 59.

10 Ibid. 61.

11 Crary would be an evident example of this approach.

12 I. Mülder-Bach, 1997, 'Cinematic ethnology: Siegfried Kracauer's *The White Collar Masses*', *New Left Review* 226, 47–8.

13 S. Kracauer, 1995, *The Mass Ornament: Weimar Essays*, trans. T. Y. Levin, Cambridge, MA: Harvard University Press, 75.

14 S. Kracauer, 1997, *The Salaried Masses: Duty and Distraction in Weimar Germany*, trans. Q. Hoare, London: Verso.

15 M. Coverley's 2006 overview includes William Blake's visions of London as New Jerusalem, Thomas De Quincey's opium-guided wanderings, Robert Louis Stevenson's *Jekyll and Hyde*, Alfred Watkin's ley lines, and more: *Psychogeography*, Harpenden: Pocket Essentials.

16 T. McDonagh, 1996, 'The dérive and situationist Paris' in L. Andreotti and X. Costa (eds), *Situationists, Art, Politics, Urbanism*, Barcelona: ACTAR, 60.

17 J. Rendell, 2006, *Art and Architecture: A Place Between*, London: I.B. Tauris, 188.

18 www.filming.networkrail.co.uk/locationlibrary/stpancrasinternational.aspx?t=1 accessed 15 November 2013.

19 J. Glover, 2007, *Modern Railways: Dictionary of Railway Industry Terms*, London: Ian Allen Publishing, 50–7.

20 www.brentcross.co.uk/visitor-info/about-the-centre/about-brent-cross accessed 15 November 2013.

21 www.completelyretail.co.uk/portfolio/Hammerson/scheme/Brent-Cross-Shopping-Centre-Brent-Cross/index accessed 15 November 2013.

22 www.blog.sciencemuseum.org.uk/insight/2013/05/04/a-great-exhibition/ accessed 15 November 2013.

23 T. Bennett, 1995, *The Birth of the Museum: History, Theory, Politics*, London and New York: Routledge; and more recently 2006, 'Civic seeing: Museums and the organisation of vision', in S. MacDonald (ed.), *Companion to Museum Studies*, Oxford: Blackwell, 263–81.

24 See A. Barry, 1998, 'On interactivity: Consumers, citizens and culture', in S. MacDonald (ed.), *The Politics of Display: Museums, Science and Culture*, London and New York: Routledge, 98–117.

25 M. Weber, 1988, 'Science as a vocation' in P. Lassman and I. Velody with H. Martins (eds), trans. M. John *Max Weber's 'Science as a Vocation'*, London: Routledge, 3–31.

26 H. Lefebvre, 2005, *Critique of Everyday Life: From Modernity to Modernism Volume 3*, trans. G. Elliot, London: Verso, 53.

27 G. Debord, 1983, *The Society of the Spectacle*, trans. K. Knabb, Detroit: Black and Red.

28 Lefebvre, 123.

29 Ibid., 127.

30 ibid., 127.

31 M. Saler, 2006, 'Modernity and enchantment: A historiographic review', *American Historical Review* 111:3, 692–716.

32 M. Pierson, 2002, *Special Effects: Still in Search of Wonder*, New York: Columbia University Press.

33 S. Cubitt, 2004, *The Cinema Effect*, Cambridge, MA: MIT Press, 19–21.

34 The work of Edgar Morin from the 1950s has only recently been translated into English and has had a belated impact on theorizing the cinematic image. For a contextualization of his writings and their reception, see the translator's introduction in E. Morin, 2005, *The Cinema, or The Imaginary Man*, Minneapolis: University of Minnesota Press, xi–xxxix.

35 Ibid. 9.

36 Ibid. 89.

37 Ibid. 85.

38 Ibid. 23.

9

Screens and Imagination: Technovisuality and Consumption in Hong Kong Urbanscapes

Felix Loi Ho Man

The concept of consumption is dependent on the use of visual signs of certain goods or objects as a meaning-bearer to consumers. Many scholars, however, have pointed out that consumption nowadays no longer means the taking of signs, as this meaning is becoming increasingly unstable in the age of media globalization. This is fundamentally linked to the mixed and prevalent use of technology, giving rise to newly emerging and differentiated global imaginations across different cultural contexts. This chapter is an attempt to look into the relationship between consumption and technology in the Hong Kong urbanscape, and explore how contemporary consumption in the local context is very much informed by a kind of global imagination specifically found in Hong Kong. It argues that technovisuality (i.e. visuality enabled by technology), embodied in our use of devices, provides us with techniques that shape the experience of consumption in a tense relation with the determinate mediations of media globalization and corporate/state interests. To demonstrate the operations of this experience of conformity and resistance, we examine screens in Hong Kong shopping malls and in a Mong Kok street; in each case, there is a specific articulation of the imagination of globality, intersecting with local interest groups and incidents, suggesting different yet mutually illuminating ways of conceptualizing the relationship between consumption and technovisuality.

Technovisuality and Imagination

Consumption, an everyday routine and experience, has long been used as a useful lens in the investigation of issues concerning the social or cultural nature of human life. Works with consumption as an analytic focus, ranging from the anthropological (Douglas) to the sociological, suggesting intricate social habitus (Bourdieu), all allow us to examine the meanings, or the sign values, of the goods being consumed within a given social context, providing us with a particular conception of social identity and leading us to a more profound understanding of everyday life.[1]

However, this general structuralist approach on the self-evidently ritualistic meaning of signs has become less applicable to contemporary globalized society, which, more than a vulgar logistic fact, has fundamentally re-defined the meaning of the social. Signs from globalized modernity, which replace *the* new with *novelties* from all around our life-world as informed by the anarchistic force of globalization, have been liberated in a spatial sense.[2] This process implies more than the expected burgeoning of complicated webs of signs, but, importantly, a qualitative change brought about by the liberation of the ordering of signs, as we shift from a practice of signs stubbornly rooted onto a normalized circuit to an *existentially globalized* world, behind which lies a permanent shift towards the labyrinth of mediation as suggested by Bruno Latour.[3] No longer can the relationship between people and the goods around us be taken organically. Instead, we need to deploy our faculty of imagination in overcoming our fundamentally necessary ignorance of the process of production, transportation and retailing of a mind-numbing variety of goods, thereby creating an imaginary 'apparent stability' in our perception of this otherwise total chaos of signs.[4] This paradigm shift, from an anthropological point of view, may be conceived as a post-Marxian realization of the idea of alienation and its overcoming.

This radical shift in the nature of the ordering of signs is, however, more complicated than the pessimistic narrative of alienation. Without resorting to the somewhat gloomy and value-laden Marxist conclusion of the loss of subjectivity, from the timely reminder of Arjun Appadurai on the social nature of globalization we know that imagination, now as a necessary totalizing agent coping with perpetual difference in the globalized local, has now become an independent social fact, which can be singled out in studies of consumption. While there is no denying that the state apparatus or corporate interests can still, with their omnipresent power, intrude into the shaping of imagination, its articulations in actual contexts are always independent of such interventions. In Appadurai's words, it is not only that '[o]rdinary people have begun to deploy their imaginations in the practice of their everyday lives',[5] but also that there lies the 'contested' nature of the imagination, which enjoys a relative autonomous status.[6]

What the common theoretical principle of the structuralist approach becomes increasingly unable to address is, therefore, not the quantitative but the qualitative change. In an age in which modernity is 'at large', the actual practice of consumption is fundamentally at variance with the simple quasi-scientific approach which structuralism has spearheaded. While consumption is desire for *the* new, its manifestation in the globalized era and its search for novelty, or the work of imagination in putting together the spontaneous presence of signs, can no longer be monopolized, nor can it be examined as a closed circuit of flow. Imagination, in this sense, is more than simply a new variable that abstracts and processes signs within the circuit of consumption; rather, it emphasizes the inherent complexity of the very situational mediation of the imagination with signs themselves. If, for the structuralists, studying consumption was the study of how the circulation of signs becomes a circuit, then now it must refocus on identifying a certain *articulation* of imagination in place during consumption. This concerns not only how exactly signs are organized by a particular imagination in the consumption process within a fixed period of time, but how the mechanism of that particular work of autonomous imagination is ultimately informed by the impossible Lacanian real or a boundless ur-imagination, in the radical search for the new.

In this new turn in the study of consumption, technology proves to be an ideal point of departure. Appadurai has identified media and migration as the two decisive factors contributing to his version of globalization,[7] but no less crucial is perhaps the role played by technology, which, to a certain extent, can even be considered as the common denominator for both media and migration. Particularly, it is the 'disenchantment of technology', by the incorporation of the awe of new technology into a new norm of life, that merits attention. This incorporation stems from, on the one hand, as Bloch has aptly pointed out, the slowing and trivialization of technological advancement after the

Industrial Revolution. On the other hand, more decisively, it resulted from the fact that the pure possibility of technological reproducibility has been systematically exploited by the logic of capitalism, which, together with instrumental rationality, turns everything into a kind of technology that can be manipulated to serve the utopian image generated by capital.[8]

This trivialization, however, has also contributed to the advancement of modernity in a spatial sense, in which '[m]odernity now seems more practical and less pedagogic, more experiential and less disciplinary'.[9] In Latour's sense, with the coming normalization of technology, the labyrinth of levels of mediation is now seen as an unnecessary complication, or, to the post-structuralists, ideology laid bare.

In late capitalist societies, as in Hong Kong, this relationship between consumption and technology is all the more riddled with tension. Very often, the corporate takes the monopolized role of the ruling regime in setting a predominant context, but the very *representational nature* of technology, which now includes everything that visualizes, does not simply reflect culturally meaningful signs offered by certain parties; rather, the articulation of our imagination is often directed by the route of visuality offered by corporate interests. On the other hand, we also observe the possibility of 'resistance', though in a sense different from the romantic conception of human resistance.[10]

The term technovisuality provides a useful embodiment of the points mentioned above. If technovisuality, the main concern of this chapter, is an appropriate point of departure in considering the consumption of signs under the impact of technology, this is because the new imagination has already taken the visual, a 'universally' translatable language, as a metaphorically and realistically appropriate candidate in explaining the compression of time and space given rise to by technology.

As part of a contribution in the investigation of the so far little-examined relationship between consumption and technology in Hong Kong, this chapter takes two consumption sites, Hong Kong shopping malls and Mong Kok streets, each representing a certain mode of interacting with the imagination of contemporary Hong Kong, alongside a particular type of technological construct, as examples to demonstrate the critical and yet elusive relationship between technology and consumption. In the first section, I want to examine how a new kind of imagination in Hong Kong urbanscape is developed from an earlier historical period of appropriating signs in the city. The emphasis in the second and third part will be, respectively, on a local shopping mall and streets of Mong Kok, exploring the possibility of alternative articulations of imagination in Hong Kong.

The public screen is selected as the point of focus in both parts, not because it is a kind of 'technology', which, strictly speaking, could be anything that can be utilized to direct our consumption process after the total instrumentalization of technology. Rather, it is selected because, compared to other less advanced technology, its manipulation produces more relatively obvious effects, especially in the past decade. Standing as an institutional tool manipulated especially by different corporate interests, and yet still holding space for uses outside of routine ones, it therefore permits us to be critical towards the manipulating powers behind the technology, whether these powers succeed or not in their use of technology.

'General Gentrification' of Hong Kong Public Space

Before turning to the two sites, we must first understand more about the emergence of the work of imagination specific to contemporary Hong Kong. As has been pointed out, Appadurai sees media and migration as the two factors key to globalization.[11] Hong Kong, in this regard, can be easily seen as a global city *par excellence*. The myth or truism of 'flow' brought about by migration, or more generally, the apparent personal mobility and the use of new media, is fully embodied in the massive change in the Hong Kong urbanscape in the last two decades, as it has become a global rather than a colonial city. Hong Kong residents, travelling from Kowloon or the New Territories to Central – regarded as the 'capital' of Hong Kong – no longer regard themselves as pilgrims, as they once did.[12] Instead, with the coming of the MTR (Mass Transit Railway) and the opening of cross-harbour tunnels in the 1970s and 1980s, intra-city travelling has become a very ordinary, convenient and affordable activity, if not a routine, for most.[13]

A less noticeable but much more decisive change of urbanscape took place in the 1970s and 1980s – the emergence of a new space and quality of consumption. If consumption is a prominent thing in a post-industrial city, then what happened at exactly the same time as the MTR and cross-harbour tunnels – namely, the gradual prohibition of hawking, as shopping malls became an increasing feature of urban space – could be regarded as much more significant. Since the 1980s, shopping malls have increasingly assumed a major, if not dominant, role in the ordering of consumption space in Hong Kong, replacing the local stores and hawking, which were the major means through which people bought and sold goods before the 1970s.[14] We may even say that this massive shift in the nature of consumption space is comparable to Haussmann's project of renovating Paris in the 1860s.[15]

We need only to compare those new shopping malls in Hong Kong with the 'suburban' shopping plazas or malls prevalent in the 1950s in the United States to get a sense of their spatial features. In Hong Kong, where malls are built above public transport hubs (MTR stations and bus stations), they seamlessly connect public transport with mall space, in such a way that the boundary difference between transport and malls has become virtually non-existent.[16] In fact, more than half of the major MTR stations are currently connected to malls in this way, and the urbanscape of Hong Kong has been radically restructured by such spaces, as Ackbar Abbas has suggestively discussed.[17]

While this façade of public space inside a corporate shopping mall is far from uniquely found in Hong Kong,[18] one must note that, in this case, it becomes virtually the only available choice. While, on the surface, many people in Hong Kong still choose not to enter such spaces, what is most significant about this development is that it amounts to a monopolization of public space, given that the MTR-mall space is in many areas the only choice left as public space. While relatively wealthy or commercial retail districts, such as Kowloon Tong Station (Festival Walk) and Kowloon Bay (Telford Plaza), have seen public space subsumed by mall space, the expansion of this kind of space has been so extensive that traditionally low-income districts, such as Wong Tai Sin (Wong Tai Sin Plaza), Tai Po (Uptown Plaza) and Chai Wan (New Jade Shopping Arcade and Hing Wah Plaza), have also been increasingly absorbed into this kind of appropriation and monopolization of space. Many of these places are immediately adjacent to stations, and public open space and street-space is increasingly made inaccessible by the use of footbridges designed to direct the flow of people through malls. In districts commonly regarded as 'new towns', such as Ma On Shan, Tseung Kwan O and Tin Shui Wai, where the difference between streets and recreational facilities has been maximized under a total compartmentalization process as part of governmental city planning, space is presented in such a way that people are required to go through the mall space in order to reach a certain destination. Though the pedestrian streets still remain, the long wait at traffic lights and the large area allocated to roads instead of pedestrians signifies that it is more advisable to walk through the mall.[19] It is, therefore, misleading to think that someone can simply choose to walk on the streets if he or she is not satisfied with the all-pervasive lure of consumption set by the mall. While in the relatively recent past, people might have naturally turned to streets as part of their daily routine, the building of poorly designed roads in new towns and the high level of air pollution means that more people are faced with the choice of whether to select streets or the new MTR-mall space as their public sphere; rather than an opportunity of freedom, this is more like the 'money or life' dilemma/false choice, presented by street muggers that Jacques Lacan relates in his Seminar XI.[20]

This radical change in urbanscape is no less than a 'general gentrification', as Neil Smith suggests,[21] of the urbanscape in Hong Kong. This change from a light industrial city to a white-collar consumer society is a story familiar to most, and the eventual gentrification is somewhat expected. However, what many may not be able to foresee is the extent of the process, and that many low-income people have to endure the high cost of daily necessities advertised as a privilege in an all-too-bright shopping centre. As Sharon Zukin rightly states, gentrification can always risk effacing the 'authenticity' of a city.[22] In the case of Hong Kong, the poor are left no choice but to turn to the chain store and the elegantly renovated shopping malls, although their disposable incomes do not really match the goods sold there. But more inauthentic is perhaps the new imagination of the social that is generated in this whole process of complicity between the Hong Kong government and corporate interests. The performative act of shopping in this kind of 'transparent' and 'mobile' urban space is too easily reduced to the articulation of imagination these two parties are trying to implant onto the population.

There is no lack of oppositional voices towards this increasingly blatant complicity between the two parties. In fact, the term 'land developer hegemony' (地產霸權) has been widely popularized in recent years across Hong Kong, as a term denoting the absolute power enjoyed by corporate land developers in the commercial scene.[23] In this connection, the 'Times Square Incident' that occurred in February 2008 was yet another instance documenting the violence of the 'developer hegemony' in Hong Kong. The incident began when complaints were made alleging that security guards in Times Square Mall had ejected people strolling round the huge open area of the square underneath the building. The space was understood to be a public area, but it was revealed that it had been illegally appropriated as part of the property of Wharf Holdings, the owners of Times Square.[24]

This sudden discovery was astonishing to the general public and immediately triggered an avalanche of debates and discussions concerning the actual rights of Wharf to the square, attracting wide attention, ranging from politicians and local media to social activists and local artists, each expressing his or her own concern about the illegal occupation of the open area by Times Square.[25] After a series of investigations, the government finally clarified that, although the area of the square belonged to Times Square, it was a designated recreational area open for the public, which meant that security guards had no right to interfere with activities performed in public, so long as they did not infringe the law. However, despite increasing public awareness towards the fundamentally questionable motive behind the less than justified collaboration between the Hong Kong government and corporate interests, public concern and dissatisfaction was still aimed at the complicity of the two parties in controlling the supply and thus the value of residential property in general; but only relatively little attention has been paid to rights to have extensive public space available to use.

Clearly, the emergence of this new public space is central to both the articulation of imagination *and* its formation, especially for the younger generation. There is thus little doubt that Hong Kong has reached a historical moment in which the work of imagination, as outlined by Appadurai, has become a social fact. However, the particular genealogy of the conception of flow in Hong Kong can and should be traced back to the beginnings of modernization in this city. To be sure, Hong Kong is fundamentally a migrant city of a special kind. Starting from the early twentieth century, it has become an important strategic point for the massive and interminable political change on the Chinese mainland. In an attempt to seek a place distanced from the political turmoil in China, many chose to move to colonial Hong Kong, treating it as no more than a relatively safe shelter away from political and economic instability.

Even after the end of World War II, Hong Kong still continued to serve as one of the most favoured sites of migration for those Chinese on the mainland who sought to escape from the rule of the Chinese

Communist Party, particularly during the Cultural Revolution in the 1960s and 1970s. As a result, the image of a migrant, if not a refugee, city hardly receded even after the 1970s, during which it was commonly said that the local consciousness started to grow.[26] The myth of contemporary Hong Kong as an international or cosmopolitan city can be seen as an attempt by the political authority to domesticate this inherently anarchistic ur-imagination of 'flow' to serve their own interest.

There is little account of how the fact of constant migration has affected the sense of space and imagination through the decades, and especially how this genealogy of flow may have given shape to the essence of the global imagination. The following two sections will be dedicated to the actual manifestation of the imagination in two different types of consumption sites in Hong Kong, in order to identify the articulation of imagination at play in a closer manner.

Screens and the Screening of Imagination in Hong Kong Shopping Malls

Malls, as a specific site of consumption, are so ubiquitous in the Hong Kong urbanscape[27] that it is possible to say it has undergone a shift in the pattern of consumption indicative of a general change in the spatial economies of Hong Kong, as a result of mall developments.

This section on the general technovisual nature of Hong Kong malls as a representative aspect of Hong Kong urbanscape contributes to a more systematic study of this phenomenon. Following a general anthropological approach referred to earlier, a historical shift in the consumption mode of Hong Kong shopping malls will first be outlined and explained with reference to the general change of consumption in malls, followed by a synchronic account of the conforming effect of screens in New Town Plaza as a major example. I will show that its then new installation of visual screens acts as part of the support required to sustain the emergent imagination of globalization. After establishing the general mutually supportive relationship between imagination and technovisuality, the chapter also considers the inherently unstable relationship between institutionalized power and technology, in the case of the popular spectacle of the Beijing Olympic Games in the Plaza as an appropriation of the screens. Additionally, the controversy around Times Square public space and artistic responses to this suggest a more versatile conception of the articulation of imagination in the face of corporate or state interests' preferred forms of visuality in mall spaces.

As already argued, the major spatial change in Hong Kong in recent decades is highly significant, and the proliferation of malls is emblematic of this change. It is notable that the early malls and department stores in Hong Kong – as sites for conspicuous consumption – considered their main target to be tourists and high income locals alike, and were much more remote to Hong Kong people than they are today.[28] In recent years, however, instead of continuing to stand as specific ritualistic areas, malls in Hong Kong are increasingly stripping themselves of the isolation characteristic of department stores and are regarded as neutral public space. This, in retrospect, is perfectly in line with the kind of change in imagination brought about by globalization. As already outlined in the previous section, the MTR as the major mass transport system is connected to malls, and malls are themselves also increasingly inter-connected, marking the completion of modernization in Hong Kong. Besides this connectivity, one may also note the spatial presentation of these new malls, which have all tried to maximize the sense of spatial visibility within their sometimes tiny space, in order to offer a sense of high transparency reminiscent of a naive conception of globalization. All in all, with these changes, Hong Kong shopping malls are increasingly being 'gentrified' as they are completely fused with the domestic public sphere, as noted in the previous section.

Clearly, the contextualization process governing consumption has changed so radically that a new way of studying malls is called for. On the one hand, there are accounts regarding the architectural construction of modern malls,[29] while on the other, there are studies on shopping malls as sites of active identity construction through consumption.[30] In other words, studies frequently focus either on the material existence of the mall or the cultural significance of malling, but not the relationship between them. In the face of the increasingly intricate setting of modern malls, it seems increasingly important to pay attention to both these factors, and restate the key question regarding consumption by locating the underlying dynamics governing the precise act of consumption, namely, our particular type of global imagination reflecting the eclectic visibility of the 'general gentrification' in Hong Kong. This can help to underline the influence of a new socio-economy, of which the historical origin and mental tendency are elaborated in the highly observant account provided by Tai-lok Lui.[31]

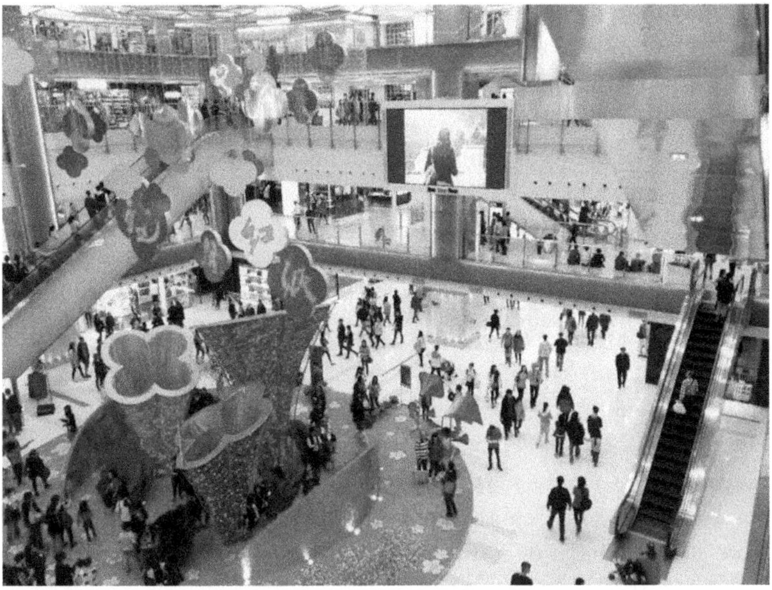

Figure 9.1. New Town Plaza.

As already argued in the previous section, technovisuality is an excellent point to start our study. Here, one may note how New Town Plaza, a mall that was built adjacent to Shatin MTR station, serves as a good example of the connectivity just discussed. Just as many other malls in Hong Kong, the Plaza, particularly Phase One, enjoys the absolute privilege of being seamlessly connected to the MTR station. What is slightly different in this case is perhaps the extensive use of screens in the mall. Among the many Hong Kong malls, New Town Plaza may be more ambitious, with its three gigantic rectangular screens installed in three areas, resulting in a long visualized corridor to Shatin Town Hall, once the landmark of the public sphere for the old Hong Kong. Sun Hung Kei Properties,[32] a private corporation, owns the mall, and it has complete control over the use of the screens; it would be revealing to analyse its use of the three gigantic screens separately, to see how the mode of consumption has been affected by screens and the route of visuality.[33]

Among the three screens, the one closest to the MTR is located in an open area with much space for strolling, and presumably this is the one that is deliberately placed to attract the attention of most people.

Different from the generous gigantic screen on Times Square in Causeway Bay, it shows not news reports but fashion shows and music videos, and this is commercially understandable if the videos are assumed to be promoting the latest fashion news. But if one tries to equip oneself with trends of fashion, then the screens become disappointing, because they are barely audible, if not completely mute, especially in peak hours. When it comes to the second much smaller screen, which broadcasts news reports, one may reasonably wonder why the reports are not on the first screen to maximize the use of news reports. And while there are different kinds of exhibitions constantly found in this central area, it seems that everything is in a good harmony.

What is more ironic, however, is that this second screen is situated *just* in front of an escalator, which means that only those taking the escalator, who would normally only watch for a few seconds, could comfortably see the reports shown on the screen. It is as if the reports were just a reminder to consumers that the world is still being reported, and thus is still running.

The third screen, the one installed above the exit of the Plaza, is much more soothing, as it is simply an advertising screen, constantly showing mute and boring images and at times images of the mall itself, making it no more than a changeable advertisement block marking the boundary of the mall. In fact, the very position of this third screen blocks the visual line of visitors walking towards Shatin Town Hall, one of the larger cultural spaces in Hong Kong and one of the more representative 'genuine' public spaces in the city. This presents a dilemma to the mall, insofar as the illusory continuity of the mobility of the public space has to be kept without, however, threatening the flow of capital by introducing a heterogeneous object. It is as if the sole *raison d'être* of this third screen, installed on the huge transparent plate of glass, is to exclude from the mall the very existence of the Town Hall, which threatens to endanger capital flow, without actually terminating the space of flow.

Seen this way, the three screens seem detached from their content.[34] Obviously, in the face of these commercially mild screens, it is too simple to assume that the malls are actively encouraging consumption by advertising. Indeed, people are not reminded to consume in the traditional sense, at least not as manifest in the soundless music videos of, for example, Avril Lavigne and news reports. That screens in Hong Kong malls are mere direct stimulants to consumption would

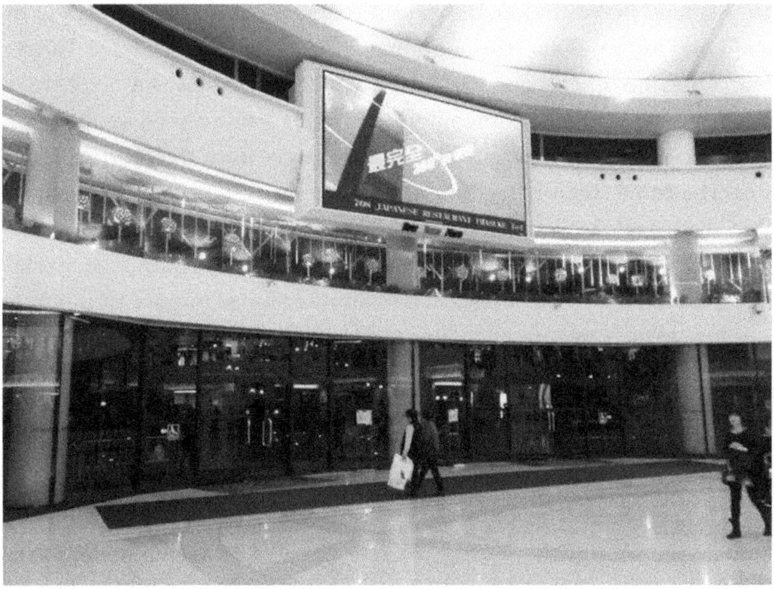

Figure 9.2. New Town Plaza, Shatin, screen near exit to Town Hall square.

thus seem unconvincing, but neither are they simply redundant; they help direct the global imagination in a certain way.

In this respect, the very geographical materiality of shopping malls may be a clue to the more concrete functioning of the screen in serving corporate interests. This examination of the spatial 'limitation' is particularly revealing in the case of Hong Kong, where the restriction of space often forces malls to configure the arrangement of space in a more nuanced way, often without being able to achieve a perfect phantasmagoric effect,[35] and this differentiates them from those in the United States, where Disneyfication of any scale can be carried out without much constraint.

In the case of New Town Plaza, which, as already mentioned, is a long visual corridor in terms of its geography, the 'constitutive gap' that inevitably exists is perhaps the space unattended by the gaze of the screens. In fact, the space of New Town Plaza, at least for Phase One, has been arranged in such a way that it is difficult *not* to feel the spatial existence of the screen. However, the middle point of the whole Phase One, situated precisely between the first and the second screen, can only be marginally considered as being infused with the ambience of the screens. Nevertheless, this critical conceptual abyss is remedied by the corridor of global cosmetic brands, such as Chanel, Estée Lauder and Dior. Their existence is perfectly justified when one explains it with regard to their profitability – this area can be seen as the most easily accessible and presentable location, away from the bustling scene near the MTR station, and thus it is only the most profitable – and visible – cosmetic stores that can afford the rent.

However, from the perspective of spatial harmony, this area, exclusively dedicated to cosmetics, serves another more important function insofar as one takes into account the previously mentioned gap. To be sure, the extreme transparency typical of the high-end cosmetic stores acts as a deterrent and yet is subtly fantasizing because of the promise of an unreachable zone that somehow fits perfectly into the imagination triggered by the screens. The kind of global imagination promoted in the Plaza is, simply put, to justify the intrusion of transnational capital.[36]

The use of gigantic screens in New Town Plaza is much more theoretically understandable in this regard. More than as advertisement blocks, they are inherently connected with an intricate network flow, ultimately resulting in an apparent transparency in line with globalization. The big soundless screen and the vertical screen showing music videos and fashion shows, for instance, trigger not the desire to consume certain designated goods, but rather to consume the ever-changing flow of information. Likewise, the seemingly misplaced screen showing news reports is simply a most effective reminder to consumers that the world is running in a globalized fashion, without distracting them with the real content of the reports. The third screen, which is half-deserted because of its inconvenient location, may be an attempt to lower the apparently huge difference between the mall and the outer world.[37] By exploiting the public socio-economic resources available, then, the government and corporate interests are collaborating in constructing a superior space of global imagination, in which freedom and equality is seemingly included but is in fact a highly eclectic form of visibility.

However, the space of the shopping mall is still different from the total technological colonization by corporate interest, described by Jonathan Crary as 'a zone of insensibility, of amnesia, of what defeats the possibility of experience.'[38] As already argued in the introduction, the technovisual appropriation of the imagination by malls is not the complete story, since it lacks the discrepancies attesting to the creative nature of the imagination. In this connection, the 2008 Beijing Olympic Games, an event dominating

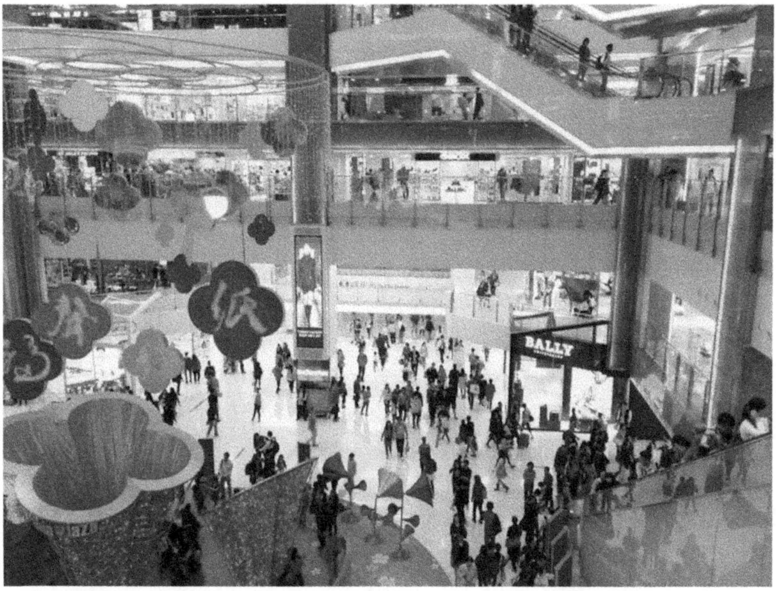

Figure 9.3. New Town Plaza, vertical screen for catwalk shows.

the media environment in Hong Kong at the time it occurred, shows us how the imagination could appropriate and articulate the route of visuality as set by corporate interests in a fascinatingly different way.

During the period of the Olympic Games, Hong Kong people gathered around the screen in New Town Plaza to watch the Olympics, effectively altering the through-flow of masses in the mall. Rather than strolling round the mall in a way more or less designated by the mall, the screen showing the Olympics attracted a huge crowd of people, stopping to indulge themselves in viewing this public event, seriously disrupting the order of the mall, while the security guards had to remain passive to keep order.[39] Contrary to easy reductionism, this gathering phenomenon was by no means the expression of support for the PRC government, but, above all, a rightful demand to utilize the designated public space. The demands of the imagination therefore resulted in the disruption of the spatial arrangements of the mall, demonstrating that the space can be occupied for uses other than the needs of consumption.[40] In a way, this forming of a crowd of onlookers is also somehow reminiscent of a refugee mentality, which is a major part of the origin of the flow imagination, as argued in the previous section.

In another more conscious appropriation, a quasi-performance artwork by a group of Hong Kong artists and social activists has shown us what we could do to this 'hegemony of imagination'. Gathering on Time Square and sitting comfortably on a sheet made by local artist Lee Kit, the artists simply treated the space as a countryside gathering. Rather than protesting about how Times Square appropriated the space for their own use, they turned themselves into a screen demonstrating how the space could be used or consumed in a way beyond the hierarchy of visuality designated by capitalist power.[41] Rather than simply an abstract live lesson teaching people in Hong Kong how to imagine the new, it is more like a way of loosening the kind of imagination that has existed all along but has increasingly been led to a point of suffocation in recent years of economic downturn.[42]

To conclude, by tracing the genealogy of the form of imagination in Hong Kong, and critically placing it within the actual context of local shopping malls, we may observe the random ruptures arising from less than perfect compatibility and begin to see how the articulated imagination is both a product of systematic corporatization between the government and corporate interests *and* a potential challenge to this exploitation.

Mong Kok and the Deconstruction of Imagination

It would have been the end of the story had Mong Kok, the most bustling consumption site in the history of modern Hong Kong, been turned into a shopping mall. But, as the busiest retail area, it stubbornly remains a district distinctly different from the clean shopping malls, yet is as busy, or even busier, than they are. Indeed, if shopping malls are the dominant type of space of consumption and gathering in Hong Kong, then one should never forget that places like Mong Kok streets are far from on the wane.[43] Although there is the presence of a malling tendency as in the case of Langham Place, which is not unlike New Town Plaza in its ability to create a space of continuity between the malls, the streets and public transport, Mong Kok remains a district which distances itself from the incorporation of governmental planning by keeping intact the noisy and disturbing street scenes, which stand in marked contrast to the normative visuality found in malls.

In this section I present a description of the current unique urbanscape of Mong Kok, comparing it to malls, followed by a discussion

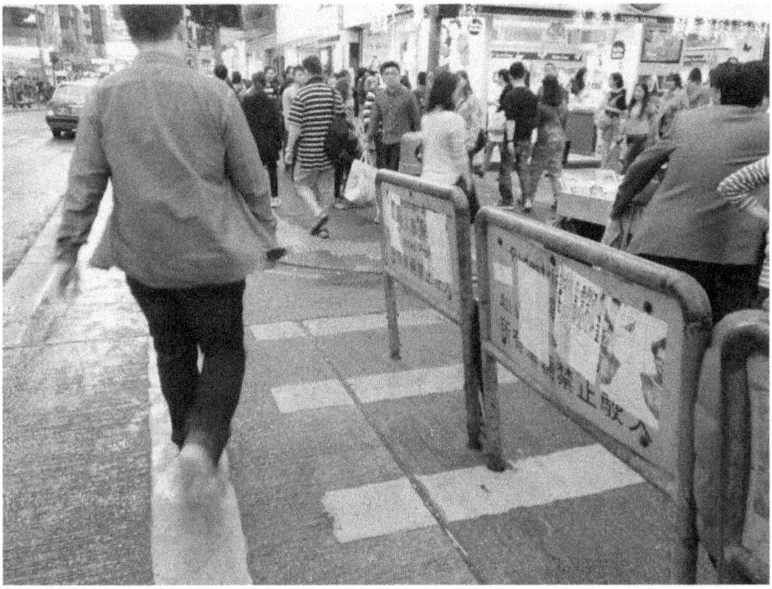

Figure 9.4. Mong Kok, road barriers demarcating pedestrian area.

of how this disparate urbanscape is connected to the same type of imagination articulated significantly differently from that of the malls, pointing to another possibility of the imagination enabled by uneven power distribution. This chapter concludes by offering an opportunity to reflect on the political implication of some significant incidents that have occurred on the street, such as the acid attacks of 2008–2010 and the Lam Wai Sze' incident of 2013, which all hint at the future of this alternative public space in Hong Kong.

The streets of Mong Kok can be regarded as an exception to the extensive coverage of malls in Hong Kong's public space. In contrast to the 'unfriendly space' of streets as distinct from malls within the gentrification of Hong Kong space, in Mong Kok pedestrians are no longer the 'hunted' and automobiles the 'privileged', as Lefebvre might see it, in the extreme cases of compartmentalization.[44] Rather, the size, or the rate of flow of the former has become so enormous that pedestrians demand more rights to the city. Particularly, around 2000, the Hong Kong government began to implement plans for pedestrian zones in Mong Kok and other areas where pedestrian traffic was already high, announcing that the Transport Department was 'committed to putting

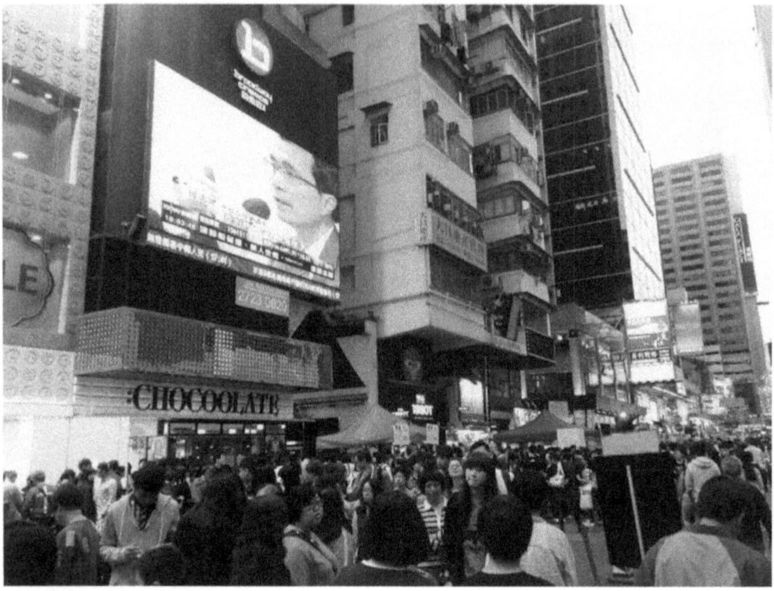

Figure 9.5. Screen above entrance to Broadway Cinemas, Sai Yeung Choi Street, Mong Kok.

more emphasis on the interests of pedestrians'.[45] Several streets in Mong Kok thus became 'part-time pedestrian streets', while two became 'traffic calming streets' in 2002 and 2003. Besides these two types of pedestrian schemes, there is a third called a 'full-time pedestrian street', representing a total change of road use. While there is no need to conjecture about the underlying governmental rationale behind the scheme, the same conformity to a kind of normative visibility seems clear. This can be seen in the quantitative description of the severity of the traffic flows and the display of before-after images for comparison – not dissimilar to those in cosmetic surgery advertisements, suggesting the government is committed to constructing an area of specific visibility.[46]

A synchronic study of the employment of technovisuality in Mong Kok helps reveal the nature of the exact articulated imagination. The different nature of screens in Mong Kok can easily be observed when one watches the news reports on the screen of Broadway Cinema on Sai Yeung Choi Street. In contrast to the news reports in New Town Plaza, the sound of this screen has been deliberately turned up, to the extent that it has virtually become a radio, especially in view of the unwillingness of pedestrians to watch the screen, which has always been hard to see because of its angle. By the same token, a nearby video store has its screen disabled by turning up the volume of the sound to an almost unbearable level, a common practice unavoidable in the narrow streets of Hong Kong crowded with pedestrians. Added to this audiovisual chaos are constant disruptions to pedestrians in Mong Kok streets. People are being constantly harassed by sales and survey interviewers, assailed by Falun Gong practitioners and their horrific images of alleged Chinese government torture of practitioners, and disturbed by street singers and drama groups. Screens can barely compete with the intensities of demanding bodies impinging on the space of passers-by.

The extreme geographical limitation of Mong Kok streets, in a way gives rise to its precise advantage over malls. It is virtually impossible to create any coherent and totalizing kind of visual route comparable to that which we observe in malls, despite, or precisely because of, its seeming disorder as compared to the unified hierarchy of visuality in malls. This disorder, however, becomes another articulation. To be sure, behind the range of street-level attention-demands, such as the broadband roll-over booths, photo-taking events as promotions for the latest products, street performances reminiscent of exotic circuses, and, above all, the 'mini malls' in Mong Kok, or even the many specialized stores, one can smell the air of globalization everywhere. Disorder, in this regard, is seen as a symbol of being extremely up-to-date. If, as Hegel has said and Benedict Anderson has quoted, the reading of a newspaper is a new prayer for the modern man, then the strolling and consumption experience in Mong Kok becomes a new experience of prayer, as it satisfies longing for a global community in a existentially stateless city, as in Hong Kong.[47]

A series of incidents demonstrates well a similar kind of imagination articulated in a different way. Between 2008 and 2010, a number of acid attacks in Mong Kok shocked people, and the subsequent response may serve as a lens onto this seeming chaos. On 13 December 2008, a plastic bottle filled with corrosive liquid was thrown onto Sai Yeung Choi Street South, hurting 46 pedestrians. Two subsequent attacks followed six and seven months later, and this prompted the government to install cameras on Mong Kok buildings. A police reward of HKD900,000 was announced and speculation on the culprit abounds, but until now, no capture or conviction has occurred. But even more notable is the fact that, even after three incidents involving a hundred victims in total, it seems that few think that Mong Kok has become a dangerous place.

On the contrary, everything remains the same, except that the police have become a more regular presence on the street. In short, people are not deterred by the incidents. Maybe it is not a lack of awareness of the danger, but precisely the awareness that danger is always present in Mong Kok, which make this less than a concern to visitors. The constant harassment and extreme density have rendered the place a somewhat transient location, in which danger is always present, but whether it really poses threats to them *here and now* is their major concern, and the answer is clear.

The precarious nature of this imagination is, in a sense, in perfect conjunction with the 'politics of disappearance' proposed by Ackbar Abbas,[48] who thinks that a form of disappearance is the very culture of Hong Kong. But we must distinguish this from the kind of 'reverse hallucination' also suggested by Abbas in pointing to a sense of the stability of Hong Kong. While malls use technology to create an illusion of the stability of ahistoricity, the use of technology in Mong Kok follows another route, arriving at a more complex network of mediation, traceable back to the socio-economic condition of Hong Kong in the 1960s and 1970s, a period many scholars have seen as the formation of a sense of Hong Kong locality.[49]

Too often the Hong Kong economic miracle is attributed to a kind of 'non-intervention' strategy said to be embraced by the Hong Kong government, which is not only incorrect, but also blurs the microscopic elements contributing to the miracle. For one thing, the core element contributing to the success is actually the flexible use of labour in production. Labour is responsible for its own production, which is organized not with an institutionalized rule but a highly contingent mobilization of labour.[50] With economic prosperity, what has disappeared in the proliferation of malls is precisely this kind of complex effort of mediation, while in Mong Kok the idea of 'disappearance', as Abbas sees it, is precisely the best manifestation of part of Hong Kong culture.[51] Here, the migrant history mentioned before may be complemented by this socio-economic history of Hong Kong.

The common economic root points to how we are to conceive of the relation between the two articulations of imaginations. By comparing the two ways of mediation, I am not denying that Mong Kok is

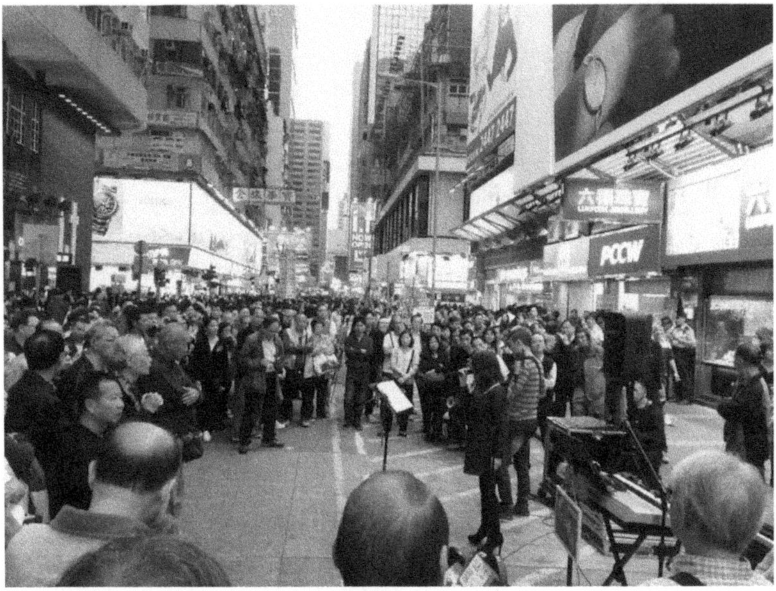

Figure 9.6. Sai Yeung Choi Street South, public performance.

preferred to malls as a historical mark in its highly resistant relation to the abstract global imagination promoted in the shopping malls, not because Mong Kok is a genuine legacy of Hong Kong culture while malls are not, as, after all, they are both part of the everyday life of Hong Kong people. Rather, what I would like to stress is how the extensive malling experience has been systematically depriving the masses of the opportunity to reflect upon their own historical position, especially in recent years. It is tempting to call this articulation of imagination a kind of proletarian one, for its opposition towards a bourgeois one. Rather than two co-existing modes of imagination, it seems that the gentrified articulation is a more developed form, while the proletarian one gives rise to more possibilities of imagination, as it involves an active deployment of imagination into different possible articulations. In Appadurai's term, Mong Kok truly witnesses the possibility of 'grassroots globalization' or 'globalization from below.'[52]

It is no accident that the space of Sai Yeung Choi Street South has become increasingly politicized and contested, as it is still beyond direct institutional control. In recent years, this street, as the central part of Mong Kok, has increasingly assumed a role as a site for political actions, especially in the form of public forums, mostly by leftist social activists and politicians. While it would be impossible to reduce their strategic use of the street to a single political motive, the common anti-establishment spirit shared between them is quite noticeable, and this points to an increasing consciousness of social injustice, evidenced in the clearly widening gap between the rich and the poor – a result of the increased narrowing of the channelling of possibilities.

This dwindling of possibilities can also be observed when we turn to another part of Mong Kok: Tung Choi St, between Boundary St and Dundas St – the so-called 'Ladies Market' or 'Ladies Street' (女人街). This has been losing its vitality under increasing governmental intervention. An officially designated street of tourism in Mong Kok, 'Ladies' Street' represents an epitome of the history of hawking in Hong Kong, providing an historical register of how the imagination of visibility can be utilized to engulf the space of the other imagination. Noted for hawkers selling a wide variety of goods, it is however the only legitimate site for such activities, with the gradual and systematic banning of itinerant hawking, long a source of economic support for many Hong Kong people before the 1970s.[53]

Governmental intervention in the control of hawker licences has undermined much of the street's vitality, so that it increasingly caters to the exotic gaze of tourists, while at the same time gradually and systematically ousting hawkers from the Hong Kong urbanscape. The insistence on keeping a unitary style of streetscape and the display of an increasingly expected range of goods has eventually made it, in some respects, the first shopping mall in Mong Kok.[54] If the pedestrian scheme is just a chance to turn it back to its original use, then this 'legitimatization' is just part of city planning in disallowing the existence of hawkers in other parts of Hong Kong, especially when one considers the fact that it is the last legal location of this form of trade.[55] The government, in a variety of ways, including its active support for the centrality of the capitalist mode, is depriving people of the chance to choose a way of life by dominating the socio-economic resources available in the formation of imagination.

Finally, one of the biggest recent scandals on the street, the so-called 'Lam Wai Sze incident', may offer us some clues as to the future of Mong Kok public space. On 14 July 2013, Lam, a primary school teacher, was recorded on video shouting obscenities at police handling a dispute between Falun Gong supporters and members of a

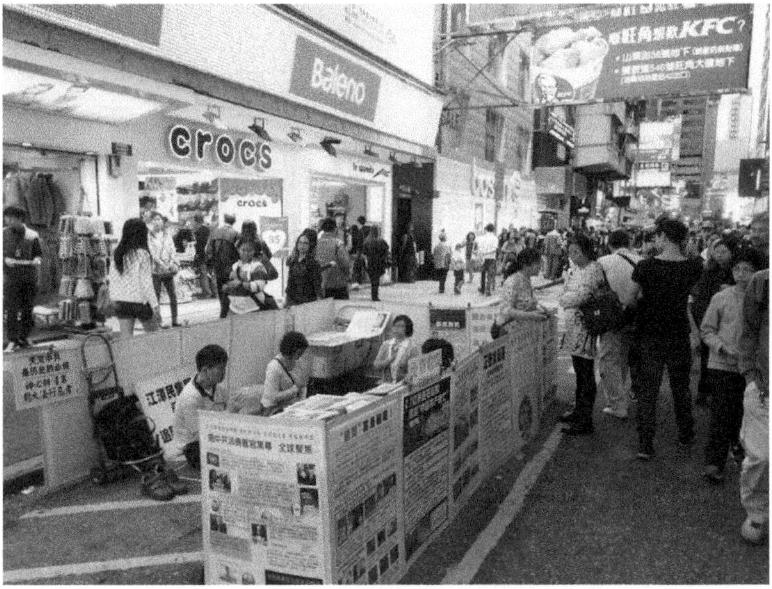

Figure 9.7. Falun Gong supporters on Sai Yeung Choi South Street.

pro-Beijing group, Hong Kong Youth Care Association, who regularly harass the Falun Gong.[56] The video was uploaded to YouTube and Lam was subsequently heavily criticized by the pro-Beijing media for not respecting the police and for using explicit language in public.[57]

To many, this incident itself clearly serves only as a means for the increasingly fierce political power struggle between the pro-democratic and the pro-Beijing parties. However, what lies behind the whole incident is not only the right of speech, but also a 'right' towards the visual, which is all the more important in a city of ultra-high population density, as in Hong Kong. Increasingly, the spatial has given way to the visual, as the latter can always convey messages in a more effective way. The extreme profusion of the use of smartphones in the Hong Kong urbanscape, for instance, testifies to how an average person may have an alternative choice in visuality. But if one wants to influence others, it is necessary to turn to space, which is often a prerequisite of the visual. As convenient and space-saving as are roll-up banners, which are everywhere found in Mong Kok and have arguably become the most commercially viable advertisement in Hong Kong because of their extremely low cost, they still need space for exhibition. The harassment

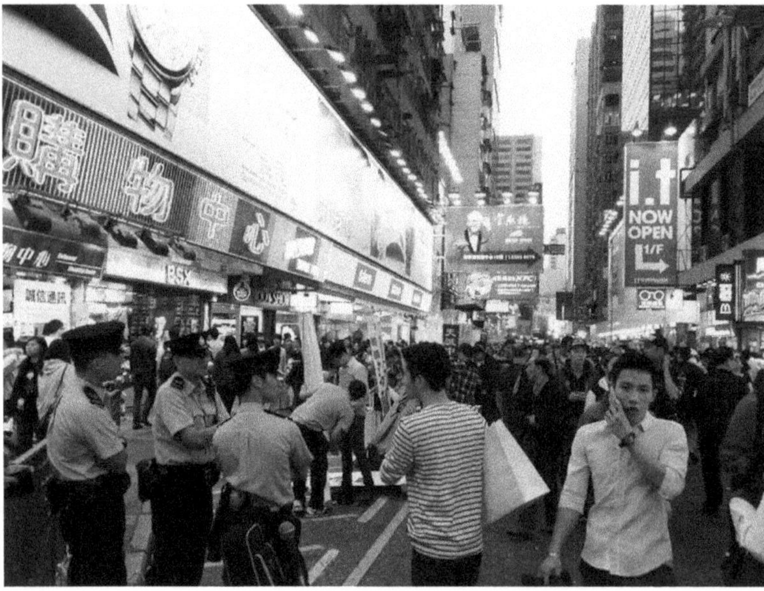

Figure 9.8. Police presence in Sai Yeung Choi Street.

of the Falun Gong by blocking their 'screens' (as represented by the booths and boards) and the reluctance of the police to defend this 'visual right' of display is particularly worrying in Hong Kong, where the possible ways to voice dissenting opinions have become more and more difficult, with increasing self-censorship of the local mass media.[58] In any case, the differential use of space on the Mong Kok streets can hardly be labelled as naturally 'liberating', but it clearly prompts local people to reconsider the possibility of a different technovisual presence, as a space for expressive possibilities within their life-world.

Such creative experiments may come to an end; the pedestrian scheme in Mong Kok underwent a major change in January 2014, when roads were reopened to traffic during weekdays under the new arrangement. This new practice looks like a regression, as it threw the baby out with the bathwater. If the infringement of rights continues, perhaps what remains to be seen is whether the Occupy Central movement,[59] as a last resort, can serve to defend what we might call the 'right to the visual'. Bodily presence is, after all, the last irreducible visual and the most primitive kind of technovisual presence, analogous to the as yet inassimilable need for sleep in 24/7 late capitalism.[60]

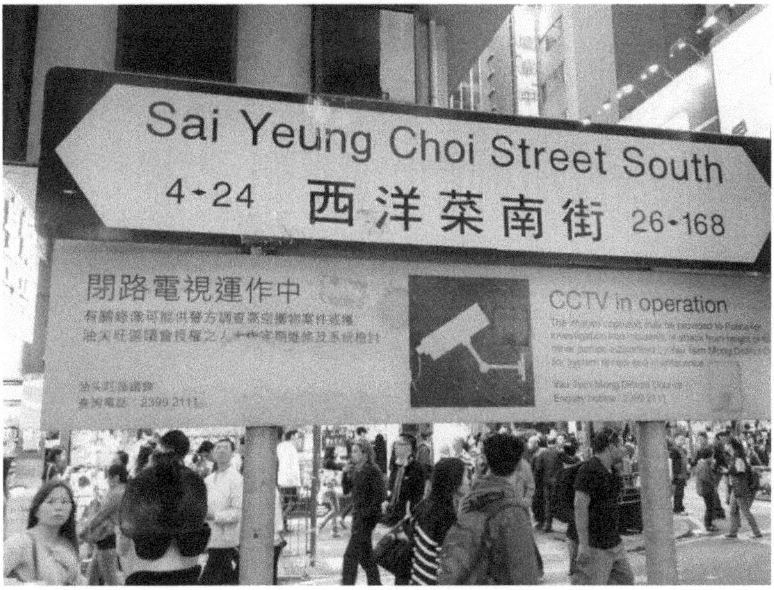

Figure 9.9. Street sign.

Conclusion

This chapter, by examining the role of imagination in consumption, by no means claims to exhaust the ways of investigating Hong Kong consumption. Rather, it is the hope that, with the contemporary role and nature of technology demonstrated, a general framework of analysis of the relationship between consumption and technovisuality can be established for further analysis.

In another less explicit yet equally important way, contemporary technology, which bears the mark of modernity, a hope to a better future, is always related to the vitality of a culture. It is the hope of this chapter that the study of consumption can lead to a more comprehensive discussion of issues concerning democracy and cultural harmony.

Notes

1 M. Douglas and B. Isherwood, 1996, *The World of Goods: Towards an Anthropology of Consumption*. London: Routledge; P. Bourdieu, 1984, *Distinction: A Social Critique of the Judgment of Taste*, trans. R. Nice London: Routledge Kegan Paul.

2 A. Appadurai, 1996, *Modernity at Large: Cultural Dimensions of Globalization* Minneapolis: University of Minnesota Press.
3 B. Latour, 1999, 'A Collective of Humans and Nonhumans' in *Pandora's Hope: Essays on the Reality of Science Studies*. Cambridge, MA: Harvard University Press, 174–215.
4 A. Appadurai, 2001, 'Grassroots globalization and the research imagination' in A. Appadurai (ed.), *Globalization*. Durham: Duke University Press, 5.
5 Appadurai, *Modernity at Large*, 5.
6 Ibid. 4. See also Appadurai 'Grassroots globalization and the research imagination', 6–7.
7 Appadurai, *Modernity at Large*, 5.
8 E. Bloch, 1995, *The Principle of Hope*, trans. N. Plaice, S. Plaice and P. Knight. Cambridge, MA: MIT Press. The concept of instrumental rationality is from M. Horkheimer and T. Adorno, 2002, *Dialectic of Enlightenment: Philosophical Fragments*, G. S. Noerr (ed.), trans. E. Jephcott. Stanford, CA: Stanford University Press.
9 Appadurai, *Modernity at Large*, 10.
10 This conception of social intervention with technology has been concisely explained by N. Dyer-Witheford in his 1999 *Cyber-Marx: Cycles and Circuits of Struggle in High-Technology Capitalism*, Urbana: University of Illinois Press, especially in the chapter on 'cycles'.
11 Appadurai, *Modernity at Large*.
12 S. M. Yau, 1997,《看眼難忘——在香港長大》*Unforgettable Glimpse: Growing Up in Hong Kong*. Hong Kong: Qing wen shu wu, 17–22.
13 Originally a company with its network limited to Hong Kong Island and Kowloon, MTR underwent a merger with KCRC (Kowloon-Canton Railway Corporation) in 2007, keeping its name MTR and extending the network to the New Territories; Shatin is one station in the New Territories. For the corporate history of the MTR, please refer to R. Yeung, 2008, *Moving Millions: The Commercial Success and Political Controversies of Hong Kong's Railways*, Hong Kong: Hong Kong University Press,.
14 K. F. Ma, 2002, 〈流行與分眾/百貨公司之死〉'Fashion and differentiation/the death of the department store' in C H. Ng and C. W. Cheung (eds), *Reading Hong Kong Popular Cultures 1970–2000*, Hong Kong: Oxford University Press, 58–68.
15 For the lasting influence of the Haussmann Project, see, for instance, W. Benjamin, 1939, 'Paris, the capital of the nineteenth century' in Benjamin, 2006, *The Writer of Modern Life: Essays on Charles Baudelaire*, Cambridge, MA: Harvard University Press.
16 There are of course some exceptions to this general ordering of the malls in Hong Kong. Consider, for instance, the relatively new malls, such as

Megabox in Kowloon Bay and HomeSquare in Shatin, both of which are comparable to the gigantic suburban car-parking malls in the United States. The functional division of labour is also evident here, as one can often find stores that sell goods which need vehicles for transportation, such as IKEA.

17 A. Abbas, 1997, *Hong Kong: Culture and the Politics of Disappearance*, Minneapolis: University of Minnesota Press, 143–4. In fact, some malls are directly managed by the MTR, including Telford Plaza in Kowloon Bay, one of the larger malls in Hong Kong. For a list of malls managed by MTR, see the website of MTR Malls: www.mtrmalls.com

18 On the idea of shopping malls as neutral public space in the United States, see E. Ralph, 1987, *The Modern Urban Landscape*, London: Croom Helm.

19 Adding fuel to this monopolization of space was the arrival of the Link Reit in Hong Kong in 2005. The Link Reit was a former Hong Kong government company managing many shopping centres and markets. It was privatized in 2005, more or less as a result of neoliberalization sweeping across the world from the 1990s. At the time of its privatization, it seemed that most Hong Kong people welcomed such a move, with the neoliberal rhetoric of efficiency and renovation works perfectly in line with the demand for spatial connectivity. However, the heavy-handed increase in rents in its many markets located in low-income districts caused a wave of closures of traditional small individually owned stores that simply could not afford the new exorbitant rents, Many of the old stores enjoyed high prestige, and served as a part of Hong Kong's intangible collective memory. Many Hong Kongers lamented how these stores were replaced by supermarkets and chain stores, and began to realize that the Link was actively destroying the nuanced cohesive force endowing the neighbourhood in the older districts with meaning.

20 J. Lacan, 1978, *The Four Fundamental Concepts of Psychoanalysis*, J.-A. Miller (ed.), trans. A. Sheridan, New York: Norton, 212. This situation in Hong Kong is all the more ubiquitous when we consider how the same is happening in the MTR and on public buses, where screens are installed and volumes turned up so that passengers are forced to watch screens as a kind of exploitation, even after paying the full fare.

21 N. Smith, 2006, 'Gentrification generalized: From local anomaly to urban "regeneration" as global urban strategy' in M. S. Fisher and G. Downey (eds), *Frontiers of Capital: Ethnographic Reflection on the New Economy*, Durham: Duke University Press, 191–209.

22 S. Zukin, 2010, *Naked City: The Death and Life of Authentic Urban Places*, Oxford and New York: Oxford University Press.

23 For the complicity between the government and land developers, and particularly on how the Hong Kong government has consistently

adopted policies strongly favouring the interests of the developers, see local bestseller A. Poon, 2005, *Land and the Ruling Class in Hong Kong*, Richmond, BC: A. Poon.

24 A variety of mass media in Hong Kong, especially newspapers and radio broadcasting companies, have reported this incident and opened up much space for further discussions. See, for instance, Anonymous, 2008, 〈時代廣場被指佔用公共空間〉 'Times Square is alleged to occupy the public space', *Apple Daily*, 7 April.

25 Illegal uses of the square by Times Square included the opening of a Starbucks coffee shop and the ejection of people roaming or sitting round the square.

26 In fact, since 1995, a quota of 150 mainland immigrants per day has been allocated, perpetuating the conception of Hong Kong as a migrant city.

27 See, for instance, T. Lui, 2001, 'The malling of Hong Kong' in G. Mathews and T. Lui (eds), *Consuming Hong Kong*, Hong Kong: Hong Kong University Press, 1–21, and L. O. Lee, 2006, *Rhapsody on Festival Walk*, Hong Kong: Oxford University Press.

28 T. Lui, 'The malling of Hong Kong'.

29 See, for instance, C. van Uffelen, 2008, *Malls & Department Stores,* Berlin: Braun.

30 See, for instance, D. Slater, 1997, *Consumer Culture and Modernity*, Oxford: Polity Press.

31 Lui has provided a useful account of bourgeois characters in Hong Kong in his several works on the bourgeois class in Hong Kong as a way to probe the political atmosphere there, especially after the handover. According to Lui, the middle classes cling to the belief that a visible and just system could eventually arrive at an ideal position, the simple belief in upward mobility. But, more importantly, he ascribes this to the postwar modernity of Hong Kong. This type of periodization is not dissimilar to the division between modernization and globalization in this paper. See, for instance, T. Lui and W. C. Chun, 2003, 《香港中產階級處境觀察》 *Observations on the Condition of Hong Kong Bourgeois Class*, Hong Kong: Joint Publishing HK or T. Lui, 2004, 《中產好痛》 *Bourgeois Class in Pain*, Hong Kong: Stepforward Press.

32 Sun Hung Kei Properties is one of the largest property companies in Hong Kong, and includes a wide variety of investments, including hotels, property management, transportation and infrastructure. So they play an influential role in shaping the urbanscape of Hong Kong, together with a small group of other influential property companies, such as Cheung Kong (Holdings) Limited, owned by Hong Kong millionaire Li Ka-shing. There is clear complicity between the Hong Kong government and these financially powerful property companies in effectively controlling the

actual design of urban space. See, for example, A. R. Cuthbert and K. G. McKinnell, 1997, 'Ambiguous space, ambiguous rights – corporate power and social control in Hong Kong', *Cities* 14:5, 295–311.

33 Screens, like everything in malls, are constantly emerging and disappearing, and New Town Plaza is no exception. For instance, in recent times, very 'experimental' three-dimensional screens were installed near the entrance of the mall, only to be removed shortly afterwards. The factor of impermanence should also be taken into consideration in the case of screens and their effects.

34 Other smaller screens in the malls are equally elusive in their function. For example, there is a vertical screen showing models on a catwalk, just opposite the first gigantic screen, and there are small screens showing knowledge channels, installed near the third gigantic screen.

35 Consider, for instance, Langham Place in Mong Kok and The One in Tsim Sha Tsui, both of which are built on very limited space. Of course, the spatial constraint does not imply that it is impossible for them to create continuity, as achieved by New Town Plaza, but that it requires a much more prudent calculation of the spatial ordering presented to visitors.

36 This change can also be understood in the light of Hong Kong's political economy in the last decade. In 2003, the Closer Economic Partnership Arrangement (CEPA) was introduced to enhance the economic cooperation between Hong Kong and mainland China, and the number of tourists from mainland China has since increased to such an extent that 71.8 per cent of tourists visiting Hong Kong in 2012 were from mainland China. So it seems that the façade of public space in Hong Kong is serving not local people but the teeming mainland tourists, many of whom have greater disposable incomes than the Hong Kong middle class. For the proportion of mainland tourists, see www.tichk.org/public/website/b5/news/2013_02_20.pdf

37 An analogy can be made between this third screen and the traditional 'screen' (*ping feng*) in Chinese domestic space, in that they both possess a material and representational nature. See H. Wu, 1997, *The Double Screen: Medium and Representation in Chinese Painting*, Chicago: University of Chicago Press.

38 J. Crary, 2013, *24/7: Late Capitalism and the Ends of Sleep*, London: Verso, 17.

39 One may rightly doubt whether it was the mall which chose to present the Olympics rather than the masses, but considering the absolute Olympic mania at that time in Hong Kong, it would have appeared even more perplexing to the masses had the malls decided not to broadcast the Games.

40 The situation of New Town Plaza was merely an example of the ways malls with screens were employed to cope with the 'Olympic

Problem', and it could even be said that it was already a less awkward one, compared with, for example, Langham Place, where a specific area for the audience had to be assigned in order to keep the mall in order, and Landmark North, where the big screen was covered just before the opening of the Olympic Games, presumably for renovation, leaving a tiny screen for the public. There were plenty of grand malls not showing the Olympic Games, but they were mostly those catering to more high-class consumers, who do not really treat the malls as public spaces.

41 This performance can be seen as a form of 'hacking' the site, appropriating technology (and in this case, space) in a way that effectively disrupts the efficacy of the network of consumption. See M. Wark, 2004, *A Hacker Manifesto*, Cambridge, MA: Harvard University Press.

42 While Hong Kong's economic stability has been constantly challenged throughout its contemporary history, the recent economic downturns, notably in 1997 and 2008, are a more serious threat to how Hong Kong's identity can be reconsidered.

43 For instance, *Apple Daily* has reported that, in peak hours, there are 14.8 people per square feet in Sai Yeung Choi Stree, which is graded 'F' – the worst grade, in the *Highway Capacity Manual*. See 級港行人密度達最劣水平F級 *Appledaily*, 2014, hk.apple.nextmedia.com/news/art/20140202/18612746. 2 February.

44 H. Lefebvre, 2003, *The Urban Revolution*, trans. R. Bononno, Minneapolis: University of Minnesota Press.

45 *Hong Kong Transport Department (Pedestrianisation)*. www.td.gov.hk/tc/transport_in_hong_kong/pedestrianisation/pedestrianisation accessed 4 February 2014. See also: Legislative Council, LC Paper No. CB(1)924/09-10 Ref: CB1/PL/PS Panel on Transport, Meeting, 22 January 2010: Background brief on improving pedestrian environment; Government Secretariat, Transport Bureau, 30 March 2000, Legislative Council Panel on Transport, Pedestrian Schemes for Mong Kok and Tsim Sha Tsui.

46 See *Hong Kong Transport Department (Pedestrianisation)*. www.td.gov.hk/tc/transport_in_hong_kong/pedestrianisation/pedestrianisation/ accessed 4 February 2014.

47 B. Anderson, 1983, *Imagined Communities: Reflections on the Origin and Spread of Nationalism*, London: Verso.

48 A. Abbas, *Hong Kong: Culture and the Politics of Disappearance*.

49 For a general social and political history of Hong Kong, see, for instance, J. Carroll, 2007, *A Concise History of Hong Kong*, Lanham: Rowman & Littlefield. For a critical introduction and reflection on Hong Kong social history, see T. Ngo (ed.), 1999, *Hong Kong's History: State and Society under Colonial Rule,* London and New York: Routledge. For an account of the

public response towards colonial rule, see S. W. K. Chiu and T. Lui (eds), 2000, *The Dynamics of Social Movement in Hong Kong*, Hong Kong: Hong Kong University Press.

50 See, for instance, K.Y. Lo and L. K. Ming (eds), 2004, *The Economy of Hong Kong in Non-economic Perspectives*, Hong Kong: Oxford University Press.

51 A detailed socio-historical account of the lives of female textile workers can be found in an oral history of the workers in the 1960s and 1970s. See P. K. Choi (ed.), 2008,《千針萬線: 香港成衣工人口述史》*Thousands of Needles and Threads: An Oral History of Hong Kong Textile Industry Workers*, Hong Kong: Stepforward Press. The account of flexible labour, however, should not be idealized as the best model of the Hong Kong miracle, which, as the book tells us, is founded on exploitation of labour by the employers.

52 Appadurai, 'Grassroots Globalization', 3.

53 Control of hawker licences has massively reduced the number of hawkers in Hong Kong since the 1970s, and this is one of the ways in which governmental intervention has decidedly shaped economic development – and the life choices of the poorest people. K. Ma, 1998,《路邊政治經濟學》*Political Economy on the Street*, Hong Kong: Shu Guang; P. Hui, 2003,《富裕中的貧乏: 香港文化經濟評論》*Lack within Affluence: Commentary on the Culture and Economy of Hong Kong*, Hong Kong: Stepforward Press.

54 A brief economic background of Hong Kong at the time of the legitimatization of hawkers in Ladies Street can be found in B.Y. Fung, 2002,《香港金融業百年》*A Century of Hong Kong Financial Development*, Hong Kong: Joint Publishing HK, 125. This legitimization of hawking activities comes with strict regulations, such as the regularities of presence and prohibitions on hiring employees, measures that suppress the original vitality of hawking activities.

55 Similarly, the re-opening of the classical hawker district in Sheung Wan called 'Tai Tat Tei' in the period of SARS is no more than a place to satisfy the nostalgia of consumers.

56 These extreme pro-establishment groups have been actively disrupting activities held by political parties belonging to the democratic side. They are known for their extreme criticism of pro-democratic public figures, and have stayed very high profile by actively organizing protests.

57 The YouTube link to the video: www.youtube.com/watch?v=OAoz4AwY6GU. accessed 4 February 2014. Some days after the uploading of this video, however, someone pointed out that it was edited in such a way that it was only telling part of the truth, and subsequently, a number of 'full version' videos were uploaded to YouTube as counter-evidence to the criticism of Lam.

58 The traditionally more reputable newspapers, such as *Economic Journal* and *Ming Pao*, have, for instance, engaged in self-censorship in order not to offend the Beijing government. At the same time, online media have become more developed, the most representative of which is Housenews.

59 The Occupy Central movement (full name 'Occupy Central with Love and Peace', or the 'Umbrella Revolution' as termed *de facto* by the media) carried out demonstrations in the autumn of 2014, as a last resort when political reforms for universal suffrage proposed by the Hong Kong government failed to live up to expectations. This movement can be distinguished from the Occupy Central movement in 2011 (in response to the Occupy Wall Street movement) by its specifically local aims and its relatively moderate commitment to principles of deliberative democracy, influenced by American constitutional law writers such as Bruce Ackerman, and deliberative democracy advocates such as James Fishkin.

60 Crary, *24/7*.

10

Multiple Modernities and the Imaging of Uselessness in Contemporary Chinese Cinema

Michelle Huang Tsung-yi and Chi-she Li

As Ulrich Beck maintains, globalization means the 'disappearance of distance and the involvement of undesirable and ineluctable forms of living'[1] How to grasp the meanings of manifold transformations in the condition of globalization has thus become an urgent issue. With this concern in mind, we examine three Chinese language films, *Mahjong* (Edward Yang, 1996), *Unknown Pleasures* (Jia Zhangke, 2002) and *Hollywood Hong Kong* (Fruit Chan, 2001). The three cinematic representations of globalizing East Asia present a similarly intense concern with large-scale urbanization and widespread consumerism. While Taipei, Datong and Hong Kong were socio-economically different during the Cold War period, in the 1990s they are likewise subject to the sway of neoliberalism.

At the core of neoliberalism is the assumption that, in an equally competitive environment, everyone can acquire maximum interests and benefits. Some of the common political-economic changes resulting from contemporary neoliberalization include: (1) urban reconstruction assuming profit-making as its founding principle; (2) the traditional function of nation-states foundering in providing the welfare of people; and (3) the policies of welfare states being replaced by strategies of privatization.[2] Arguably, *Mahjong*, *Unknown Pleasures* and *Hollywood Hong Kong* are cultural texts produced in societies facing critical structural transformations, representing the directors' attempts to comprehend how the politico-economic changes reshape individuals' social relations and everyday life. In other words, all of these films reveal the disorganization of cultural identity and identification. From a comparative perspective, we will tease out these cultural representations as distinctive consequences of economic globalization and, in so doing, illustrate what Meaghan Morris refers to as 'transnational imagination in cinema'.[3]

A particular emphasis will be placed on the complex relations between trans-Asian modernity and its representation, as well as the extent to which the cinematic texts and their shared narrative mode epitomize what Arjun Appadurai describes as the traumatic experiences of deterritorialization.[4] We also seek to expound on what we call 'anti-*bildung* narratives' found in all of these artistic representations, metaphorizing the drastic 'dispossession' of the human capacity of labour brought about by the globalizing changes in East Asia during the past two decades. Although the anti-*bildung* narrative reveals the process of disillusionment of a given young protagonist, equally important, we would like to argue, is the attempt on the part of the three film directors in employing films – a technovisual form of representation – to render trenchant a dominant myth of capitalism which Richard Sennett terms 'the specter of uselessness';[5] simply put, social imaging of apprehension at the prospect of being forced outside of the reproductive workforce and reduced to worthlessness during unruly transformation of social structures.

Before undertaking the narrative analysis of the film narratives, it is useful to clarify 'multiple modernities', a critical concept in use here. Marshall Berman's definition of modernity serves as our point of departure:

> To be modern is to find ourselves in an environment that promises us adventure, power, joy, growth, transformation of ourselves and the world – and, at the same time, that threatens to destroy everything we have [...]. Modern environments and experiences cut across all boundaries of geography and ethnicity, of class and nationality, of religion and ideology: in this sense, modernity can be said to unite all mankind. But it is a paradoxical unity, a unity of disunity: it pours us all into a maelstrom of perpetual disintegration and renewal, of struggle and contraction, of ambiguity and anguish. To be modern is to be part of a universe in which, as Marx said, 'all that is solid melts into air'.[6]

Based on Berman's definition of the illusory promises of renewal and non-stop destruction, we accentuate the contemporary stage of modernity, usually coded in the term 'globalization', not as another singular form of modernity but as multiple modernities. Scholars such as S. N. Eisenstadt[7] and Göran Therborn,[8] for example, argue that modernity or late modernity as a term is insufficient, since it may falsely imply global homogenization or idealization of the universal. They value the concept of 'multiple modernities' for its analytical capacity. Indeed, once we cast modernity into plural forms, we are able to identify subtle differences and also complications as a derivative result of the found differences. First of all, multiple modernities as a concept could render clear different formations in different geo-historical contexts. This concept would not just accentuate subtle differences generated from interpretation, adaptation, partial appropriation, reinvention, and so on, of social institutions practiced in Western Europe between the eighteenth and nineteenth century. Furthermore, it crystallizes what Göran Therborn identifies as 'entangled modernities', as he precisely maps two major forms of such configurations, including the incomplete modernity as it is entangled with the non-modern past and mutual, or interacting or overlapping influences of modern practices among different 'geo-historical' contexts.[9] Finally, 'multiple modernities' also bring to light historical sedimentation, we might add, of different modern forms of social practices, conventions, institutions, apparatuses, which is sometimes observable in one geographical location or in one social event. We would like to note in passing that, as a term, multiple modernities also allows for the possibility of so-called 'alternative modernities' (even though this is not a focus of our discussion). As Gaonkar sees it, the 'combination and recommendations' of 'societal modernization and cultural modernity' would be the breeding ground of almost infinite possibilities.[10]

In a classical definition, globalization is the consequence of modernity exercised to an extreme. As Anthony Giddens emphasizes, the scope and speed of modernity have reached new heights: '[g]lobalization can thus be defined as the intensification of worldwide social relations which link distant localities in such a way that local happenings are shaped by events occurring many miles away and vice versa'.[11] Giddens further specifies that one of the impacts globalization exerts upon everyday life is 'disembeddedness': the ever-changing experience of time and space in daily life constantly leads individuals to live in a condition disembedded from their temporal-spatial environment.[12] If modernity denotes a special kind of collective living experiences in falsely promising a space of constant renewal, then 'multiple modernities' can be understood as the historical result of the reinforcement, aggravation and dissemination of modernity, with changes of different periods overlapping in one locale. To be specific, 'multiple modernities' is not structural in nature nor does it intend to (re-)categorize modernity. Rather, this term is an analytic one, which, by putting modernity into a context of convergent histories, yields the understanding of disjunction of different layers of modernity instead of a very long and seemingly homogenized periodization that could stretch more than four hundred years, or even much longer in some instances. It is true that, since sixteenth-century Western colonization, different forms of modernity have widely interacted with local cultures. The concept of 'multiple modernities' foregrounds an accelerated interaction between modernity with its operating logic of capital globalization and different temporal-spatial cultures, and thus illuminates the complex interpenetration of diverse modernized institutions in East Asia.

Two major historical forces contribute to the making of contemporary East Asian multiple modernities in the three cases under discussion: Mainland China, Hong Kong and Taiwan. First, there is their complex and multiple histories of Westernizing/colonizing modernity. Communism in China, British colonization in Hong Kong, and Japanese imperialism and Kuomintang rule in Taiwan, all play crucial roles in instituting and sustaining modernity, albeit in different ways. The second major historical factor is neoliberal globalization dating back to the 1970s. The economic reform of China allows East Asia to be fully saturated with capitalist economy. The promoters of global capitalism in this area – be they government at all levels, transnational enterprises or real estate agencies – are devoted to capital accumulation and expansion. In what follows, we will first analyse how the three films lead us to unravel the complexity of East Asian multiple modernities, and then move to interpret anti-*bildung* narrative as a possible critique of capital globalization.

Mahjong: The Kingdom of Desire in the Global Urban Glamour Zone[13]

After the release of *A Brighter Summer Day* 牯嶺街少年殺人事件 (1991), Edward Yang once again features adolescent protagonists, in his 1996 film, *Mahjong*. With a mixture of a detached gaze and a mocking tone, Yang in *Mahjong* examines the imbrications of the global and the local, and directs the gaze of the camera to the variegated problems ushered in by the relentless and invasive manipulations of desire. As Olivier Assayas argues, *Mahjong* is 'a snapshot taken during the chaos of the transformation [of Taiwanese society]'. Yang shows us 'the collapse of the society in which he grew up, and of its reformulation as a new world, with a new urbanism, a new architecture, and a new circulation of capital imposed on it'.[14] By virtue of post-modern narratology, namely, the indetermination of reality and fantasy, as well as the predominance of coincident happenings, Yang highlights the difficulty of a cognitive mapping of multiple modernities against the backdrop of continuous transformation, fragmentation and annihilation. The catchphrase recurrent in *Mahjong* – 'None of us knows what we really want; we are merely waiting for others to tell us' – implies this predicament.

The story is set in Taipei in the early 1990s when the city was undergoing a massive transit overhaul with the construction of the Muzha Line, the first line of the Taipei Rapid Transit System (or the MRT), by a French company, Matra. The establishing shot of the film shows the main teenage character, Red Fish, driving on the Fuxing South Road, where one section of the Muzha Line above the road is located in the *mise en scène*. In addition, the fact that the heroine Marthe is from France, and hence is nicknamed Matra, is by no means accidental. This construction at the time embodied the collective yearning to transform Taipei into a modern urban space, typically marked by fast thoroughfares. From the very beginning of the film, the director suggests the MRT is the commanding symbol of modernity and a transnational space *par excellence*.[15]

As well as the MRT, Yang portrays Taipei's entertainment space embodied in the international chain Hard Rock Café, to give the audience a better picture of Taipei's global space. In the hip and chic Hard Rock, on whose walls are numerous placards of the Beatles, English pop songs are played loudly, and everyone chats in English.[16] Yang suggests that such a typical space is crowded with opportunist transnationals. For instance, Ginger, a white sex worker in Taipei, cannot wait to pimp Marthe the moment she lays eyes on her, 'advising' the newcomer that '[t]his city is like the Wild West. You look really smart (and for sure you are going to make a lot of money here).' Angela from Hong Kong, a sociable courtesan, represents another type of foreign opportunist. In Yang's gallery of gold-diggers, the Englishman Markus deserves more critical attention. Promoting himself as a much sought-after architect in Taipei, Markus comes to Taiwan simply because he cannot land any job in London. The caricature of Markus can be seen as the director's cynical gaze at the space of multiple modernities. In this scene, Markus tries to impress Marthe with his insider tips on the locals:

> These people are unbelievably rich. In ten years, this place will become the center of the world. The future of the Western civilization lies right here. [...] As we have learned in history class, the nineteenth century is renowned for the glory of imperialism; just wait for the coming of the twenty-first century. This is why Matra is here, why I am here. How lucky I am to discover this place. I won't tell my fellows in the hometown that Taiwan is the dreamland for gold-seekers – this is the secret we have to keep.

Here Yang implies that Taiwan's economic success in the 1980s attracts profit-driven foreigners for quick and easy money.

Mahjong pivots around a detective plot involving four teenagers: Red Fish, Hong Kong, Toothpaste (Little Buddha) and Luen-Luen. Using the mahjong game as a dominant metaphor, the film relates their experiences of pleasures, conflicts, losses and bewilderments in configuring the space of multiple modernities in Taipei. At the beginning, the film tells the audience the framework of the story: 'Chen, a mogul in Taipei, is missing. It is rumored that he owes ten billion and becomes the target of gangsters. They think the best way to get him is to get his son first.' Here Yang plays with the detective motif of looking for the missing person, hinting that those who look for others are, in fact, the target wanted. The gangsters seeking Chen turn Red Fish into a scapegoat for his father. Meanwhile, the son is seeking his father to solve the problem and to learn tips for a comeback in business. Within this detective framework, *Mahjong* describes how the adolescent figures (mis)understand capital accumulation, exemplified by their imitation and internalization of certain social behaviours and values. The condition of multiple modernities results in the misperception of space as a container of vast potential for all kinds of desire to be fulfilled. At the core of this notion lies another fantasy for the young heroes: these 'exotic' places like Hard Rock Cafe, T.G.I. Friday and Fashion Hairdressers are where even the wildest dreams may come true.

Red Fish worships his father as a ruthless hero, good at making money, and is proud of his father being 'the most shameless person in this shameless country'. Everything Red Fish has been doing is to duplicate his father's business tricks. If his father can turn into a parvenu so easily ('an earning of thousands of millions!'), Red Fish assumes he must have a mysterious knack of commanding the capital flow. Red Fish is eager to learn more from his father: 'I always think that he withholds new tricks from me for he thinks I am still too young.' Red Fish often preaches his father's opportunitism to Luen-Luen: 'nowadays, to be successful, you have to be smart rather than emotional. Once you get emotional, you will lose your mind. This is not about morality. Perhaps once he understands this, it will be us fooled by him.'

Obsequiously following the missing father's footsteps, the young hero turns fraudulence into an enterprise via the organization of a gang to manipulate people around him: the other three in their gang have different 'expertise': the tall, handsome Hong Kong is the lure for women; the dark-skinned Little Buddha with a foul mouth pretends to be the Feng Shui master; the new member Luen-Luen is Red Fish's driver and interpreter, and they conspire to swindle others. After picking up the targets (Jay and Angela), the gang of four vandalize the victims' car. Then, Little Buddha professes to be able to tell fortunes, predicting an unpleasant accident to the car and claiming the supernatural ability to help them avoid disasters to come. The victims are thus entrapped and defrauded by Little Buddha's fake 'advice' on Feng Shui.

Ironically, toward the end of the film, these street-smart teenagers have to take a reality check and pay for their misconceptions and wrong-doings. At one moment we see Hong Kong repeating Toothpaste Jay's contempt for the foreigners as if he knew better: 'Foreigners are nothing but scumbags who come here simply for dirty money.' It does not take too long to see that Hong Kong knows much less than he thinks he does. Taking Red Fish's instruction to compete with Markus, Hong Kong accomplishes his tasks of having sex with Alison and seducing Angela. However, in the end the handsome playboy turns out to be the women's plaything. When Angela takes two girl friends back to the teenagers' apartment, Hong Kong is treated as their sex toy. Their physical and verbal exploitation brings the young man to the verge of breakdown, leaving him alone crying in the restroom.

Red Fish is no less frustrated than Hong Kong. For all his efforts to show everyone that he is mature and sophisticated like all those grown-ups around him, in reality Red Fish naively reduces the key to success in business to simply cool-headed if not cold-hearted calculation and social networking (e.g. gangs). As the narrative unfolds, the golden rules passed down from the revered father are put to a severe test of credibility when Red Fish finds out that his father has committed suicide with his mistress, breaking the fundamental rule of being smart and not emotional. In shock, Red Fish shouts beside his father's body: 'Do you really have to tell me [your big secret] this way?'

Appalled at his father's death, Red Fish still has no idea of his own ignorance until he meets President Chiu, his father's old pal in some shady business practices. A loser bankrupt in business, Chiu sinks so low as to ask Red Fish and Little Buddha to help him with a fraud. He even sounds the note similar to his father's: 'No one really knows what he or she wants; everyone is waiting for others to tell him or her.' At this moment, he becomes in a sense a mirror reflecting Red Fish's naivety. Red Fish thus comes to realize that his father is nothing more than a scheming little-time rascal like Chiu, and the father's golden rule of life is merely a shared guideline of rogues and conmen. Disturbed by the belated knowledge and the loss of the authoritative father figure, Red Fish shoots at this partner of his father.

The wounded President Chiu then reveals another truth that is even harder for Red Fish to swallow – the Angela upon whom he intends to avenge himself is not the one who has made his father bankrupt: 'Do you know how many Angelas there are in Hong Kong?' Stunned and mortified, Red Fish finally comes to understand that his revenge play has an absurd end. Unable to face his own foolishness, the traumatized teenager loses control and kills President Chiu. The last shot of the film shows Red Fish kneeling down beside the body of Chiu crying alone helplessly.

Unknown Pleasures: A Melancholic Gaze at China in Transformation

Nominated for the *Palme d'Or* (the Golden Palm) in the 55th Annual Cannes Film Festival (2002), *Unknown Pleasures,* following *Xiao Wu* (1997) (小武 *Pickpocket*) and *Platform* (2000) (站台), is the final of Jia Zhangke's 'Hometown Trilogy'. Like its prequels, this film is shot in the style of documentary realism. Set in 2001 in Datong, Shanxi, an industrial mining town, *Unknown Pleasures* hinges its narrative upon the encounter and struggle of the adolescents Xiao Ji and Bin Bin, when China plunges into the global laissez-faire economy, no longer upholding the model of centralized industrial production. As Jia once remarked, '[t]he reason why I made *Unknown Pleasures* is that I want to capture the industrial ambience of Datong, Shanxi. The Chinese economy is under transformation; even the buildings of the past look lonely and suggest a strong sense of depression. Radical transformations of the urban areas render traditional lifestyle obsolete.'[17]

More than once, *Unknown Pleasures* emphatically refers to the establishment and initiation of the Jingda Expressway in Shanxi. The first gaze takes place when Xiao Ji has his hair cut, as the news shows the launching of the Jingda Expressway on TV. The barber, whose hometown is Zhangjiakou, rejoices that hereafter it will take her only one hour to get home. When Xiao Ji asks if she will take Iveco (a middle-size bus) to go back to Zhangjiakou, the barber excitedly replies in English: 'Yes!' The language used and the agitation in her tone show people's high hopes for urban modernization.

The space of everyday life in *Unknown Pleasures* is also inscribed with traces of urbanization. All the roads seem to be under construction, recalling the ghostly image of ruins in the reconstructed Paris of the nineteenth century.[18] Many times the heroine Qiao Qiao walks across the same macadam to wait for a bus, the same road that later causes Xiao Ji's scooter to break down. Jingda Expressway, the landmark infrastructure project that symbolizes modernization, shows up a second time at the end of the film. When Bin Bin is interrogated by the policemen of the Xingjian South Road squad for robbing the bank, the news anchor once again reports the initiation of the Jingda Expressway, emphasizing it as the milestone of the development of the West. At this point, the contrast between a progress symbolic of multiple modernities and the arrested protagonist is nothing if not ironic.

Against the backdrop of massive urban transformation, the film represents the effects of multiple modernities mainly in the reconfiguration of interpersonal relationships in a consumerist city. As Desmond Lok observes, the primary theme of *Unknown Pleasures* is the manifold conflicts that have become a prominent feature of consumerist China.[19] The film begins with the penetrating presence of consumerism and social aspiration, in the public broadcast of a lottery commercial. While the teenage protagonists Xiao Ji and Bin Bin are fooling around at the train station, the public announcement system in the background, having previously been used for revolutionary education, not only instructs people how to win but propagates the fantasy of becoming rich overnight – 'Wish you could win the jackpot.' The repeated jingle brainwashes the passers-by.

This symbolic opening is further developed by showgirl Qiao Qiao's story. The commercial refrain promoted by Qiao Qiao, 'Buy the Mongolian King [a brand of liquor] to win the US dollars', further dramatizes the way consumerist space creates the illusion of easy capital – if many have become rich, the next lucky guy might just be you. Out of curiosity, Xiao Ji buys the liquor for his father and finds a US-dollar bill attached inside the screw top. With no idea of the value of US currency, when a passer-by casually suggests that 'ten USD are worth one thousand RMB', Xiao Ji and his father are led to believe that they have been dealt a better hand and their impoverished life can be mended by that dollar bill. When Xiao Ji's father goes to the bank to exchange the one dollar bill for RMB, he is told that currency exchange is only available in the [People's] Bank of China. In perplexity, Xiao Ji's father asks the clerk 'Isn't this a bank of China?' The US dollar is nothing more than a cunning promotional package, having no substantial connection with him or his daily life.

In a dramatic twist, though, the dollar bill later becomes valuable bait in initiating a sexual transaction. Xiao Ji's father puts RMB on the table to hook up with Qiao Qiao, who nevertheless turns a cold shoulder to him, replying, 'You cannot afford me. Just leave.' In response, he takes out the US bill as his trump card. Then the camera moves to the scene in which Xiao Ji watches the news about the bank robber Zhang Jun and asks his father 'Why are you so excited today?' The scene suggests Qiao Qiao buys into the immense value of the dollar bill and the sex deal has taken place between Xiao Ji's father and Qiao Qiao.

In *Unknown Pleasures*, a different and complicated theme related to the consumerist space centres on Qiao Qiao. The film twice shows her in a dance with a studied gaze. No doubt, Qiao Qiao's performances present what Jia describes as the ubiquity of the showgirl figures promoting commodities in contemporary China; but Jia's melancholy stance toward show girls in the consumerist society accounts for a complexity of Qiao Qiao's performance: on the one hand, flamboyant yet empty toadying; on the other, respectful and graceful, even, in the service of vulgar consumerism. In her first promotion show for the Mongolian king, Qiao Qiao performs a rousing and gaudy modern dance to the pop song 'Unknown Pleasure', the theme song of the Mongolian King. After fighting with Qiao San for Xiao Ji, she dances for the second time. Standing beside the highway, she performs a folk dance with calmness, contentment and dexterity. To some extent, Qiao Qiao's performance is the way Jia grants, in an experimental manner, esteem and subjectivity to a female even under the control of consumerism. Here the object of the camera gaze, namely the woman subjugated to consumerist activities, represents the body under the melancholic gaze of modernity.

The leading characters, Bin Bin and Xiao Ji, are adolescents. Their experiences of frustration and loss accentuate the conflicts inherent in the consumerist society of multiple modernities. Unlike Red Fish in *Mahjong*, the adolescents in *Unknown Pleasures*, who do not have resources at their disposal or a rogue father figure to emulate, find real-life gangsters their models for imitation in a society where prevalent social conflicts inspire their impromptu learning.

Through the perspective of Bin Bin, the camera reveals the KTV and the train station, which are pertinent examples of the alien space of modernity. In a shabby KTV booth, Bin Bin grumbles to his girlfriend, who is preparing for the National Higher Education Entrance Examination: 'WTO? Isn't that all about making money?' Learning that his girlfriend wants to major in international business, the hero comments, 'What those specialized in international business do is no more than collect rabbits and pigs and then sell them to Ukraine.' The teenager's oversimplified imagination of globalization highlights his outdatedness (that is more about trade within the communist bloc), which partly accounts for why he is jilted by his girlfriend and symbolically jettisoned by the multiple modernities of contemporary China. Later, before the unenthusiastic girlfriend heads for Beijing, they meet for the last time at the Datong station, a place of departure that stands for the protagonist's loss of love. When the girlfriend shows up, she obviously appears more fashionable than in her previous schoolgirl attire. Knowing that their relationship has come to an end, Bin Bin borrows 5,000 yuan (an obviously extraordinary sum for the standard of living) to buy a cell phone as a farewell gift. The same old Bin Bin takes out the cell phone, saying: 'It will be useful for you when you study international business in Beijing.' The lukewarm girlfriend now gladly accepts the gift and makes an empty promise: 'It will be convenient for you to contact me.' While Bin Bin is reluctant to leave, his girlfriend quickly bids farewell. The ending of the puppy love suggests Bin Bin's girlfriend is on the track of welcoming globalization, as if riding on the Jingda Expressway to a new future, while Bin Bin is a left-behind loser, and thus not too different from the old station in the sense of being unable to 'keep up with the time'.

Bin Bin's story helps to elaborate Jia's perception of multiple modernities in China. In an interview he relates modernity, the radical transformations of urban space, to the resulting nostalgia in his films, by making the connection between modernity and his cinematic themes:

> The modernization of cities is for sure a trend. It's unstoppable but just too cruel. The development we go through is unnatural; it's a *movement* and it's highly destructive. Streets can serve as the best example. In Fengyang, I cannot find any streets where I used to play around in childhood; all of them have been demolished. Everything that contains your memories is gone and you have a strong sense of loss. In the meantime, our culture is ruptured. The power of disruption is so vehement that a lot of people are left behind. I hope whatever is good and warm in our cultural tradition can be saved, such as promises, love, trust, etc. Yet, what we are undergoing is *revolutionary* and can change everything overnight (emphasis added).[20]

This remark echoes Walter Benjamin's mourning for urban modernization. Jia's extraordinary expressions are noteworthy – he borrows the experiences of the mid-twentieth-century national modernization to broach the capitalist globalization at the end of the twentieth century, using the Maoist diction ('movement' and 'revolution') to describe the 'breaching' impact caused by global modernity. As Chris Berry suggests, Jia's cinema 'is neither in-the-now loss of history nor modern linear progress, but instead an uneasy in-the-now (and then) that invokes history and questions the present'.[21] In reference to the modern history of China, Jia indicates that globalization remains a glamorous and superficial promise of modernity, whereas in the dramatically transformed spaces, many essential values have vanished, among them, the nobility of community and the dignity of humanity.

The space of multiple modernities holds the illusion of infinite possibilities in consumerist China; nonetheless, these adolescents seem to have nothing in their hands, be it cash, spatial mobility, stable jobs or social capital. The ideal of a dignified ambition, the stimuli of consumerist spaces, and the sense of loss in real life together lead the adolescent figures to easily identify with Xiao Wu and Qiao San, the gangsters around them.[22] Such identification is made possible by the medium of popular culture, particularly Hollywood films. For example, the gangster

Xiao Wu alludes to the hero and a frustrated pickpocket in Jia's earlier work, *Xiao Wu* (1997). At the beginning of the film, Xiao Wu is caught by the police. After doing time in jail, he runs across Bin Bin, who asks him, 'Brother Xiao Wu, aren't you still behind bars?' Instead of being offended, Xiao Wu laughs it off: 'It's all about coming and going, *just like watching a movie*' (emphasis added). Another excellent example is Xiao Ji, who not only identifies with Zhang Jun, a real-life high-profile robber covered in the TV news, but the bank robbers in the Hollywood film *Pulp Fiction*. At one point, Xiao Ji tries to show off to Qiao Qiao his macho aspiration '[i]t is a pity that I was born in Datong. If I were an American, I would have robbed all the banks there.'

This boast later turns into a real thing – Xiao Ji and Bin Bin perform what they see on the screen, robbing a bank together with fake grenades. Their impromptu learning suggests the naivety typical of juvenile delinquents. The robbery scene is nothing more than a farce. Despite their serious attempt at disguising themselves as robbers, Xiao Ji and Bin Bin look like kids playing a silly game. The rehearsal is already hilarious. Uncertain if the robbers with fake grenades look intimidating, these two take turns posing as a robber in front of the mirror for the other to make comments. Bin Bin remarks to Xiao Ji, '[t] he bombs on you look real, but you don't'. Xiao Ji tells Bin Bin: 'Neither you nor your grenades look real.' Nonetheless the two reckless teenagers still decide to try their luck. Xiao Ji's part is to play the point man, riding the motorcycle outsides and watching out for the police. Bin Bin goes inside the bank to play the tough guy. Upon hearing Bin Bin's 'hands up', the security just walks to him, toying with the fake grenade, and tells Bin Bin in a sarcastic tone: 'At least you should get yourself a lighter.'

The subsequent scenes show Bin Bin interrogated by a police officer, asking him if he knows bank robbery is a capital punishment. The protagonist answers: 'No way! It's only an attempted robbery.' Finding his optimistic reply amusing, the officer then asks him to sing his favourite song and Bin Bin sings 'Unknown Pleasures', which is also the song he and his girlfriend sang hand-in-hand in the KTV booth. Jia does not tell us what happens to Bin Bin after this bizarre interrogation scene. But the end of the film provides some clue of his partner's Plan B. Xiao Ji rides to the expressway, suggesting that he is going to Xining to buy a pistol. But nothing comes easily. It begins to rain heavily and the motorcycle breaks down, and the last shot of Xiao Ji shows him walking on the highway in the rain alone.

The denouement of *Unknown Pleasures* suggests bewilderment caused by the condition of multiple modernities. The contrast between the rashly planned robbery and the longing to leave ultimately adds a touch of melancholy and sadness to the irony of the plot. With the theme song 'Unknown Pleasures', Jia attempts to reveal the conflicts concomitant with the rapid growth in Chinese economy and, to some extent, speak for those who are left behind by their time. He explains why the song is chosen to express the sentiment of the narrative:

> This song by Richie Ren is very popular in China and I am particularly touched by the line 'A true hero doesn't care about his low birth.' To compete with other countries for survival, China faces the widening gap between the rich and the poor and an alarming rate of unemployment. Young people in particular lead a stressful life. To me this line is like a 'manifesto of fury'.[23]

When analysed further, the lyrics of 'Unknown Pleasures' neatly correspond to the problems inherent in multiple modernities, and offer an insight to the breach between the prosperity promised by globalization and the deprivation of those who fall behind, like Bin Bin and Xiao Ji. Esther M. K. Cheung observes that Jia's cinema embodies an appeal, 'a plea to invite both Chinese and global audiences to be more sympathetic toward those who are historically residual and who are being forgotten in the epic-historical vacuum'.[24] For Kent Jones, the signature move of the film is 'back and forth, the frustration of pushing and pulling and getting nowhere'.[25] At first glance, everything seems possible ('A true hero doesn't care about his low birth / with a high ambition he can be proud and dignified').

However, the ultimate freedom in the open space promised vaguely ('Rambling freely with the wind around the world') amounts to nothing but an illusive dream: in reality life is packed with unspeakable frustration and loss ('Just let me suffer / Or just let me feel exhausted'; 'Just let me feel sad / Or just let me regret / Regret that heaven can never understand'; and 'Just let me get drunk / Or just let me sleep / Let me forget all the sorrows and troubles').

The open space is neither the unknown pleasures of Chuang Tzu in his philosophy of 'the use of uselessness' nor the imaginary freedom enjoyed by the Monkey King – and the title, *Unknown Pleasures*, is an allusion to Chuang Tzu's work. Instead, it conceals the ideology of capital accumulation and a large-scaled reterritorialization of living space.

Hollywood Hong Kong: The Journey to the West in the Form of Black Comedy

If Jia's *Unknown Pleasures* is a realistic, melancholy representation of Chinese modernity, Fruit Chan's *Hollywood Hong Kong* is a black comedy of lower class Hong Kong in the post-1997 period. The story narrates what happens to several Tai Hom Village residents, mainly a teenager Chi Keung Wong and local pork vendors, the Chu family, after they meet the Northern (Chinese) prostitute Hung Hung. After having sex with practically every man in the Tai Hom Village, the nymph-like Hung Hung professes to be underage and extorts Wong and the Chu family. In a post-colonial perspective and sometimes surrealistic style, the film limns out the multiple modernities of the twenty-first-century Hong Kong and demonstrates how the everyday life of lower class Hong Kong people is displaced and dislocated by the space of global modernity.

The major setting of the film, the Tai Hom Village, is of paramount significance in this film for contextualizing multiple modernities. The Village, demolished in 2001, in reality had been a large squatter site in postwar Hong Kong. Dating its history back to the Qing dynasty, it was later renamed Diamond Hill after Kowloon was leased to the United Kingdom – and implied in the irony of the title is that early Hong Kong film studios were also located there. With the growth of the Hong Kong economy and the decline of agriculture, the vegetable farms were gradually replaced by iron-clad and wooden houses. During the 1970s, the colonial government began to reclaim the neighbouring lands, with a plan to wipe out these squatter areas. The 1980s and 1990s then witnessed a myriad of Chinese migrants moving into the Village, and more and more iron-clad, wooden and stone houses being built to accommodate the new immigrants.[26] The Tai Hom Village was thereby densely populated, with houses in simple structures entwined with one another by cables, pipes, clotheslines, as well as tortuous lanes and alleys. The village is literally a labyrinth in the city.[27]

To fully grasp Chan's allegory of Hong Kong's multiple modernities represented by the last chapter of the urban squatter village, it is useful to situate the story in its geopolitical context. *Hollywood Hong Kong* was produced when the momentum of Hong Kong's economy began to depend much more on China, a socio-economic reality interestingly reincarnated by the Chinese characters in the film. As early as the 1970s, Hong Kong developed into a prominent global city in East Asia and is hence accustomed to imagining China as the synonym of belated modernity, if not a socio-economic backwater.

Nonetheless, with the takeover of the political sovereignty of Hong Kong, along with its rapid economic growth and rising global competitiveness, China has been transformed into the main agent, politically and economically, in charge of the former British colony, thereby undermining Hong Kong's long-term status as a seemingly autonomous global city in the region. Both its significant function of trading and singular niche of capital investment in the global system are challenged, due to the fast development of Shenzhen, Guangzhou and, above all, Shanghai.

This new geopolitical dynamic drives Hong Kong to recognize the need to reposition itself in the global system so as to maintain its competitive edge. As Huang has elsewhere argued, one way to understand the transformation of the geopolitical hierarchy is to consider the impact on Hong Kong people's imagination of identity.[28] Hong Kong used to stand at the top of a supranational network but now has to compete and cooperate with other cities in the region for resources, and so its inhabitants see new immigrants from China in a different light. Recounting the dwellers' lives in the Tai Hom Village due for demolition, the film represents Hong Kong's multiple modernities by portraying how modern urbanization compresses the lived space of the lower class and how China has replaced the United Kingdom as the agent of modernity after the handover.

In *Hollywood Hong Kong*, the demolition and relocation of the Tai Hom Village not only exemplifies the process of urban reconstruction, but offers Chan a feature case to characterize what Hong Kong has to wrestle with in the twenty-first century – everyday life is now in the hands of those newly empowered, who in the film, ironically, have no clear idea of global modernity or the Western ways of life that Hong Kong people have enjoyed for the past few decades. Through the interaction between locals and newcomers in the Tai Hom Village during its last days, Chan allegorizes the cultural impact brought about by the arrival of a new power and key agent of multiple modernities: specifically, the female immigrants from China.

To some extent, Hong Kong's imagination of China is refracted through Chinese migrant women in the film. Both Doctor Liu and Hung Hung allegorize the anxiety of the Hong Kong (male) subject towards the transfer of not so much sovereignty but the agent of modernity. For example, Chan portrays the displaced power of modernity by the middle-aged Chinese quack doctor's exaggerated and overzealous scientific rhetoric. Doctor Liu once asks Mr Chu to help her with an experiment of planting fertilized eggs into his mother pig and having her give birth to human beings. Detecting Mr Chu's suspicion, she tries to enlighten him by saying 'Mr Chu, you don't believe in Jesus? But you cannot doubt science. Science is marvellous.' To persuade Chu, Doctor Liu even cites successful cases from the West (the model of modernity) to support her argument. The scientific fantasy of the quack doctor reflects a sarcastic view of Chinese modernity. What originally seems to be a Frankensteinian experiment becomes simple and banal in her account of modern science, echoing much of the science propaganda of the communist regime in the 1950s and 1960s.

If Liu is the witch-doctor spokesperson for the Chinese communist bent for modern science, the mysterious 'northern girl' Hung Hung typifies two of the most prominent features of multiple modernities, flexibility and mobility. Throughout the film, the camera over and again characterizes her as an enchanting succubus with changing identities. The allegorical allusions to *The Journey to the West* embedded in the film suggest the heroine's multiple identities as the spider demoness incarnated. She calls herself 'Angel of Shanghai', and at the same time Hung Hung (her self-denomination to Chi Keung Wong), Tung Tung (to the Chu family) and Fang Fang (to Peter). She says, 'call me whatever you want to and I am that person'. Her shape-shifting echoes the spider demoness' capacity of metamorphosis. The phantasmagoric scene of Hung Hung playing on the swing further superimposes her with the image of succubus. In reality, she traps her preys like a spider.

Hung Hung personifies the longing for translocal and upward mobility as well as the imagination of flexibility. In this sense, her repeated attempts for an aerial vantage point are not coincidental. After having sex with Chi Keung, Hung Hung climbs up the hill to overlook the Tai Hom Village with the five skyscrapers in the Hollywood square as a sharp contrast in the background. The second time she stands on the swing outside the Chus'. Excited with the swing going higher and higher, Hung shouts in a language suggesting sexual climax, 'I see the rooftop! I am so high! Get higher!' Later, when the heroine plays with Tiny Chu, the youngest child of the Chu family, she stands by the window of the apartment in one of the Hollywood skyscrapers, using a red flag to signal to him down below in the Tai Hom Village. Last, in one of the most surrealistic scenes of the film, we see Hung Hung command a panoramic and dominant perspective again. This particular scene shows her dressed in red playing on the swing right outside the window of the Chus', with the monotonous, creaking sound of the swing in the background. The image of a spider woman waiting for her prey again looms large.[29]

The film manages an overt symbolic identification between Hung Hung and Hollywood, and thus coldly points to her role as the winner in multiple modernities, successfully managing to lay claim to both material and symbolic capital. In the film this *femme fatale* not only lives in a luxurious development (called Plaza Hollywood) situated in the Hong Kong Square overlooking the squalid Tai Hom Village, but ultimately moves to Hollywood, California. Hung Hung once tells Tiny Chiu that 'I want to go to the United States, a huge land with Hollywood, Disneyland, and a lot of universities.' She also says to Peter: 'Take me to the United States.' Clearly, the mobility of reaching Hollywood and the US is a synonym of ultimate success, an idiosyncratic utopian projection of global modernity. Unlike the Chu family, who are forced to move out of the Tai Hom Village, and Chi Keung Wong, who seemingly disappears at the end of the film, Hung Hung has her American dream come true. She is the one capable of manipulating the power and resources of multiple modernities, represented by the lofty building where she stays (Hollywood Hong Kong) and her mobility (leaving for the real Hollywood).

Like Jia, Chan borrows the tale of *The Journey to the West* to allegorize the juvenile subjects in the village. The leading teenage characters are Chi Keung Wong and Ah Ming, the eldest son of the Chu family. Both of them reside in the Tai Hom Village; these 'boyz n the hood' are obliterated by the space of multiple modernities underscoring mobility and development. The 18-year-old Chi Keung Wong is an original resident of the old Tai Hom Village and, like Chung Chau, the hero of *Made in Hong Kong*, a typical young gangster in Chan's films. Such a character is to some degree the epitome of everyman. (At one point, Tiny Chu looks up the yellow page and says in surprise: 'There are so many Chi Keung Wongs in Hong Kong!')

Chi Keung Wong is also the incarnation of Monkey King: the bony, seemingly parentless protagonist who desires to leave the Water-Curtain Cave (i.e. the Tai Hom Village) for an adventure in the outside world. Soon after the film begins, Chi Keung says to his girlfriend/prostitute in excitement: 'When I make enough money here, let's venture to Mong Kok together [to run a real whore house]!' The limited knowledge of the young hero makes him believe that the world outside the Tai Hom Village simply means Mong Kok, the well-known red-light district in Hong Kong.

Chi Keung's facile understanding of the outside world is also demonstrated in contrast to Hung Hung's supposedly worldly point of view. After having sex, Chi Keung confesses that he has been living in the old Tai Hom Village all his life. Hung Hung rejoins, 'You are more miserable than I. You were born in a poverty-stricken place and are being overshadowed all day by the high-rise cluster of Hollywood Hong Kong. It feels so uncomfortable.' And she adds: 'You have never been to Shanghai? Now it is a very beautiful place, even more beautiful than Hong Kong.' Here the heroine's comparison on the one hand shows her superiority to Chi Keung and the Tai Hom Village, and on the other suggests the young man's parochial upbringing and thus prepares his role as a victim duped by Hung Hung. In the same scene, the heroine stretches out her right hand to match the five pillar-like apartment complexes in front of them, mentioning in passing that these high-rises are just like Five Finger Mountain. Hung Hung's metaphor points to the heart of the Monkey King allegory and the theme of entrapment of the Chinese monkey myth – neither the street-smart Chi Keung nor the seemingly dim-witted Ah Ming ever escape from the Buddha's hand. The latter's lack of confidence betrays his lack of determination, experiences and socialization. Before having sex with Ah Ming, the heroine Hung Hung teases him, saying that he is cute. All Ah Ming can say is that 'Everyone calls me Pigsy.'

Fruit Chan dramatizes the teenage subjects' desire and uncertainty towards an intimate relation (sex) with the manipulative mediator of modernity (Hung Hung). For example, set up by Hung Hung to have sex with her, Chi Keung is extorted by gangsters. Upset and panicky, the only thing he can do is to smash his desktop computer, the only symbolic linkage between him and the outside world of multiple modernities. The interesting twist is that, even later, when he is mutilated by the gangsters by mistake, Chi Keung still fantasizes about sleeping with Hung Hung: a fantasy represented by an eerie image of a roast pigling in the oven at the Chus', with a phallus-like object looming in the fire, implying the dangerous cost of sexual pleasure. Recounting the adolescent characters' complicated feelings for sex, a mixture of longing, fear and guilt, Chan suggests the ambivalent perception of modernity, uncertain if what they face is a blessing in disguise or a sugar-coated disaster. When the cinematic narration comes to its closure, the Chus end up broke and Wong mutilated.

In this regard, *Hollywood Hong Kong* can be seen as a traumatic anti-*bildungsroman*, without prospect and progression. Although Chi Keung finally comes to see through Hung Hung's deception, such awareness does not lead to the hero's elevation or progression, as the convention of *bildungsroman* dictates. Here the concept of the *bildungsroman* in the film can be better elucidated, as argued, by the allusion of *The Journey to the West*. The Monkey King is the archetype of a rebellious teenager, and the demons challenging him in his pilgrimage to the West are the ordeals he must undergo to become mature and wise. Yet, Chan's allusion delivers a strong sense of irony. The trials and tribulations in the Monkey King and Pigsy's journey pave the way for their elevation (at the end of the story, the former is converted to Buddhism and entitled the Sage of Heaven).

By contrast, the Monkey King (Chi Keung Wong) and Pigsy (Ah Ming) in the Tai Hom Village are duped and downgraded, so to speak. With two left hands and no right hand, the devastated Chi Keung asks Ah Ming to take avenge on the spider demon. (The hand grafted back by Dr Liu is someone else's left hand, not Chi Keung's right hand, the one cut off by the gangsters). Finding Hung Hung gone, Chan's Monkey King in desperation begs Pigsy to cut off his wrongly grafted hand. At the end of *Hollywood Hong Kong*, the Monkey King is missing; the family of Pigsy move out of the Tai Hom Village with their pig. In terms of social mobility, the film hints that neither of them manages to escape from the Buddha's grasp.

The Visions of Disappearance and the Spectre of Uselessness

After we align in the previous discussion the three films in terms of multiple modernities, it becomes apparent that they tell stories of some surprising similarities, in spite of their relatively different production periods and places in East Asia: all of them exhibit impossible visions of unchanged everyday life against technological triumphalism. The three films, consciously motivated by the inevitable and drastic reconfiguration of everyday life induced by larger-than-the-local-scale capitalism, capture how human beings have been effectively enclosed in the technological reconstruction of the global space. The component of social realism literally dominates in the *mise en scène* of elevated trains, highways or highrises, and the resulting associations with uncongenial people from the outside. The technological achievements are taunted as progress of urbanization but, more importantly, felt by local characters to be unprepared displacement and menaces. In the case of the three films, a technological irony prevails: The technology of cinematic gaze zooms in on the immediate transition into the annihilated neighborhood, brought about by the technology of creating artificial topographies. In consequence, these films are able to sustain the vision of everyday life as 'the space of disappearance',[30] to borrow a term of Akbar Abbas.

This irony exists because the three films also explore extensively the narrative capacity of cinema to attempt to grasp the global changes in East Asia in terms of connectedness. The films relate how the local characters, such as Red Fish, Xiao Ji, Bin Bin and Chi Keung Wong, fight back after their presumed local autonomy is removed by the imposed opening-up of their neighbourhoods and how they do so unsuccessfully. All of the main characters anticipate the ways in which they thrive by assuming that they are the heroic figures who see the connectedness of a mythological picaresque (such as gangster-roaming and the adventures of Monkey King) with the invitation to leisure and fun in the capitalist culture. However, the films expose that they are the victims of their own various illusions of a coherent world of adventures. In this way, the three films all distinguish the seemingly voluntary participation in modernities as a contradiction in itself.

In these three films, gangster characters function as agents undertaking to make ad hoc use of very limited resources and knowledge, tackling the immense gaps and disjunction between the escalating capitalized society and the gradually outmoded cultural values adolescents have acquired from pre-globalization modernity. To the teenagers in the films, how the gangsters accumulate capital seems to be the way global capital operates – in a mechanism dissociated from the original social order, most of the time at the cost of social justice and equity in the course of accumulation. From their perspective, the gang leaders deserve respect not so much for their recklessness as for their resourcefulness in a fast changing society. That is what makes them idols in their neoliberal entrepreneurship of know-how and social networking.

In the films, the disconnection of the *bildung* experiences of adolescents from their space of daily life dramatizes the problem with the predominance of multiple modernities. Albeit unlike the classical *bildung* narrative, whose protagonists go through their rites of passage and emerge with knowledge about themselves, *Mahjong*, *Unknown Pleasures*, *Hollywood Hong Kong* assume the grand narrative of the *bildungsroman* that seeks to solve the social problems associated with teenagers. Here we can borrow Richard Sennett's premise of 'the specter of uselessness'[31] to further illuminate the significance of modernity in anti-*bildung* stories. What Sennett means by 'uselessness' refers to the dropouts and the unemployed, that is, the historical products of the large-scale transformations of social structure and unprecedented destruction brought about by modernity. With unlimited global capital expansion, related phenomena such as the management of global labour's demand and supply, automatization and aging are structural factors for a malfunctioned society and the consequent unemployment.

As Sennett asserts, modern society usually neglects the structural factors of unemployment and instead focuses upon *Bildung* and education as the solution to the problem of uselessness. In other words, uselessness poses a fundamental threat that modern society desires to eradicate, but in vain. As the term 'specter' suggests, uselessness is the inextricable nightmare of modern society. While Sennett's thesis is developed within the framework of sociology, it provides important insights into interdisciplinary studies. Drawing on Sennett, uselessness can be essentially grasped as a symbolic sign that simultaneously uncovers and conceals the destructive changes derived from modernity. In this regard, uselessness is the created nightmare of modernity. As Sennett points out, in the 1930s recession of the United States, the queues of unemployed people incarnate the spectre of uselessness itself. In the context of globalization, 'the specter of uselessness' is embodied by the children of developing countries, who have to leave family and drop out of school so as to work in sweatshops.

The anti-*bildung* narratives of the three films are not only a metaphor for a daily life penetrated by multiple modernities but a vivid exemplification of the myth of 'the specter of uselessness'. If social success is the key factor in the conventional *bildung* narrative, it is misleading to think of the anti-*bildung* narration of the three cinematic texts as social deviance. That is, the 'anti' of the 'anti-*bildung*' does not indicate anti-social; rather, it refers to the fundamental conflict implicit in the ever-changing society of multiple modernities. Here we can come back to the gangster figures in the film to understand the conflicts. The local gangsters personify the idea of anti-*bildung* and thus point to the inherent challenge facing teenagers, the oscillation between yearning and frustration. On the one hand, these characters reflect the useless class in society, who wander around in the street and contribute nothing to social production. On the other, they are the vehicle for the directors to show the ignorance and confusion of their juvenile protagonists, who fall for the myth of capital accumulation, a game of social networking and recklessness, showcased by the gangsters around them. All the while, these young heroes turn a blind eye to the transformations of social structures brought about by multiple modernities. Dramatizing the existent social relations mediated through signs and images in the context of the radical transformations attributed to the expansion of global capital, *Mahjong*, *Unknown Pleasures* and *Hollywood Hong Kong* as artistic representations shed light on the complexity of East Asian multiple modernities. Anti-*bildung* narratives in these three films thus reveal the bafflement as to what kind of *bildung* in our day can help to exorcise the other side of the global prospect of increased productivity, the global-scale changes of rendering individual human labourers useless.

Notes

1 U. Beck, 2000, *What is Globalization?* trans. P. Camiller. Malden, MA: Polity Press, 30.

2 See D. Harvey, 2005, *A Brief History of Neoliberalism* New York: Oxford University Press; N. Brenner and N. Theodore (eds), 2002, *Spaces of Neoliberalism* Oxford: Blackwell.

3 M. Morris, 2004, 'Transnational imagination in Action Cinema: Hong Kong and the making of a global popular culture', *Inter-Asia Cultural Studies,* 5:2, 181–99.

4 A. Appadurai, 1996, *Modernity at Large: Cultural Dimensions of Globalization.* Minneapolis: University of Minnesota Press, 42–4.

5 R. Sennett, 2006, *The Culture of the New Capitalism* New Haven: Yale University Press.

6 M. Berman, 1983, *All That Is Solid Melts into Air: The Experience of Modernity.* New York: Penguin, 15.

7 S. N. Eisenstadt, 2000, 'Multiple modernities', *Daedalus*, 129:1, 129; Eisenstadt, 2009, 'Multiple modernities in an age of globalization', *Canadian Journal of Sociology/Cahiers canadiens de sociologie,* 24:2, 283–95.

8 G. Therborn, 2003, 'Entangled modernities', *European Journal of Social Theory* 6:3, 293–305; see also, S. J. Tambiah, 2000, 'Transnational movements, diaspora, and multiple modernities', *Daedalus* 129:1, 163–94; B. Wittrock, 2000, 'Modernity: One, none, or many? European origins and modernity as a global condition', *Daedalus* 129:1, 31–60.

9 Ibid. 95.

10 D. P. Gaonkar, 1999, 'On alternative modernities', *Public Culture* 11:1, 1–18.

11 A. Giddens, 1990, *The Consequences of Modernity.* Cambridge: Polity Press, 64.

12 Ibid. 33–4.

13 We borrow Saskia Sassen's term 'urban glamour zone' to delineate the global space of Taipei. See S. Sassen, 1998, *Globalization and its Discontents* New York: New Press, xxxiii.

14 O. Assayas, 2008, 'Modern time', *Film Comment* 244, January/February, 48–56.

15 For the modernization of Taipei's urban space, see Y. Chiou, 2006, 'Hengchang yu wuchang: lun Tien-Hsin Chu's *Gu Du* zhong de kongjian, shenti, yu zhengzhijingjixue' 'Mutability and immutability: space, body, and political economy in Tien-Hsin Chu's "Ancient Capital" ', *Zhongwai wenxue* (*Chung-wai Literary Monthly*), 35:4, 57–94.

16 Through the media reproduction and replaying of certain cultural products, the Hard Rock Café illustrates Appadurai's delimitation of transnational imagination: 'a social imaginaire built largely around reruns' (30).

17 Z. Jia and X. Tu (塗翔文). 'Kancheng yingzhan tebie baodao (《坎城影展特別報導》: 賈樟柯 影像「逍遙」 主題「感傷」 The special report on the Cannes Film Festival: Zhangke Jia – the image of 'unknown pleasures' with the topic of 'melancholia').' *Ziyou dianzi xinwenwang* (自由電子新聞網 *Liberty Times* website), 24 May 2002.

18 For an account of how ruins function in Jia's films as 'semiotic reconstruction and cinematic interpretation' of the historical process of globalization, see H. Zhang, 2009, 'Ruins and grassroots: Jia Zhangke's cinematic discontents in the age of globalization' in S. H. Lu and J. Mi (eds) *Chinese Ecocinema: In the Age of Environmental Challenge*, Hong Kong: Hong Kong University Press. In *Unknown Pleasures*, Zhang argues, ruins start to spread in public space, and the whole city of Datong is a wasteland except for the new highway (138–9).

19 D. Lok, 2014, (洛謀) 'Xiaofeizhuyi xia de shiluozhongguo (消費主義下的失落中國 — 賈樟柯《任逍遙》The China lost in consumerism – Zhangke Jia's *Unknown Pleasures*' *Xianggang jiaoyucheng* (香港教育城 HKEdCity.net). 25 September 2003.

20 Y. Lu (綠妖) and Z. Jia, 2002, 'Jia Zhangke: Xingzouzai duanleizhong de yingxiangshiren (賈樟柯：行走在斷裂中的影像詩人 Zhangke Jia: the imagist poet walking in disjunctured landscapes)' *Wangyi* (網易 NetEase) 26 September.

21 C. Berry, 2009, 'Jia Zhangke and the temporality of postsocialist Chinese cinema: In the now (and then)', *Futures of Chinese Cinema*. Bristol: Intellect.

22 For the role gang organizations play mediating China's conversion from socialism to capitalism, see G. R. Barmé, 1999, *In the Red: On Contemporary Chinese Culture*. New York: Columbia University Press, Chapter 4.

23 Zia and Tu, Special report on the Cannes Film Festival.

24 E. M. K. Cheung, 2010, (張美君) 'Realisms within conundrum: The personal and authentic appeal in Zhangke Jia's accented films', *China Perspectives* 1, 11–20.

25 K. Jones, 2002, 'Out of time', *Film Comment* 212 (September/October), 43–7.

26 K. Leung, 2001, (梁廣福). *Qingtianyutian dakancun: xianggang zuidayige liaowucun de cangsang suiyue* 晴天雨天大磡村：香港最大一個寮屋村的滄桑歲月(Tai Hom village – be it sunny or rainy – the hard time of the largest squatter village in Hong Kong). Hong Kong: Mingchuang, 158–9.

27 Ibid. 76–80.

28 For more on this point, see T. M. Huang, 2008, (黃宗儀). 'Quanqiu chengshi quyuzhili zhiwai: xianggang de kuajing shenfen lunshu yu zaixian (全球城市區域治理之外：香港的跨境身份論述與再現 Beyond the governance of global city-regions: Discourses and representations of Hong Kong's cross-border identities)' *Dili xuebao* (地理學報 *Journal of Geographical Science*) 52, 1–30.

29 For Hung Hung's role as a femme fatale, see P. C. Feng, 2004, 'Huoshui hongyan (Femme fatale: The gender and national narrative in *Hollywood Hong Kong*)' *Yingpingren jikan* (*Film Critics Quarterly*) 25, 11–14.

30 A. Abbas, 1997, *Hong Kong: Culture and the Politics of Disappearance*. Hong Kong: Hong Kong University Press/Minneapolis: University Of Minnesota Press.

31 Sennett, *The Culture of the New Capitalism*, 88.

Bibliography

'Lam Wai Sze Incident' http://www.youtube.com/watch?v=OAoz4AwY6GU.

Abbas, A., 1997, *Hong Kong: Culture and the Politics of Disappearance*. Minneapolis: University of Minnesota Press.

Acland, C. R. (ed.), 2007, *Residual Media*. Minneapolis: University of Minnesota Press.

Alliez, E., 2004, *The Signature of the World: 'What is Deleuze and Guattari's Philosophy?'* trans. E. R. Albert and A. Toscano. New York: Continuum.

Anderson, B., 1983, *Imagined Communities: Reflections on the Origin and Spread of Nationalism*. London: Verso.

Anonymous, 2008, 〈時代廣場被指佔用公共空間〉 'Times Square is alleged to occupy the public space', *Apple Daily*, 7 April.

Appadurai, A., 1996, *Modernity at Large: Cultural Dimensions of Globalization*. Minneapolis: University of Minnesota Press.

——, 2001, 'Grassroots globalization and the research imagination' in *Globalization*, A. Appadurai (ed.). Durham: Duke University Press.

Assayas, O., 2008, 'Modern time', *Film Comment* 244, January/February.

Austin, J. L., 1962, *How to do Things with Words*. Cambridge, MA: Harvard University Press.

Badiou, A., 1997, *Deleuze: La clameur de l'Être*. Paris: Hachette.

——, 1999, *Manifesto for Philosophy*, trans. N. Madarsz. Albany: State University of New York Press.

Bailey, P., 2007, *Think of an Elephant: Combining Science and Spirituality for a Better Life*. London: Watkins.

Bains, P., 2002, 'Subjectless subjectivities' in B. Massumi (ed.), *A Shock to Thought: Expression after Deleuze and Guattai*. London and New York: Routledge.

Banquet, J. P., 1972, 'EEG and meditation', *Electroencephalography and Clinical Neurophysiology* 33.

Barmé, G. R., 1999, *In the Red: On Contemporary Chinese Culture*. New York: Columbia University Press.

Barron, N. (ed.), 2004, *Anatomy of Wonder*. 5th edn. Westport, CT: Libraries Unlimited.

Barry, A., 1998, 'On interactivity: consumers, citizens and culture' in S. MacDonald (ed.), *The Politics of Display: Museums, Science and Culture*. London and New York: Routledge.

Barthes, R., 1977, 'The grain of the voice' in *Image-Music-Text: Selected Essays*, trans. Stephen Heath (ed.). London: Fontana.

Baudrillard, J., 1983, *Simulations*, trans. P. Foss, P. Patton and P. Beitchman. New York: Semiotext(e).

Beck, U., 2000, *What is Globalization?* trans. P. Camiller. Malden, MA: Polity Press.

Bell, D., 2007, *Cyberculture Theorists: Manuel Castells and Donna Haraway*. London: Routledge.

Belting, H., 2008, 'Arab mathematics and renaissance Western Art', *European Review* 16: 2.

Benjamin, W., 1939, 'Paris, the capital of the nineteenth century' in W. Benjamin (ed.), trans. H. Eiland, E. Jephcott, R. Livingston and H. Zohn *The Writer of Modern Life: Essays on Charles Baudelaire*. Cambridge, MA: Harvard University Press (2006).

Bennett, J., 2001, *The Enchantment of Modern Life: Attachments, Crossings, and Ethics*. Princeton, NJ, and Oxford: Princeton University Press.

Bennett ,T., 1995, *The Birth of the Museum: History, Theory, Politics*. London and New York: Routledge.

——, 2006, 'Civic seeing: museums and the organisation of vision' in S. MacDonald (ed.), *Companion to Museum Studies*. Oxford: Blackwell.

Bergson, H., 1911, *Creative Evolution*, trans. A. Mitchell. New York: Henry Holt.

——, 1988, *Matter and Memory* trans. N. M. Paul and W. S. Palmer. New York: Zone Books.

——, 1991, *Matter and Memory*. New York: Zone Books (1896).

Berman, M., 1981, *The Reenchantment of the World*. Ithaca, NY: Cornell University Press.

——, 1982, *All That is Solid Melts into Air: The Experience of Modernity*, 2nd edn. New York: Penguin.

——, 1983, *All That is Solid Melts into Air: The Experience of Modernity*. New York: Verso.

Berry, C., 2009, 'Jia Zhangke and the temporality of postsocialist Chinese cinema: In the now (and then)' in *Futures of Chinese Cinema*. Bristol: Intellect.

Berzin, A., 1997, *Taking the Kalachakra Initiation*. Ithaca, NY: Snow Lion Publications.

Bey, H., 1991, *T.A.Z.: The Temporary Autonomous Zone, Ontological Anarchism, Poetic Terrorism*. New York: Autonomedia.

Blackford, R., 2005, 'Greg Egan' in D. Seed (ed.), *A Companion to Science Fiction*. Oxford: Blackwell.

Bloch, E., 1995, *The Principle of Hope*. Cambridge, MA: MIT Press.

Boehm, G. and W. J. T. Mitchell, 2009, 'Pictorial versus Iconic Turn: Two letters', *Culture, Theory and Critique*, 50:2–3, 103–121

Bogue, R., 2003a, *Deleuze on Cinema*. New York and London: Routledge.

——, 2003b, *Deleuze: On music, painting, and the arts*. New York: Routledge.

——, 2010, 'To choose to choose – to believe in this world' in D. N. Rodowick (ed.), *Afterimages of Gilles Deleuze's Film Philosophy*. Minneapolis: University of Minnesota.

Bolter, J. D. and Grusin, R., 2000, *Remediation: Understanding New Media*. Cambridge, MA: MIT Press.

Bonta, M. and J. Protevi, 2004, *Deleuze and Geophilosophy: A Guide and Glossary*. Edinburgh: Edinburgh University Press.

Boundas, C.V., 2005, 'Intensity' in A. Parr (ed.), *The Deleuze Dictionary*, New York: Columbia University Press.

Bourdieu, P., 1984, *Distinction: A Social Critique of the Judgment of Taste*, trans. R. Nice. London: Routledge & K. Paul.

Brauen, M., 2009, *Mandala: Sacred Circle in Tibetan Buddhism*. Stuttgart: Arnoldsche Art Publishers.

Brautigan, R., 1968, 'All watched over by machines of loving grace' in *The Pill Versus the Springhill Mine Disaster*. New York: Delta.

Brenez, N., 1998, *De la figure en general et du corps en particulier: L'invention figurative au cinema*. De Boeck Université.

Brenner, N. and N. Theodore (eds), 2002, *Spaces of Neoliberalism*. Oxford: Blackwell.

Bryant. B., 1992, *The Wheel of Time: Sand Mandala*. Ithaca, NY: Snow Lion Publications.

Buchanan, I., 2008, *Deleuze and Guattari's anti-Oedipus*. London and New York: Continuum.

—— and L. Gregg (eds), 2005, *Deleuze and Space*. Edinburgh: University of Edinburgh Press.

Buchloh, B., 1999, 'Gerhard Richter's *The Atlas.* The anomic archive', *October* 88: Spring.

Buckley, J. H., 1974, *Season of Youth: The Bildungsroman from Dickens to Golding.* Cambridge, MA: Harvard University Press.

Butler, J., 1993, *Bodies that Matter: On the Discursive Limits of 'Sex'.* London: Routledge.

Buxton, W. A. S., 1997, 'Living in augmented reality: Ubiquitous media and reactive environments' in K. E. Finn, A. J. Sellen and S. Wilber (eds), *Video Mediated Communication.* Hillsdale, NJ: Erlbaum.

Canetti, E., 1984, *Crowds and Power.* New York: Farrar, Straus and Giroux.

Carroll, J., 2007, *A Concise History of Hong Kong.* Lanham: Rowman & Littlefield.

Cartwright, L., 1995, *Screening the Body: Tracing Medicine's Visual Culture.* Minneapolis: University of Minnesota Press.

Casetti, F., 2007, 'Theory, post-theory neo-theories: Changes in discourses, changes in objects', *Cinémas: revue d'études cinématographiques/Cinémas: Journal of Film Studies* 17: 2–3, Spring.

Chakravartty, P. and K. Sarikakis, 2006, *Media Policy and Globalization.* Edinburgh: Edinburgh University Press.

Cheung, E. M. K. 張美君, 2010, 'Realisms within conundrum: The personal and authentic appeal in Jia Zhangke's accented films', *China Perspectives* [Online], 2010/1: http://chinaperspectives.revues.org/5048.

Chiou, Y. 邱彥彬, 2006, 'Hengchang yu wuchang: lun Tien-Hsin Chu's *Gu Du* zhong de kongjian, shenti, yu zhengzhijingjixue 恆常與無常：論朱天心《古都》中的空間、身體與政治經濟學 (Mutability and immutability: space, body, and political economy in Tien-Hsin Chu's "Ancient Capital")' *Zhongwai wenxue* 中外文學 *Chung-wai Literary Monthly* 35:4.

Chiu, S. W. K. and T. Lui (eds), 2000, *The Dynamics of Social Movement in Hong Kong.* Hong Kong: Hong Kong University Press.

Choi, P. K. (ed.), 2008,《千針萬線：香港成衣工人口述史》*Thousands of Needles and Threads: An Oral History of Hong Kong Textile Industry Workers.* Hong Kong: Stepforward Press.

Chow, R., 2004, 'Towards an ethics of postvisuality: Some thoughts on the recent work of Zhang Yimou', *Poetics Today* 25:4.

Cohen, G. A., 1978, *Karl Marx's Theory of History: A Defence.* Princeton: Princeton University Press.

Colebrook, C., 2006, *Deleuze: A Guide for the Perplexed.* London and New York: Continuum.

Coverley, M., 2006, *Psychogeography.* Harpenden: Pocket Essentials.

Crary, J., 2001, *Suspensions of Perception: Attention, Spectacle, and Modern Culture*. Cambridge, MA: MIT Press.

Crary, J., 2013, *24/7: Late Capitalism and the Ends of Sleep*. London: Verso.

Csicsery-Ronay, I., Jnr, 1992, 'The sentimental futurist: Cybernetics and art in William Gibson's *Neuromancer*', *Critique: Studies in Contemporary Fiction* 33:3, Spring.

——, 2005, 'Science/fiction criticism,' in D. Seed (ed.), *A Companion to Science Fiction*. Oxford: Blackwell.

——, 2008, *The Seven Beauties of Science Fiction*. Middletown, CT: Wesleyan University Press.

Cubitt, S., 2004, *The Cinema Effect*. Cambridge, MA: MIT Press.

——, 2005, *EcoMedia (Contemporary Cinema 1)*. Amsterdam and New York: Rodopi.

Cuthbert, A. R. and K. G. McKinnell, 1997, 'Ambiguous space, ambiguous rights – corporate power and social control in Hong Kong', *Cities* 14:5.

Daston L. and P. Galison, 2010, *Objectivity*. New York: Zone Books.

Dawkins, R., 1989, *The Selfish Gene*. Oxford: Oxford University Press.

De Certeau, M., 1984, *The Practice of Everyday Life*. Berkeley: University of California Press.

De Landa, M., 2002, *Intensive Science and Virtual Philosophy*. London and New York: Continuum.

Debord, G., 1983, *The Society of the Spectacle*. Detriot: Black and Red.

Deikman, A. J., 1966, 'De-automatization and the mystic experience', *Psychiatry* 29.

Deleuze, G., 1983, *Nietzsche and Philosophy*, trans. H. Tomlinson. New York: Columbia University Press.

——, 1984, *Kant's Critical Philosophy*, trans. H. Tomlinson and B. Habberjam. Minneapolis: University of Minnesota Press.

——, 1986, *Cinema 1: The Movement-image*, trans. H. Tomlinson and B. Habberjam. Minneapolis: University of Minnesota Press.

——, 1988, *Spinoza: Practical Philosophy* trans. R. Hurley. San Francisco: City Lights Books.

——, 1989, *Cinema 2: The Time-image* trans. H. Tomlinson and R. Galeta. Minneapolis: University of Minnesota Press.

——, 1990, *The Logic of Sense* trans. Mark Lester with C. Stivale (ed.), and C.V. Boundas. New York: Columbia University Press.

——, 1991, *Bergsonism*, trans. C. Boundas. New York: Zone Books.

——, 1992, 'Postscript on the societies of control', *October* 59, Winter.

——, 1993, *The Fold: Leibniz and the Baroque*. Minneapolis: University of Minnesota Press.

——, 1994, *Difference and Repetition* trans. P. Patton. New York: Columbia University Press.

——, 2000, 'The brain is the screen: An interview with Gilles Deleuze' in G. Flaxman (ed.), *The Brain is the Screen: Deleuze and the Philosophy of Cinema.* Minneapolis and London: University of Minnesota Press.

—— and F. Guattari, 1977, *Anti-Oedipus* trans. R. Hurley, M. Seem and H. R. Lane. Minneapolis: University of Minnesota Press.

—— and C. Parnet, 1987, *Dialogues II* trans. H. Tomlinson. London and New York: Continuum.

—— and F. Guattari, 1987, *A Thousand Plateaus* trans. B. Massumi. Minneapolis: University of Minnesota Press.

—— and F. Guattari, 1994, *What Is Philosophy*? trans. H. Tomlinson and G. Burchell. New York: Columbia University Press.

Derrida, J., 1982, *Margins of Philosophy* trans. with Introduction by A. Bass. Chicago: University of Chicago Press (French edn 1972).

——, 1995, *Archive Fever: A Freudian Impression.* Chicago: University of Chicago Press.

Dougherty, S., 2012, 'Embodiment and Technicity in Geoff Ryman's *Air*', *Science Fiction Studies* 39:1, March.

Douglas, M. and B. Isherwood, 1996, *The World of Goods: Towards an Anthropology of Consumption.* London: Routledge.

Due, R., 2007, *Deleuze.* Cambridge, UK: Polity Press.

Dyer-Witheford, N., 1999, *Cyber-Marx: Cycles and Circuits of Struggle in High-Technology Capitalism.* Urbana: University of Illinois Press.

Eagleman, D. M., 2010, 'How does the timing of neural signals map onto the timing of perception?' in R. Nijhawan and B. Khurana (eds), *Space and Time in Perception and Action.* Cambridge, UK: Cambridge University Press.

Easterbrook, N., 2005, 'Estrangement' in G. Westfahl (ed.), *The Greenwood Encyclopedia of Science Fiction and Fantasy: Themes, Works, and Wonders*, vol. 1 . Westport, CT: Greenwood.

——, 2008a, 'Giving an account of oneself: ethics, alterity, *Air*', *Extrapolation* 49:2.

——, 2008b, review of *No Maps for These Territories* DVD, *Science Fiction Film and Television* 1:1, Spring.

Eco, U., 1994, *Apocalypse Postponed*, Robert Lumley (ed.). Bloomington: Indiana University Press.

Egan, G., 2001, *Schild's Ladder.* London: Gollancz.

——, 2008, *Incandescence.* San Francisco, CA: Night Shade.

Eisenstadt, S. N., 2000, 'Multiple Modernities', *Daedalus*, 129:1.

——, 2009, 'Multiple Modernities in an Age of Globalization', *Canadian Journal of Sociology/Cahiers canadiens de sociologie* 24:2.

Eisenstein, S. N., 1929, 'The cinematic principle and the ideogram in film form' in *Film Form*. Orlando: Harcourt, Brace & Company (1949).

——, 1987, *Nonindifferent Nature: Film and the Structure of Things*, trans. H. Marshall. Cambridge, UK: Cambridge University Press.

Erb, C., 1998, *Tracking King Kong: A Hollywood Icon in World Culture*. Detroit: Wayne State University Press.

Ernst, W., 2000, M.edium F.oucault. Weimarer Vorlesungen über Archive, Archäologie, Monumente und Medien, Weimar (Verlag & Datenbank für Geisteswissenschaften, Reihe Medien, Bd. 4)

——, 2002, *Das Rumoren der Archive. Ordnung aus Unordnung.* Berlin: Merve.

Ervin L., 2006, *Science and the Reenchantment of the Cosmos: The Rise of the Integral Vision of Reality*. Rochester, VT: Inner Tradition.

Faulkner, K. W., 2006, *Deleuze and the Three Syntheses of Time*. New York: Peter Lang.

Feng, P. 馮品佳, 2004, 'Huoshui hongyan 禍水紅顏:《香港有個荷里活》中的性別與國族論述 Femme fatale: The gender and national narrative in *Hollywood Hong Kong*', *Yingpingren jikan* 影評人季刊 *Film Critics Quarterly* 25.

Flaxman, G. (ed.), 2000, *The Brain is the Screen: Deleuze and the Philosophy of Cinema*. Minneapolis and London: University of Minnesota Press.

——, 2000, 'Introduction' in G. Flaxman (ed.), *The Brain is the Screen: Deleuze and the Philosophy of Cinema*. Minneapolis and London: University of Minnesota Press.

Flusser, V., 2000, *Towards a Philosophy of Photography.* London: Reaktion Books.

——, 2002, 'Line and Surface' in Ströhl, A. (ed.), *Writings*. Minneapolis: University of Minnesota Press.

Forster, E. M., 1909, 'The Machine Stops', *Science Fiction: The Science Fiction Research Association Anthology* in P. S. Warrick, C. G. Waugh and M. H. Greenberg (eds). New York: Harper and Row (1988).

——, 1910, *Howards End*. London: Edward Arnold.

Foster, H., 2004, 'An Archival Impulse', *October* 110.

Foucault, M., 1969, *Archaeology of Knowledge*. London: Routledge (1989).

——, 1977a, 'La vie des hommes infâmes', *Les cahiers du chemin,* 29: January.

——, 1977b, *Discipline and Punish: The Birth of the Prison*, trans. A. Sheridan. London: Allen Lane, Penguin.

Froomkin, A. M., 2003, 'Habermas@Discourse.net: Toward a critical theory of cyberspace', *Harvard Law Review*. 116, January.

Fung, B.Y., 2002,《香港金融業百年》*A Century of Hong Kong Financial Development*. Hong Kong: Joint Publishing HK.

Galison, P. L., 1997, *Image and Logic: A Material Culture of Microphysics*. Chicago: University of Chicago Press.

Galloway, A. R., 2004, *Protocol: How Control Exists After Decentralization*. Cambridge, MA: MIT Press.

Gaonkar, D. P., 1999, 'On Alternative Modernities' *Public Culture* 11.1.

Gardner, J. N., 2003, *Biocosm: The New Scientific Theory of Evolution: Intelligent Life is the Architect of the Universe*. Makawao: Inner Ocean.

Garfield, J. L., 1995, *The Fundamental Wisdom of the Middle Way: Nagarjuna's Mulamadhyamakakarika*. Oxford: Oxford University Press.

Gentle, N., 2008, 'Mall sued over public space rents', *South China Morning Post* 18 June

Gibson, W., 1984, *Neuromancer*. New York: Ace.

——, 2003, *Pattern Recognition*. New York: Putnam's.

Giddens, A., 1990, *The Consequences of Modernity*. Cambridge, UK: Polity Press.

Glover, J., 2007, *Modern Railways: Dictionary of Railway Industry Terms*. London: Ian Allen Publishing.

Grace, H., 2007, 'Monuments and the face of time: Distortions of scale and asynchrony in postcolonial Hong Kong', *Postcolonial Studies* 10:4.

Graham, D., 1979, *Video-Architecture-Television: Writings on Video and Video Works 1970–1978*. Halifax: Press of Nova Scotia College of Art and Design; New York: New York University Press.

Gualandi, A., 1998, *Deleuze*. Paris: Les Belles Lettres.

Guattari, F., 1996, 'Subjectivities: For better and for worse' in G. Genosko (ed.), *The Guattari Reader*. Oxford: Blackwell.

Guenther, H.V., 1977, *Tibetan Buddhism in Western Perspective: Collected Articles of Herbert V. Guenther*. Emerville, CA: Dharma Publishing.

Hall, D., S. J. Fifer and D. Bolt (eds), 2005. *Illuminating Video: An Essential Guide to Video Art*. New York: Aperture Foundation.

Hansen, M., 2000, *Embodying Technesis: Technology beyond Writing*. Ann Arbor: University of Michigan Press.

——, 2006, *New Philosophy for New Media*. Cambridge, MA: MIT Press.

Haraway, D., 1991, 'A cyborg manifesto: Science, technology, and socialist-feminism in the late twentieth century' in *Simians, Cyborgs and Women: The Reinvention of Nature. New York: Routledge.*

Hartley, H., 1994, 'In images we trust: Hal Hartley interviews Jean-Luc Godard', *Filmmaker* 3:1, Autumn.

Hartmann, H., 1958, *Ego Psychology and the Problem of Adaptation*. New York: International University Press.

Harvey, D., 2005, *A Brief History of Neoliberalism*. New York: Oxford University Press.

Hayward, J. W. and F. J. Varela, 1992, *Gentle Bridges: Conversation with the Dalai Lama on the Sciences of Mind*. Boston and London: Shambhala.

Heidegger, M., 1977, *The Question Concerning Technology and Other Essays*. New York: Harper and Row.

Hirai, T., 1960, 'Electroencephalographic study of Zen Meditation (Zazen): EEG changes during the concentrated relaxation', *Psychiatrica et Neurologia Japanica*, 62.

His Holiness the Dalai Lama, 1985, 'Foreword: Concerning the Kalachakra' in R.J. Geshe Lhundub Sopa (ed.), *The Wheel of Time: The Kalachakra in Context*. Ithaca, NY: Snow Lion Publications.

——, 2005a, *The Universe in a Single Atom: The Convergence of Science and Spirituality*. New York: Morgan Road Books.

——, 2005b, 'The Four Noble Truths' in N. Ribush, *Teachings from Tibet: Guidance from Great Lamas*. Boston: Lama Yeshe Wisdom Archive.

Hollinger, V., 2006, 'Stories about the future: From patterns of expectation to pattern recognition', *Science Fiction Studies* 33:3, November.

Hong Kong Transport Department, http://www.td.gov.hk/tc/transport_in_hong_kong/pedestrianisation/pedestrianisation/ accessed 4 February 2014.

Hopkins, J., 1999, 'The Kalachakra Tantra: Introduction' in *Kalachakra Tantra: Rite of Initiation*, His Holiness the Dalai Lama (ed.). Boston: Wisdom Publications.

Horkheimer, M. and T. Adorno, 2002, *Dialectic of Enlightenment: Philosophical Fragments*, G. S. Noerr (ed.), trans. E. Jephcott. Stanford, CA: Stanford University Press.

Huang, T. M. 黃宗儀, 2008, 'Quanqiu chengshi quyuzhili zhi wai: xianggang de kuajing shenfen lunshu yu zaixian 全球城市區域治理之外：香港的跨境身份論述與再現 Beyond the governance of global city-regions: Discourses and representations of Hong Kong's cross-border identities.' *Dili xuebao* 地理學報 *Journal of Geographical Science* 52.

Hui, P., 2003,《富裕中的貧乏：香港文化經濟評論》*Lack within Affluence: Commentary on the Culture and Economy of Hong Kong.*, Hong Kong: Stepforward Press.

——, 2008, 'Luxury estate owners demand "public" podium back', *South China Morning Post* 14 April.

Husserl, E., 1991, *On the Phenomenology of the Consciousness of Internal Time 1983–1917*, trans. J. Brough. Dordrecht: Kluwer Academic Publishers.

Ihde, D., 1979, *Technics and Praxis*. Dordrecht, Holland and Boston: D. Reidel Publishing Company.

——, 1999, *Expanding Hermeneutics: Visualism in Science*. Evanston, IL: Northwestern University Press.

Ivins, W. M., Jnr, 1953, *Prints and Visual Communication*. Cambridge, MA: MIT Press.

Jäger, J., G. Knapstein and A. Hüsch (eds), 2006, *Beyond Cinema: The Art of Projection. Films, Videos and Installations from 1963 to 2005*. Ostfidern: Hatje Cantz.

Jakobson, R., 1957, 'Shifters and verbal categories' in L. R. Waugh and M. Monville-Burston (eds), *On Language*. Cambridge, MA: Harvard University Press (1990).

Jameson, F., 2005, 'Fear and loathing in globalization' in *Archaeologies of the Future: The Desire Called Utopia and Other Science Fictions*. London: Verso.

Jay, M., 1993, *Downcast Eyes: The Denigration of Vision in Twentieth-Century French Philosophy*. Oakland, CA: University of California Press.

——, 2009, 'Magical Nominalism: Photography and the Re-enchantment of the World' in *Culture, Theory and Critique*, 50: 2–3 (special issue).

Jia, Z. and X. Tu 塗翔文, 2002, 'Kancheng yinzhan tebie baodao《坎城影展特別報導》: 賈樟柯 影像「逍遙」 主題「感傷」 *Ziyou dianzi xinwenwang* 自由電子新聞網 *Liberty Times* website, 24 May.

Newman J. R., 'A Brief History of the Kalachakra' in *The Wheel of Time: The Kalachakra in Context*. Ithaca, NY: Snow Lion Publications.

Jones, K., 2002, 'Out of time', *Film Comment* 212, September/October.

Jones, S. E., 2006, *Against Technology: From the Luddites to Neo-Luddism*. New York: Routledge.

Jung, C., 1972, *Mandala Symbolism*, trans. R. Hull. Princeton, NJ: Princeton University Press.

Kahn, D., 1999, *Noise, Water, Meat: A History of Sound in the Arts*. Cambridge, MA: MIT Press.

Kearnes, M., 2006, 'Chaos and control: Nanotechnology and the politics of emergence' in John Marks (ed.), *Deleuze and Science. Paragraph*, 29: 2.

Kittler, F., 1985, *Discourse Networks 1800/1900*. Stanford, CA: Stanford University Press (1990).

——, 1986, *Gramophone, Film, Typewriter*. Standford, CA: Stanford University Press (1999).

——, 2006, 'Number and numeral' in *Theory, Culture & Society*. London, Thousand Oaks; New Delhi: Sage. 23:7–8.

Komparu, K., 1983, *The Noh Theatre: Principles and Perspectives*, trans. J. Corddry and S. Comee. New York/Tokyo: Weatherhill.

Koolhaas, R., 1995, 'The generic city' in R. Koolhaas, B. Mau, J. Sigler and H. Werlemann (eds), *S, M, L, XL*. New York: Monacelli.

Kracauer, S., 1960, *Theory of Film*. New York: Oxford University Press.

——, 1995, *The Mass Ornament: Weimar Essays*, trans. T. Y. Levin. Cambridge, MA: Harvard University Press.

——, 1997, *The Salaried Masses: Duty and Distraction in Weimar Germany*, trans. Q. Hoare. London: Verso.

Kristeva, J., 2003, 'The future of a defeat: Interview with Arnaud Spire'. *Parallax* 9: 2, first published *L'Humanite´* 2 July 2001.

Kurtz, B., 1976, 'The present tense' in I. Schneider and B. Korot (eds), *Video Art: An Anthology*. New York: Harcourt Brace Jovanovich.

Kurzweil, R., 2005, *The Singularity is Near: When Humans Transcend Biology*. New York: Penguin (2006).

Lacan, J., 1978, *The Four Fundamental Concepts of Psychoanalysis*, J.-A. Miller (ed.), trans. A. Sheridan. New York: Norton.

Lambert, G., 2002, *The non-philosophy of Gilles Deleuze*. New York: Continuum.

Laszlo, E., 2006a, *Science and the Re-enchantment of the Cosmos: The Rise of the Integral Vision of Reality*. Rochester, VT: Inner Traditions.

——, 2006b, *Science and the Akashic Field: An Integral Theory of Everything*. Rochester, VT: Inner Traditions.

——, 2008, *Quantum shift in the global brain: How the new scientific reality can change us and our world*. Rochester, VT: Inner Traditions.

Latour, B., 1999, 'A collective of humans and nonhumans' in *Pandora's Hope: Essays on the Reality of Science Studies*. Cambridge, MA: Harvard University Press.

——, 2005, *Reassembling the Social: An Introduction to Actor-Network-Theory*. Oxford: Oxford University Press.

Lee, L. O., 2006, *Rhapsody on Festival Walk*. Hong Kong: Oxford University Press.

Lefebvre, H., 2005, *Critique of Everyday Life: From Modernity to Modernism Volume 3*, trans. G. Elliot. London: Verso.

——, 2003, *The Urban Revolution*, trans. Robert Bononno. Minneapolis: University of Minnesota Press.

Leidy, D. P. and R. Thurman, 2000, *Mandala: The Architecture of Enlightenment*. New York: Tibet House.

Leung, K., 梁廣福, 2001, *Qingtianyutian dakancun: xianggang zuidayige liaowucun de cangsang suiyue* 晴天雨天大磡村：香港最大一個寮屋村的滄桑歲月 Tai 'Hom Village – be it sunny or rainy – the hard time of the largest squatter village in Hong Kong'. Hong Kong: Mingchuang.

Levin, D. M. (ed.), 2003, *Modernity and The Hegemony Of Vision*. New York: University of California Press.

Livingston, I., 2006, *Between Science and Literature: An Introduction to Autopoetics*. Urbana and Chicago: University of Illinois Press.

Lo, K.Y. and K. M. Lee (eds), 2004, *The Economy of Hong Kong in Non-economic Perspectives*. Hong Kong: Oxford University Press.

Loh, C., 2008, 'Reclaiming the city', *South China Morning Post* 10 April.

Lok, D. 洛謀, 2014, 'Xiaofeizhuyi xia de shiluozhongguo 消費主義下的失落中國 — 賈樟柯《任逍遙》The China lost in consumerism – Zhangke Jia's *Unknown Pleasures*' *Xianggang jiaoyucheng* 香港教育城 HKEdCity. net. 25 September 2003, accessed 21 January 2014. http://www. hkedcity.net/ article/culture_movie/030925-003/.

Lopez , D. S., Jnr, 2008, *Buddhism & Science: A Guide for the Perplexed*. Chicago and London: University of Chicago Press.

Lu, S. H. and M. Jiayan (eds), 2009, *Chinese Ecocinema in the Age of Environmental* Challenge. Hong Kong: Hong Kong University Press.

Lu, Y. 綠妖 and Z. Jia, 2002, 'Jia Zhangke: Xingzouzai duanleizhong de yingxiangshiren 賈樟柯：行走在斷裂中的影像詩人 Zhangke Jia: the imagist poet walking in disjunctured landscapes' *Wangyi* 網易 NetEase 26 September, 2002 accessed 1 October 2004. http://ent.163.com/ edit/ 020926/020926_1357251. html.

Lui, T., 2001, 'The malling of Hong Kong' in G. Mathews and T. Lui (eds), *Consuming Hong Kong*. Hong Kong: Hong Kong University Press.

——, 2004,《中產好痛》*Bourgeois Class in Pain*. Hong Kong: Stepforward Press.

—— and W. C. Chun, 2003,《香港中產階級處境觀察》*Observations on the Condition of Hong Kong Bourgeois Class*. Hong Kong: Joint Publishing HK.

Lyotard, J. F., 1971, *Discours, Figure*. Paris: Klincksieck.

Ma, K. F., 1998,《路邊政治經濟學》*Political Economy on the Street*. Hong Kong: Shu Guang.

——, 2002,〈流行與分眾/百貨公司之死〉'Fashion and differentiation/the death of the department store' in C. H. Ng and C. W. Cheung (eds), *Reading Hong Kong Popular Cultures 1970–2000*. Hong Kong: Oxford University Press.

MacCormack, P., 2008, 'An ethics of spectatorship: Love, death and cinema' in I. Buchanan and P. MacCormack (eds), *Deleuze and the Schizoanalysis of Cinema*. London and New York: Continuum.

Mackenzie, A., 2006, *Cutting Code: Software and Sociality*. New York: Peter Lang.

McDonagh, T., 1996, 'The Dérive and situationist Paris' in L. Andreotti and X. Costa (eds), *Situationists, Art, Politics, Urbanism*. Barcelona: ACTAR.

Mallin, S. B., 1979, *Merleau-Ponty's Philosophy*. New Haven and London: Yale University Press.

Manovich, L., 2003, 'Metadating the image' in A. Adriaansens (ed.), *Making Art of Databases*. Rotterdam: V2 Publishing.

Mansfield, N., 2000, *Subjectivity: Theories of the Self from Freud to Haraway*. New York: New York University Press.

Marks, J., 2006, 'Introduction' in J. Marks (ed.), *Deleuze and Science. Paragraph* 29:2.

Marx, K., 1973, *Grundrisse : Foundations of the critique of political economy* .trans. M. Nicolaus. London: Allen Lane/New Left Review.

Massumi, B. (ed.), *A Shock to Thought: Expression after Deleuze and Guattai*. London and New York: Routledge.

Mendlesohn, F., 2003, 'Introduction: Reading science fiction' in E. James and F. Mendlesohn (eds), *The Cambridge Companion to Science Fiction*. Cambridge, UK: Cambridge University Press.

Merewether, C. (ed.), 2006, *The Archive*. Cambridge, MA: MIT Press.

Merleau-Ponty, M., 1962, *Phenomenology of Perception*, trans. Colin Smith. London and New Jersey: Routledge.

——, 1964, 'Eye and mind', in J. M. Edie (ed.), trans. C. Dally *The Primacy of Perception*. Evanston: Northwestern University Press.

Michelson, A. (ed.), 1984, *Kino-Eye: The Writings of Dziga Vertov*, Oakland, CA: University of California Press.

Mitchell, W. J., 1992, *The Reconfigured Eye. Visual Truth in the Post-Photographic Era*. Cambridge, MA: MIP Press.

Mitchell, W. J. T., 2005, *What Do Pictures Want? The Lives and Loves of Images*. Chicago: University of Chicago Press.

Moacanin, R., 1986, *Jung's Psychology and Tibetan Buddhism: Western and Eastern Paths to the Heart*. Boston: Wisdom Publications.

Morin, E., 2005, *The Cinema, or The Imaginary Man*, trans. L. Mortimer. Minneapolis: University of Minnesota Press.

Morris, M., 2004, 'Transnational imagination in Action Cinema: Hong Kong and the making of a global popular culture', *Inter-Asia Cultural Studies* 5:2.

Moylan, T., 2000, *Scraps of the Untainted Sky: Science Fiction, Utopia, Dystopia.* Boulder, CO: Westview Press.

MTR Malls. http://www.mtrmalls.com.

Mülder-Bach, I., 1997, 'Cinematic ethnology: Siegfried Kracauer's *The White Collar Masses*', *New Left Review*, 226.

Murphie, A., 2002. 'Putting the virtual back into VR' in B. Massumi (ed.), *A Shock to Thought: Expression after Deleuze and Guattari.* New York and London: Routledge.

Nash, M., 1990, interview with Bill Viola, *Journal of Contemporary Art*, 3:2.

Nelmes, J., 2003, *An Introduction to Film Studies.* London: Routledge.

Newman, J. R., 1985, 'A Brief History of the Kalachakra' in *The Wheel of Time: The Kalachakra in Context.* Ithaca, NY: Snow Lion Publications.

Ngo, T. (ed.), 1999, *Hong Kong's History: State and Society under Colonial Rule.* London and New York: Routledge.

O'Sullivan, S., 2006, *Art Encounters Deleuze and Guattari: Thought Beyond Representation.* New York: Palgrave Macmillan.

Owens, C., 1980, 'The allegorical impulse. Toward a theory of postmodernism. I–II', *October* 12 and 13.

Palmer, M. and E. Breuilly (trans.), 1996, *The Book of Chuang Tzu: A New, Complete Translation of the Classic Taoist Text.* Arkana: Penguin Books.

Parisi, L., 2009, 'Technoecologies of sensation' in B. Herzogenrath (ed.), *Deleuze/ Guattari & Ecology.* London: Palgrave Macmillan.

Parr, A. (ed.), 2005, *The Deleuze Dictionary.* New York: Columbia University Press.

Pearson, K. A., 1999, *Germinal life: The difference and repetition of Deleuze.* London: Routledge.

Pierson, M., 2002, *Special Effects: Still in Search of Wonder.* New York: Columbia University Press.

Pold, S., 2005, 'Interface realisms: The interface as aesthetic form', *Postmodern Culture* 15:2, January.

Poole, S., 2003, 'Tomorrow's man', interview with W. Gibson, *The Guardian*, 3 May 2003. http://www.theguardian.com/books/2003/may/03/sciencefictionfantasyandhorror.william gibson accessed 30 October 2013.

Poon, A., 2005, *Land and the Ruling Class in Hong Kong.* Richmond, BC: Alice Poon.

Preston, M. and M. Hill, 2006, 'Grooming, animating & rendering fur for "King Kong" ', *ACM SIGGRAPH 2006 Sketches*, ACM, New York.

Prigogine, I. and I. Stengers, 1984, *Order out of Chaos: Man's New Dialogue with Nature.* New York: Bantam.

Prucher, J. (ed.), 2007, *Brave New Words: The Oxford Dictionary of Science Fiction*. Oxford: Oxford University Press.

Qui, J. L., 2009, *Working-Class Network Society: Communication Technology and the Information Have-Less in Urban China*. Cambridge, MA: MIT Press.

Quine, W. V., 1953, 'Mr. Strawson on Logical Theory', *Mind*, New Series, 62:248, October.

Rabinbach, A., 1990, *The Human Motor: Energy, Fatigue and the Origins of Modernity*. New York: Basic Books; Berkeley: University of California Press.

Ralph, E., 1987, *The Modern Urban Landscape*. London: Croom Helm.

Rancière, J., 2007, *The Future of the Image*. London: Verso.

Rayns, T., n.d. cited on *The Andy Warhol Museum, The Warhol: resources and lessons* website http://edu.warhol.org/aract_screentest.html accessed January 2014.

Rendell, J., 2006, *Art and Architecture: A Place Between*. London: I.B. Tauris.

Ricard, M., 2000, 'Introduction to the purpose of symbolism of the Mandala in Tibetan Buddhism' in D. P. Leidy and R. Thurman (eds), *Mandala: The Architecture of Enlightenment*. New York: Tibet House.

Robson, J., 2005, *Natural History*. New York: Bantam.

Rodowick, D. N., 1997, *Gilles Deleuze's Time Machine*. Durham and London: Duke University Press.

——, 2001, *Reading the Figural, or, Philosophy after the New Media*. Durham, NC: Duke University Press.

——, 2014, *Elegy for Theory*. Cambridge, MA: Harvard University Press.

Rosenblum, B. and Kuttner, F., 2006, *Quantum Enigma: Physics Encounters Consciousness*. Oxford: Oxford University Press.

Røssaak, E., 2005, *Selviakttakelse: En tendens i kunst og litteratur.* Oslo and Bergen: Norsk kulturråd.

——, 2010, *The Archive in Motion*, Oslo: Novus Press.

Ruyer, R., 1952, *Néo-finalisme*. Paris: Presses Universitaires de France.

Ryman, G., 2004, *Air (or, Have Not Have)*. New York: St Martin's Griffin.

——, 2007a, 'The Mundane Manifesto', *The New York Review of Science Fiction* 226, June.

——, 2007b, 'Take the third star on the left and on til morning!', *The New York Review of Science Fiction* 226, June.

Sadakata, A., 2004, *Buddhist Cosmology: Philosophy and Origins*, trans. G. Sekimori. Tokyo: Kosei Publishing.

Saler, M., 2006, 'Modernity and enchantment: A historiographic review', *The American Historical Review* 111:3.

Sassen, S., 1998, *Globalization and its Discontents*. New York: New Press.

Schalow, F., 2006, *The Incarnality of Being: The Earth, Animals, and the Body in Heidegger's Thought*. Albany: State University of New York Press.

Sekula, A., 1986, 'The Body and the Archive', *October* 39, Winter.

Sennett, R., 2006, *The Culture of the New Capitalism*. New Haven: Yale University Press.

Shapiro, D., 1960, 'A Perceptual Understanding of Color Response' in M. A. Rickers-Ovsiankina (ed.), *Rorschach Psychology*. New York: Wiley.

Slater, D., 1997, *Consumer Culture and Modernity*. Oxford: Polity Press; Cambridge, MA: Blackwell Publishers.

Smith, N., 2006, 'Gentrification generalized: From local anomaly to urban "regeneration" as global urban strategy' in M. S. Fisher and G. Downey (eds), *Frontiers of Capital: Ethnographic Reflection on the New Economy*. Durham: Duke University Press.

Snyder, G., 1971, *The Back Country*. London: Fulcrum Press.

Sobchack, V., 1994, 'The Scene of the Screen' in *Materialities of Communication*, H. U. Gumbrecht and K. L. Pfeiffer (eds). Stanford: Stanford University Press.

Sopa, R.J. Geshe Lhundub (ed.), 1985, *The Wheel of Time: The Kalachakra in Context*. Ithaca, New York: Snow Lion Publications.

Spiegel, S., 2008, 'Things made strange: on the concept of "estrangement" in science fiction theory', *Science Fiction Studies* 35:3, November.

Spieker, S., 2008, *The Big Archive: Art from Bureaucracy*. Cambridge, MA: MIT Press.

Spielmann, Y., 2008, *Video: The Reflexive Medium*. Cambridge, MA: MIT Press.

Spigel, L., 2005, 'Designing the smart house: Posthuman domesticity and conspicuous consumption', *European Journal of Cultural Studies* 8:4.

Stagoll, C., 2005, 'Event' in A. Parr (ed.), *The Deleuze Dictionary*. New York: Columbia University Press.

Stivale, C. J., 2005, *Gilles Deleuze: Key Concepts*. Ithaca, NY: McGill-Queen's University Press.

Strogatz, S., 2003, SYNC: *The Emerging Science of Spontaneous Order*. New York: Hyperion.

Ströhl, A. (ed.), 2004, *Vilém Flusser: Writings*. Minneapolis: University of Minnesota Press.

Stross, C., 2008, *Halting State*. New York: Ace.

Suvin, D., 1979, *Metamorphoses of Science Fiction: On the Poetics and History of a Literary Genre*. New Haven: Yale University Press.

Tambiah, S. J., 2000, 'Transnational movements, diaspora, and multiple modernities', *Daedalus* 129:1

Tarthang T., 1990, *Knowledge of Time and Space*. Berkeley: Dharma Publishing.

Therborn, G., 2003, 'Entangled Modernities', *European Journal of Social Theory* 6:3.

Thurman, R., 1997, 'Mandala: The architecture of enlightenment' in *Mandala: The Architecture of Enlightenment*. London: Thames and Hudson.

Trungpa, C., 1991, *Orderly Chaos: The Mandala Principle,* S. Chodzin (ed.). Boston and London: Shambhala.

Tucci, G., 1961, *The Theory and Practice of the Mandala: With Reference to the Modern Psychology of the Unconscious*, trans. A.H. Brodrick. Mineola, NY: Dover Publications.

Tulku, T., 1994, *Dynamics of Time and Space: Transcending Limits on Knowledge.* Berkeley: Dharma Publishing.

Van Campen, C., 2008, *The Hidden Sense: Synesthesia in Art and Science.* London: MIT Press.

Van Uffelen, C., 2008, *Malls & Department Stores*. Berlin: Braun.

Varela, F. J., Thompson, E. and Rosch, E., 1991, *The Embodied Mind: Cognitive and Human Experience*. Cambridge, MA and London: The MIT Press.

Vasseleu, C., 1998, *Textures of Light: Vision and Touch in Irigaray, Levinas and Merleau-Ponty*. Abingdon: Routledge.

Vinge, V., 1993, 'The coming technological singularity.' http://www.faculty.english.vt.edu/Collier/4874/pdfs/vinge_1993.pdf .

Vint, S., 2007, *Bodies of Tomorrow: Technology, Subjectivity, Science Fiction*. Toronto: University of Toronto Press.

Wallace, B. A., 2007, *Contemplative Science: Where Buddhism and Neuroscience Converge*. New York: Columbia University Press.

Wallace, V. A., 2001, *The Inner Kalacakratantra: A Buddhist Tantric View of the Individual.* Oxford and New York: Oxford University Press.

Walsh, J. (ed.), 2003, *Bill Viola: The Passions. Exhibition Catalogue.* Los Angeles.

Wang, R. (trans.), 1999, *Zhuangzi I.* Hunan: Hunan People's Publishing House.

Warhol, A., 1975, *The Philosophy of Andy Warhol From A to B & Back Again*. New York: Harcourt Brace Jovanovich.

Wark, M., 2004, *A Hacker Manifesto*. Cambridge, MA: Harvard University Press.

Watson, B. (trans.), 1968, *The Complete Works of Chuang Tzu*. New York: Columbia University Press.

Weber, M., 1946, 'Science as a Vocation' in trans. H. H. Gerth and C. Wright Mills (eds), *From Max Weber: Essays in Sociology*. New York: Oxford University Press.

——, 1988, 'Science as a vocation' in P. Lassman and I. Velody with H. Martins (eds), *Max Weber's Science as a Vocation*, London: Routledge.

——, 2009, *From Max Weber: Essays in Sociology*. Abingdon: Routledge.

Wees, W. C., 1993, *Recycled Images: The Art and Politics of Found Footage Films.* New York: Anthology Film Archives.

Werner, H., 1957, *Comparative Psychology of Mental Development.* New York: International University Press.

Westfahl, G. (ed.), 2005, *Science Fiction Quotations: From the Inner Mind to the Outer Limits.* New Haven: Yale University Press.

Williams, J., 2003, *Gilles Deleuze's Difference and Repetition: A Critical Introduction and Guide.* Edinburgh: Edinburgh University Press.

Williams, W. C., 1946, Book 1 in *Paterson.* New York: New Directions (1963).

Wittrock, B., 2000, 'Modernity: One, none, or many? European origins and modernity as a global condition', *Daedalus* 129:1.

Wong, K. Y., 1986, 'Negative-positive dialectics of the Chinese sublime' in Chou Ying-hsiung (ed.), *The Chinese Text.* Hong Kong: Chinese University Press.

——, 1989, 'Temporalization of spatial experience in classical Chinese landscape poetry' in *Essays in Commemoration of the 30th Anniversary of the United College.* Hong Kong: Chinese University of Hong Kong.

Wong, O. and Ng, J., 2008, 'Bid to resolve conflict over open space', *South China Morning Post* 27 August.

Wu, H., 1997, *The Double Screen: Medium and Representation in Chinese Painting.* Chicago: University of Chicago Press.

——, 2008, 'Developers back review of policies covering public space', *South China Morning Post* 23 April.

Yau, S. M., 1997, 《看眼難忘——在香港長大》*Unforgettable Glimpse: Growing up in Hong Kong.* Hong Kong: Qing wen shu wu.

Yeung, R., 2008, *Moving Millions: The Commercial Success and Political Controversies of Hong Kong's Railways.* Hong Kong: Hong Kong University Press.

Yip, W. L. (trans.), 1972, *Hiding the Universe: Poems by Wang Wei.* New York: Grossman.

Zepke, S., 2005, *Art as Abstract Machine: Ontology and aesthetics in Deleuze and Guattari.* New York and London: Routledge.

Zhang, H. 張洪兵, 2009, 'Ruins and Grassroots: Jia Zhangke's Cinematic Discontents in the Age of Globalization' in S. H. Lu and J. Mi (eds), *Chinese Ecocinema: In the Age of Environmental Challenge.* Hong Kong: Hong Kong University Press.

Zittrain, J., 2008, *The Future of the Internet and How to Stop it.* London; Allen Lane.

Zourabichvili, F., 2000, 'The eye of montage: Dziga Vertov and Bergsonian materialism', in G. Flaxman (ed.), trans. M. McMahon *The Brain is the Screen*. Minneapolis: University of Minnesota Press.

Zukin, S., 2010, *Naked City: The Death and Life of Authentic Urban Places*. Oxford and New York: Oxford University Press.

港行人密度 達最劣水平F級 'The Density of Sidewalks in Hong Kong has Reached The Worst Level of F'. *Apple Daily* http://hk.apple.nextmedia.com/news/art/20140202/18612746.

Filmography

Hollywood Hong Kong, Xianggang yougehelihuo 香港有個荷里活, 2001, Fruit Chan, 陳果, Nicetop Independent Ltd.

Majiang 麻將 *Mahjong*. Yang, E., 楊德昌, 1996, Taipei: Atom Films.

Unknown Pleasures. Jia, Z., 賈樟柯, 2002, New Yorker Films.

Index

www.ingramcontent.com/pod-product-compliance
Ingram Content Group UK Ltd.
Pitfield, Milton Keynes, MK11 3LW, UK
UKHW020205290926
15470UKWH00001B/17

9 781784 530341